NEW AFRIC*N THINKERS

CONSIDERING PEACE AND DEVELOPMENT IN AFRICA

Edited by Rodney Managa | Check Achu | Vuyo Mjimba

Africa Institute
of South Africa
Development Through Knowledge

First Published in 2025 by AISA Press
Private Bag X41
Pretoria 0001
South Africa
ISBN (soft cover) 978-0-7983-0540-2
ISBN (PDF) 978-0-7983-0539-6

© 2025 Human Sciences Research Council
The views expressed in this publication are those of the authors. They do not necessarily reflect the views or policies of the Human Sciences Research Council (the Council) and those of the Africa Institute of South Africa (the Institute) or indicate that either the Council or the Institute endorses the views of the authors. In quoting from this publication, readers are advised to attribute the source of the information to the individual author concerned and not to either the Council or the Institute.

The publishers have no responsibility for the continued existence or accuracy of URLs for external or third-party websites referred to in this book and do not guarantee that any content on such websites is, or will remain, accurate or appropriate.

Copy edited by Jen Stern
Typeset by Andy Thesen
Cover design by Shaun Andrews
Printed by CTP Printers, Cape Town

Distributed in Africa by Blue Weaver
Tel: +27 (021) 701 4477; Fax Local: (021) 701 7302; Fax International: 0927865242139
www.blueweaver.co.za

Distributed worldwide (except central and southern Africa)
by Lynne Rienner Publishers, Inc.
Tel: +1 303-444-6684; Fax: +1 303-444-0824; Email: cservice@rienner.com
www.rienner.com

No part of this publication may be reproduced, stored in a retrieval system, or transmitted by any form or by any means, electronic, mechanical, photocopying, recording or otherwise, without prior permission from the copyright owner.

To copy any part of this publication, you may contact DALRO for information and copyright clearance.

Tel: 086 12 DALRO (or 086 12 3256 from within South Africa); +27 (0)11 712-8000
Fax: +27 (0)11 403-9094
Postal Address: P O Box 31627, Braamfontein, 2017, South Africa
www.dalro.co.za

Any unauthorised copying could lead to civil liability and/or criminal sanctions.

Suggested citation: Managa R, Achu C, Mjimba V (2025). *New African Thinkers: Considering Peace and Development in Africa*. Pretoria: AISA Press

Contents

Tables v
Figures vi
Preface vii
Acronyms viii

PART 1: Conflict resolution, peacebuilding and good governance 1

1. Dimensions of peacebuilding and development in Africa 3
   Nicasius Achu Check, Lavhelesani R Managa and Vuyo Mjimba

2. The resurgence of coups d'état in West Africa and the Sahel 14
   Collin Olebogeng Mongale and Keaobaka Tsholo

3. Silencing the guns in Somalia 36
   Jacqueline Nakaiza

4. Measuring Nigerians' willingness to talk to police on duty 52
   Oluwaseun Ayomipo, Babatunde Raphael Ojebuyi, Oluwabusolami Oluwajulugbe, Oluwafunmilayo Olarewaju Aminu and Ridwan Abiola Kolawole

5. Good governance remains key to Africa's sustainable development 65
   Boikanyo C Nkwatle

PART 2: Africa's sustainable development and regional integration 83

6. Attributes of community leaders for sustainable development 85
   Awelani J Nemathithi, Joseph Francis, Lufuno R Kone and Phellecy Lavhelani

7. African continental free trade potential for South Africa's renewable energy 98
   Phemelo Michelle Mashamaite

8. Sustainable food systems transformation in South Africa 118
   Lavhelesani R Managa

9. The role of technology for marketers in Africa 139
   Winfrida Thadei Kobero

10 Survival strategies of Nigerian youth when things fall apart   164
    Oluwafunmilayo Olarewaju Aminu, Babatunde Raphael Ojebuyi,
    Oluwabusolami Oluwajulugbe, Oluwaseun Ayomipo
    and Ridwan Abiola Kolawole

11 Assessing the efficiency of indigenous soil and water conservation
    methods   188
    Gideon Monday

About the authors   207
Index   209

Tables

Table 4.1	Demography of the respondents 56
Table 4.2	Study scales and Cronbach alpha values 57
Table 4.3	Exploratory factor analysis results 59
Table 4.4	Correlation analysis results 60
Table 6.1	Community-perceived ideal attributes of ward committee members 91
Table 7.1	Critical minerals required for rooftop solar PV panels 104
Table 7.2	A snapshot of South Africa's mineral security for solar panels 105
Table 8.1	Black farmers' share of agricultural outputs in South Africa: 2015 to 2019 123
Table 8.2	Proportion of post-harvest losses in South Africa 124
Table 8.3	Challenges and potential solutions for sustainable urban agriculture in South Africa 130
Table 9.1	World internet users 145
Table 9.2	The mean, median and mode for each variable 150
Table 9.3	Frequencies and percentages of responses 151
Table 11.1	Description of silt traps installed in the project area 192
Table 11.2	Water quality analysis 203
Table 11.3	Annual soil erosion rates for micro catchments 1, 2, 3 and 4 203
Table 11.4	Annual sediment yield in micro catchments 1, 2, 3 and 4 204
Table 11.5	Trapping efficiency of indigenous soil and water conservation measures 204

Figures

Figure 4.1	Confirmatory factor analysis results	59
Figure 8.1	Selection procedure used for the literature review	120
Figure 9.1	Technology acceptance model	141
Figure 9.2	Research framework	148
Figure 11.1a–d	Soil erosion (a), river flooding (b, c) and water pollution (d) in the study area	189
Figure 11.2	Map of Kisoro District showing the study area	190
Figure 11.3	Micro catchment delineation	192
Figure 11.4	Runoff plots at representative sites	193
Figure 11.5	Installation of silt traps on plots	193
Figure 11.6	In-situ sampling in the troughs	194
Figure 11.7	Multi-parameter water quality meter	194
Figure 11.8a	Age of respondents	196
Figure 11.8b	Duration of stay in the study area	196
Figure 11.9a–d	Soil erosion control by tree planting (a), fallowing (b), ridging (c)and contour bunds (d)	197
Figure 11.10a–d	Traditional rainwater harvesting tank (a), rainwater harvesting pond (b), clay pot (c) and wooden trough (d)	198
Figure 11.11a	Gently sloping bare land	199
Figure 11.11b	Gently sloping grassland	200
Figure 11.11c	Gently sloping cultivated land	200
Figure 11.11d	Steeply sloping cultivated land	201
Figure 11.11e	Steeply sloping bare land	201
Figure 11.11f	Steeply sloping grassland	202

Preface

The African continent stands at a pivotal juncture, where the pursuit of peace and development is intricately woven into the fabric of its diverse societies. *Considering Peace and Development in Africa* seeks to explore the complex interplay between conflict resolution, peacebuilding, good governance, sustainable development, and regional integration. Through a comprehensive examination of these themes, the book aims to provide a nuanced understanding of the challenges and opportunities that define Africa's path towards a prosperous future. It is divided into two parts and consists of eleven individual chapters.

Part 1, Conflict Resolution, Peacebuilding and Good Governance, delves into the foundational elements necessary for establishing lasting peace and stability on the continent. The introductory chapter sets the stage by advocating for a multidimensional approach to peacebuilding and development, recognising the interconnectedness of these efforts. Subsequent chapters explore the critical issues of the resurgence of coups d'état in West Africa and the Sahel, the African Union's initiatives to combat terrorism in Somalia, and the importance of fostering trust between citizens and law enforcement in Nigeria. This section concludes by emphasising the indispensable role of good governance in ensuring Africa's sustainable development.

Part 2, Africa's Sustainable Development and Regional Integration, shifts the focus towards the continent's economic and social advancement. It highlights the significance of grassroots leadership in sustainable development, the potential of the African Continental Free Trade Area (AfCFTA) in enhancing mineral security and renewable energy initiatives, and the transformation of food systems to be more inclusive and sustainable. Additionally, this section examines the role of information and communication technology in facilitating trade, the resilience of Nigerian youth amidst infrastructural challenges, and the effectiveness of indigenous soil and water conservation methods in Uganda.

This book is a collection of papers presented at the 17th Africa Young Graduates and Scholars Conference held in March 2023 in Pretoria, South Africa. The conference was organised by the Human Sciences Research Council and the Partnership for African Social and Governance Research. It was held at a critical time when the African Union was assessing the first 10-year implementation plan of Agenda 2063. This book is a testament to the resilience and ingenuity of African societies as they navigate the complexities of peace and development. We hope the insights and analyses presented herein will contribute to the ongoing discourse and inspire actionable strategies for the more peaceful and prosperous Africa we want.

Acronyms

AAMP	Agriculture and Agro-Processing Master Plan
AfCFTA	African Continental Free Trade Area
AGA	African Governance Architecture
AMISOM	African Union Mission in Somalia
APRM	African Peer Review Mechanism
ATMIS	African Transition Mission in Somalia
AU	African Union
B2B	business to business
B2C	business to consumer
C2C	consumer to consumer
COP 15	15th Conference of the Parties to the United Nations Convention on Biological Diversity
ECOWAS	Economic Community of West African States
EFA	exploratory factor analysis
ESG	environment, society, and governance (of mining)
FAO	Food and Agriculture Organization
FGS	Federal Government of Somalia
GDP	gross domestic product
ICT	information and communication technology
IRENA	International Renewable Energy Agency
ISWAP	Islamic State of West Africa Province
ITU	International Telecommunications Union
JNIM	Jama'a Nusrat al-Islam wal Muslim
NDP	National Development Plan
OAU	Organisation of African Unity
OCHA	Office for the Coordination of Humanitarian Affairs (UN)
PV	photovoltaic
R2P	responsibility to protect
RDP	Reconstruction and Development Programme
REDZ	Renewable Energy Development Zone
REIPPPP	Renewable Energy Independent Power Producers Procurement Programme
RET	renewable energy transition
SADC	Southern African Development Community
SAPP	Southern African Power Pool
SDG	Sustainable Development Goal
SEZ	special economic zone

SPSS	Statistical Package for Social Scientists
SNF	Somali National Forces
SWC	soil and water conservation (systems)
TFG	Transitional Federal Government (Somalia)
UNFCCC	United Nations Framework Convention on Climate Change
UNDP	United Nations Development Program
UNSC	United Nations Security Council
UPDF	Uganda People's Defence Forces
WTCWPOD	willingness to communicate with police on duty

PART 1

CONFLICT RESOLUTION, PEACEBUILDING, AND GOOD GOVERNANCE

1 Dimensions of peacebuilding and development in Africa

Nicasius Achu Check, Lavhelesani R Managa and Vuyo Mjimba

Background

The African continent, with its rich tapestry of cultures, languages, and histories, stands at a pivotal juncture in its pursuit of sustainable peace and development. Despite the remarkable progress made in recent decades, Africa grapples with many challenges that prevent it from reaching its full potential. These challenges are multifaceted, encompassing political instability, economic disparities, social inequalities, and environmental vulnerabilities. As such, a multidimensional approach to peacebuilding and development is required to address the continent's complex and interrelated issues.

The current global conflagration in Ukraine in the international political and security arena suggests a deficiency in peacebuilding and conflict-resolution strategies adopted soon after the fall of the former Soviet Union. The persistence of conflicts in many places where peacebuilding has been tried, as witnessed currently in Europe and Africa, illustrates how difficult it is to establish conditions for peace so that communities can thrive. Knight (2010) posits that the fact that conflicts persist despite significant efforts to prevent them shows that subregional organisations and – more so – the United Unions, whose main objective is to avoid conflicts, have failed in this regard. The world has witnessed several intra-state disputes and significant political instability since the end of the Cold War. These all require some form of post-conflict and peacebuilding intervention. The many organisations that were involved in such interventions intended not only to stem the upsurge in civil conflicts but also to prevent a relapse when these conflicts ended (Knight 2010). Many have argued that a peacebuilding strategy is a strategy to prevent a country, especially one that is recovering from a conflict situation, from descending into the anarchy of more political and social instability.

As well as a concerted and obvious strategy for conflict prevention, a classical approach to peacebuilding would include early warning systems for potential conflicts. However, in this chapter we focus on the multidimensional aspects of peace-building on the continent, on what has been done and what can be done differently to ensure that African countries do not relapse into conflict. While attention will be paid to disarmament, demobilisation and reintegration, post-conflict reconstruction, human rights, justice, the role of women, religion, humanitarian intervention, and grassroots organisations, the emphasis will equally be on why local remedies for conflict prevention and resolution fail. Indigenous knowledge has played an important role in addressing fundamental societal challenges in several African societies, so our approach will ensure that such strategies are harnessed for the good of the continent.

Historically, development efforts in Africa have often been narrowly focused, emphasising economic growth without adequately addressing the underlying social and political dynamics. However, recent shifts in global development paradigms highlight the importance of integrating various dimensions to achieve sustainable and inclusive growth. This chapter underscores the need to adopt a multidimensional framework that takes into account the diverse challenges and opportunities across the continent. For instance, economic development remains a cornerstone of progress, but it must be pursued alongside efforts to improve governance, enhance social cohesion, and protect the environment. Political stability and effective governance are crucial for creating an enabling environment for development, while social factors such as education, health, and gender equality play a vital role in empowering communities. Additionally, environmental sustainability is essential to ensure that resource depletion and climate change do not undermine development gains.

Conceptualising armed conflicts in Africa

Despite gaining independence over 50 years ago, many African countries still experience sectarian conflicts and lack strategic frameworks to address developmental challenges. These issues are exacerbated by volatile global economic conditions, weakening governance institutions, and the emergence of asymmetric conflicts, such as those brought about by Boko Haram in Nigeria. Boko Haram, founded in 2002, initially opposed Western education but has since evolved into a more aggressive insurgency, capturing towns and creating Islamic caliphates (BBC 2014) – a situation that calls for new security strategies on the continent.

The Central African Republic (CAR) also faces significant challenges, with conflicts between SELEKA rebels and the Anti-Balaka group leading to humanitarian crises and economic decline (International Crisis Group 2014). The CAR's struggles are rooted in a lack of nation-building and reliance on foreign approval, particularly from France. The proliferation of small arms and the demobilisation of militia members have further destabilised the region.

Insecurity linked to armed conflict is a major obstacle to development, as it discourages investment and destroys infrastructure and livelihoods. The economic crisis of the 1980s, the end of the Cold War, and the proliferation of small arms have all contributed to the unravelling of Africa's political and security landscape. The inability of post-colonial elites to address state building has left many countries vulnerable to conflict.

Asymmetric conflicts, characterised by power disparities between belligerents, have become more prominent (Mack 1974). These conflicts often involve unconventional warfare tactics, as seen with Boko Haram and other groups like al-Shabaab and ISIS. In Nigeria, the Boko Haram insurgency is driven by religion, corruption, poverty, and political struggles. The Niger Delta insurgency, on the other hand, stems from environmental concerns and demands for a fair distribution of oil wealth.

Foreign interference and the military's political involvement further complicate the situation in the CAR. The proliferation of small arms and the impact of climate change on fragile ecosystems also contribute to instability. Addressing these challenges requires a comprehensive approach to peacebuilding and development in Africa.

Building peace on the continent: A multidimensional approach

It has been argued that the continent should adopt a neo-functional approach in its multilateral conversations to address its current governance, peace, and security challenges. In Africa, the neo-functional paradigm owes much of its intellectual and policy direction to Kwame Nkrumah, who advocated for a federative model of political unity on the continent by forming supranational institutions (Fagbayibo 2018). The formation of the Organisation of African Unity (OAU) in May 1963 and the subsequent transformation of the organisation to the African Union (AU) in 2001, reflect the aspirations of the leaders of the Casablanca and Monrovia blocs in establishing some form of a supranational institution that will guide the political and socioeconomic development trajectory of the continent.

Over the years, the OAU and the AU, in their attempts to achieve this important milestone, have created policy frameworks, institutions, and agencies to help fulfil this critical mandate. One such policy framework is the AU Agenda 2063. Conceived in 2013 and debated for two years, the AU Agenda 2063 is an African Union Commission development blueprint for a prosperous, people-driven, integrated Africa based on inclusive growth, good governance, democracy, respect for human rights, peace, security and political unity based on the ideals of Pan-Africanism.

The seven aspirations of Agenda 2063 (African Union Commission 2015) emphasise the importance of inclusive growth, peace, and security, but the difficulty of engaging with political leaders and the changing power dynamics on the global stage compel us to regularly evaluate what has been done and what we as a people still need to do to achieve all our seven aspirations by the year 2063. In as much as we recognise the fact that missed development opportunities are due to the fundamental problem of democratic governance deficit, there is no gainsaying that weak governance and its associated political instability, insecurity, and lack of peace continue to hinder economic, social and cultural development on the continent (Nwebo 2018). Thus, for Africa to achieve all the aspirations outlined in Agenda 2063, we must prioritise democratic governance and strong institutions. Agenda

2063 outlines the short-, medium-, and long-term steps necessary to achieve these aspirations. However, challenges persist.

In the short term, i.e., 2014–2023, Agenda 2063 had set goals and priority areas for the first ten-year implementation plan, including:
- an integrated high speed train network connecting all African capitals;
- an African virtual e-university;
- a community strategy;
- an annual African forum;
- establishment of a continental free trade area by 2017;
- the African Passport to facilitate free movement of people;
- implementation of the Grand Inga Dam Project;
- the Pan-African E-Network;
- silencing the guns by 2020;
- the Africa outer space strategy to strengthen Africa's use aerospace industry;
- a single African air transport market; and
- an integrated African financial institution (African Union Commission 2015).

It was unlikely that all the first ten-year implementation plan goals would be achieved in the given time frame – and they were not. However, the key was not necessarily to achieve all these milestones but to ensure that mechanisms are in place to monitor and evaluate the implementation plan. In recognising the enormity of tracking the implementation plan, the AU, during its 2017 Heads of State Summit, decided to expand the mandate of the African Peer Review Mechanism (APRM) to include the monitoring the implementation of Agenda 2063 and the Sustainable Development Goals (SDGs) by 2030 (Corrigan & Gruzd 2017).

Many have lauded expanding the mandate of the APRM to include the monitoring and evaluation of Agenda 2063 and SDGs 2030 but there is a growing concern that its current structure is not suitable. Three key issues are at play here. First, the APRM was explicitly conceived as a tool for policy reform so it may not have the technical expertise to monitor, for example, the execution of grand public works projects such as the high-speed train or the Grand Inga Dam. AUDA-NEPAD may be the appropriate AU agency to carry out this important task. It is, therefore, essential that the appropriate policy ensures that specialised Agencies of the AU monitor the Agenda 2063 goals with proper expertise and competence. Second, any monitoring system must be able to deliver timely reports on all countries within its remit (Corrigan & Gruzd 2017). With more than 54 African countries, it is unrealistic to expect a timely report on implementing the immediate goals of Agenda 2063 and SDGs 2030. The third challenge is the absence of non-state actors in the monitoring process of implementing Agenda 2063 and SDGs 2030. While civil society organisations played important roles in formulating the various aspirations of Agenda 2063 and SDGs 2030, their role in monitoring their implementation is fluid and, at best, lacking. It is therefore, important to consider the role that non-state actors could play in monitoring the implementation of the various aspirations of Agenda 2063 and SDGs 2030.

Renewed democracy and political governance approach

One of the fundamental pillars of the AU is the entrenching of a solid democratic and political governance framework for Africa. Despite enormous efforts to consolidate democratic and political governance gains, challenges remain. As noted elsewhere, the level of compliance and implementation of the various governance frameworks on the continent is concerning (Wachira 2014). Recognising this fundamental challenge, the AU established the African Governance Architecture (AGA) and the African Governance Platform, which work closely with the APRM to enhance democracy and political governance on the continent (Wachira 2014). The goals of AGA are to connect, empower, and build the capacities of AU organs, regional economic communities, and stakeholders to enhance good governance and democracy in Africa. However, as the APRM notes, democracy and political governance should not be separated from accountability in the management of the democratic and political events in member states, transparency, the rule of law, and unhindered exercise of individual rights as enshrined in the African Charter on Human and People's Rights (African Union n.d.). Therefore, democracy and political governance touch on the fundamental rights of the citizenry and the accountability of governments to the governed to guarantee relative peace and stability on the continent (African Union n.d.).

It is, therefore, crucial to note that democracy and good political governance should be primary considerations if we are to drastically reduce poverty and attain sustainable development as envisaged in Agenda 2063 and SDGs 2030. For this to happen, four critical policy directions need to be considered, namely regularity, fairness, and plurality of the democratic and political process; a free press and transparency in the management of the political process; strong institutions and the rule of law; and access to the judiciary.

One of the pillars of the consolidation of democracy and the entrenchment of the political process in Africa, on which the AU has been uncompromising, is the regularity, fairness, and plurality of the democratic and political process.

The second variable that is necessary for effective democratic and political governance to flourish is a free press and transparency in the management of the political process. A free press is essential for exposing corruption in the political process. Corrupt political practices such as election rigging, bribing the electorate and the people managing the electoral process, and stuffing ballot boxes are usually exposed by the press. The methodological approach that the AU should adopt would be to ensure that members of the media are given the necessary powers to do their job and to take seriously their views on the credibility of the political process. The press needs to be free to perform its job of sensitising and informing the people.

The third variable that needs to be considered is the strength of the institutions of member countries and the rule of law. While the international community has intervened repeatedly to rebuild state institutions after the collapse of one-party state systems, there are instances in which robust, transparent, and accountable state institutions have been internally fashioned and capacitated (Ottaway 2002). However, for any state to establish strong institutions of which the population can claim some form of ownership, the de facto rather than the de jure form of the state must be well established. De jure states usually exist by a fiat of the international community, which recognises them as sovereign entities, while de facto states are those in which the people occupying the territory are organised under an effective government (Ottaway 2002). Because most African states can be classified as de jure, the international community must validate the building and recognition of state institutions. This has made it very difficult for states to develop viable and workable indigenous strong institutions that have the buy-in of the international community.

However, a primary focus in formulating a new methodology and ensuring standardised national programmes of action would be to ensure that institutions that are representative of a broad sector of the population of a particular country should be strengthened and supported. What matters most is not whether the international community recognises a specific institution but, significantly, whether the institution is an organic and unique structure that can resolve local socioeconomic and political challenges. The key is to ensure that the indigenisation approach of institutions is taken into consideration and that uniquely African institutions are strengthened. Evidence from countries such as Rwanda and Uganda have shown that institutions that are rooted in African culture are resilient, and are generally accepted by most of the people.

The last critical concern that the democracy and political governance thematic thrust would focus on is the rule of law and accessibility of the judiciary to the people. It has been argued that the effectiveness of legal institutions is of critical importance to legal scholars, academics, politicians, and policymakers primarily because the rule of law is intricately connected to the entrenchment of democracy (Joireman 2001). African countries in real need of a democratic process that responds to their complex contextual realities will benefit from the effective rule of law and free access to legal institutions for all. Thus, for an effective democracy and political governance process, the rule of law must be practical and accessible to all who may feel aggrieved in any electoral or political process. Conversely, a country that can assure physical protection and equal treatment under the law for its citizens is less likely to be engaged in violent internal conflict (Joireman 2001). Therefore, the laws of all African countries must be fair and responsive to the legal needs of all.

Multidimensional approach in the context of sustainable development

In the context of sustainable development, a multidimensional approach involves considering various interconnected factors that contribute to the overall well-being of society. This approach recognises that development is not just about economic growth, but also includes social, environmental, and cultural dimensions (Li et al.

2021). Sustainable development is all about finding a balance between economic growth, environmental protection, and social equity to ensure that we meet the needs of the present without compromising the ability of future generations to meet their own needs. This concept was popularised in the Brundtland Report (United Nations 1987), which emphasised the interconnectedness of these three pillars. Numerous frameworks and goals, such as the United Nations' Sustainable Development Goals (SDGs), provide a blueprint for achieving sustainable development by 2030. The 17 SDGs cover many issues, from poverty and hunger to clean energy and climate action. It's a comprehensive approach that requires collaboration across sectors and borders to create a sustainable future for all. Africa has made progress towards achieving the SDGs, but many challenges remain. Some of the key areas in which Africa is focusing its efforts include poverty reduction, improving access to education and healthcare, promoting gender equality, and addressing climate change. However, significant infrastructure, governance, and economic development gaps still need to be addressed to fully achieve the SDGs by 2030.

Fostering a multidimensionality approach to development in Africa

In Africa, a multidimensional approach to development is essential for fostering inclusive growth and ensuring that development benefits reach all segments of society, particularly marginalised groups such as women, youth, and rural communities. This approach recognises that development is not a one-size-fits-all process. Instead, it requires a comprehensive strategy that addresses various social, economic, and environmental factors. For instance, empowering women is a critical component of a multidimensional approach. African women often face significant barriers to education, healthcare, and economic opportunities. By promoting gender equality and providing women with access to education and resources, societies can unlock the potential of half their population, leading to increased productivity and economic growth. Initiatives such as microfinance programmes, vocational training, and legal reforms to protect women's rights can play a pivotal role in this empowerment (Mayoux 2000). Focusing on youth is also vital, given that Africa has one of the youngest populations in the world. Investing in education and skills development for young people can equip them with the tools needed to participate actively in the economy and contribute to innovation and entrepreneurship. Programmes that support youth employment, mentorship, and leadership development are crucial for harnessing the energy and creativity of this demographic.

Rural communities are often isolated from the benefits of urban development, so they require targeted interventions to improve their living standards. Infrastructure development, such as roads, electricity, and internet connectivity, can significantly enhance access to markets, education, and healthcare. Additionally, supporting sustainable agricultural practices and providing access to financial services can help rural populations improve their livelihoods and reduce poverty. Moreover, environmental degradation is a major factor that negatively impacts development in

Africa. Africa is particularly vulnerable to the impacts of climate change, which can exacerbate existing challenges such as food insecurity and water scarcity. Integrating environmental considerations into development planning, promoting renewable energy, and supporting climate-resilient agriculture is essential for ensuring long-term sustainability (Jaiswal et al. 2022; Bathaei & Štreimikienė 2023).

To foster inclusive economic growth, African nations must move beyond dependence on a limited range of commodities or sectors, such as oil or agriculture, and work towards developing a more diverse economic base. This involves investment in strategic manufacturing, technology, and services to build more resilient and sustainable economies. While countries like South Africa, Egypt, Morocco, and Tunisia are often highlighted for their diversified economic development, many other African nations have also embraced economic diversification with notable success. For instance, Senegal has made significant strides by utilising special economic zones to attract manufacturing investment, and it is actively developing new tourism hubs to position itself as a major tourist destination (Delechat et al. 2024). In contrast, Mauritius has excelled in producing and marketing high-end agricultural value-added products and has established duty-free shops that sell condiments and seasonings, enhancing its economic profile (Rahardja & Swaroop 2024). Countries such as Burkina Faso, Kenya, Malawi, and Sierra Leone have diversified their service sectors, with the top three service sectors accounting for approximately 65 per cent of total service exports (UNCTAD 2022). This indicates a broader range of economic activities contributing to their economies. Conversely, other countries – like Benin, for example – face challenges in strengthening their economies, primarily because they lack lucrative natural resources, which hampers their ability to diversify effectively (OECD/United Nations 2011).

AU initiatives to promote multidimensional approaches to development in Africa

The AU has been instrumental in shaping development strategies across the African continent, focusing on a holistic and integrated approach to addressing the diverse challenges faced by its member states. The AU has prioritised development as a key component of its agenda, recognising that sustainable growth is essential for peace, stability, and prosperity in Africa. One of the AU's primary frameworks for development is Agenda 2063, a strategic blueprint that envisions a prosperous and integrated Africa driven by its own citizens. Agenda 2063 outlines several key aspirations including inclusive economic growth, sustainable development, good governance, and peace and security (African Union Commission 2015). It emphasises the importance of regional integration, infrastructure development, and women and youth empowerment as critical drivers of progress.

The AU collaborates with various regional economic communities to harmonise policies and initiatives promoting trade, investment, and economic cooperation. By fostering partnerships with international organisations, development partners, and the private sector, the AU aims to mobilise resources and expertise to support its development goals. In addition to economic development, the AU addresses social and environmental dimensions through initiatives such as the Comprehensive Africa Agriculture Development Programme and the African Continental Free Trade Area (AfCFTA). These initiatives seek to enhance food security, boost intra-African trade, and create jobs, contributing to the continent's overall development. Furthermore, the AU strongly emphasises peacebuilding as a foundation for development. Through its Peace and Security Council, the AU works to prevent and resolve conflicts, promote human rights, and support post-conflict reconstruction efforts. The AU strives to create a stable environment conducive to sustainable growth and prosperity for all Africans by integrating peace and development.

Overcoming challenges to implementing comprehensive development strategies in Africa

Implementing comprehensive development strategies in Africa is hampered by numerous challenges, including governance issues like political instability, corruption, and weak institutions. Economic disparities, poverty, and inadequate infrastructure hinder progress despite the continent's rich resources. Social factors such as cultural diversity and ethnic tensions complicate efforts, while environmental challenges like climate change exacerbate existing problems. Additionally, reliance on unpredictable foreign aid and global economic fluctuations can disrupt development plans.

Therefore, efforts to implement development strategies in Africa should focus on strengthening local institutions through training and improved governance, fostering regional cooperation to tackle transnational issues, and enhancing infrastructure via initiatives like the AfCFTA and the Programme for Infrastructure Development in Africa. Inclusivity should be prioritised by addressing inequalities and promoting opportunities for marginalised groups, including rural women and youth. African countries need to leverage technology and innovation to address socioeconomic and environmental challenges and develop comprehensive policy frameworks aligning national efforts with global agendas like the SDGs and Agenda 2063. Securing funding remains a challenge, and more efforts are needed to mobilise resources from domestic and international sources to finance Africa's development projects,

Conclusion

Africa is critically pursuing sustainable peace and development, which requires a comprehensive, multidimensional approach. The continent must move beyond a sole focus on economic growth to integrate governance, social cohesion, and environmental sustainability into its strategies. The many persistent conflicts highlight the need for innovative security and peacebuilding efforts that leverage local remedies and promote participatory democracy to resolve political disputes. Equally, strong democratic institutions, equality before the law, and a well-functioning civil service, army, and police are essential to maintain stability and peace on the continent. The African Union's Agenda 2063 provides a vital framework for inclusive growth and good governance, but its implementation faces challenges like governance issues, economic disparities, and environmental threats. To address these, African nations must strengthen local institutions, enhance regional cooperation, and harness technology and innovation, aligning with global agendas like the SDGs. Empowering marginalised groups, promoting gender equality, and addressing environmental concerns are essential for equitable development. By fostering a collaborative and inclusive approach, Africa can build resilient economies and achieve lasting peace and prosperity.

References

African Union (n.d.) *Revised Country Self-Assessment Base Questionnaire for the African Peer Review Mechanism.* Accessed 6 December 2024, https://au.int/en/organs/aprm

African Union Commission (2015) *Agenda 2063: The Africa we want; Framework document.*

Bathaei A & Štreimikienė D (2023) Renewable energy and sustainable agriculture: Review of indicators. *Sustainability* 15(19): 14307. Accessed 6 December 2024, https://www.mdpi.com/2071-1050/15/19/14307

BBC (2014) *Boko Haram put Maiduguri under siege.* Accessed 6 December 2024, http://www.bbc.com/news/world-africa-29155529

Corrigan T & Gruzd S (2017) *Can the APRM be an effective tool to monitor Agenda 2063 and the SDGs?* Occasional Paper 251. South African Institute of International Affairs. Accessed 6 December 2024, https://saiia.org.za/wp-content/uploads/2017/02/Occasional-Paper-251.pdf

Delechat CC, Melina G, Newiak M, Papageorgiou C & Spatafora N (2024) *Economic diversification in developing countries: Lessons from country experiences with broad-based and industrial policies, Departmental Paper 2024/006.* International Monetary Fund. Accessed 6 December 2024, https://www.imf.org/en/Publications/Departmental-Papers-Policy-Papers/Issues/2024/07/20/Economic-Diversification-in-Developing-Countries-Lessons-from-Country-Experiences-with-532135

Fagbayibo B (2018) Nkrumahism, Agenda 2063, and the role of inter-governmental institutions in fast-tracking continental unity. *Journal of Asian and African Studies* (53)4: 630

International Crisis Group (2014) *The Central African crisis: From predation to stabilisation, Report No. 219.* Accessed 6 December 2024, https://www.crisisgroup.org/africa/central-africa/central-african-republic/central-african-crisis-predation-stabilisation

Jaiswal KK, Chowdhury CR, Yadav D, Verma R, Dutta S, Jaiswal KS & Karuppasamy KSK (2022) Renewable and sustainable clean energy development and impact on social, economic, and environmental health. *Energy Nexus*, (7): 100118. Accessed 6 December 2024, https://www.sciencedirect.com/science/article/pii/S2772427122000687?via=hub

Joireman S (2001) Inherited legal systems and effective rule of law: Africa and the colonial legacy. *Journal of Modern African Studies* (39)4: 572

Knight WA (2010) Linking DDR and SSR in post-conflict peacebuilding in Africa: An overview. *African Journal of Political Science and International Relations* 4(1): 29–54

Li D, He G, Jin H & Tsai FS (2021) Sustainable development of African countries: Minding public life, education, and welfare. *Frontiers in Public Health* (9): 74884. Accessed 6 December 2024, https://www.frontiersin.org/journals/public-health/articles/10.3389/fpubh.2021.748845/full

Mack A (1974) Why big nations lose small wars: The politics of asymmetric conflict. *World Politics* 27(2): 175–200

Mayoux L (2000) *Micro-finance and the empowerment of women: A review of the key issues.* ILO Working Paper no. 23. Accessed 6 December 2024, https://www.ilo.org/publications/micro-finance-and-empowerment-women

Nwebo O (2018) The African Union Agenda 2063 and the imperative of democratic governance. *Law and Development Review* (11)2: 259–276

OECD/United Nations (2011). Experiences in national economic diversification in Africa. In *Economic diversification in Africa: A review of selected countries.* OECD Publishing. Accessed 20 February 2025, https://www.oecd.org/content/dam/oecd/en/publications/reports/2011/04/economic-diversification-in-africa_g1g1209f/9789264096233-en.pdf

Ottaway M (2002). Rebuilding state institutions in collapsed states. *Development and Change* (33)5: 1002

Rahardja S & Swaroop V (2024) What can sub-Saharan Africa learn from Mauritius's successful development? *Africa Can End Poverty.* World Bank Blogs. Accessed 6 December 2024, https://blogs.worldbank.org/en/africacan/what-can-sub-saharan-africa-learn-from-mauritius-s-successful-afe-0324

UNCTAD (2022) Rethinking the foundations of export diversification in Africa: The catalytic role of business and financial services. *Economic Development in Africa Report 2022.* Accessed 6 December 2024, https://unctad.org/system/files/official-document/aldcafrica2022_en.pdf

United Nations (1987) *Our common future (The Brundtland Report).* Accessed 6 December 2024, https://www.brundtland.co.za/wp-content/uploads/2022/08/Brundtland-Report-1987-Our-Common-Future.pdf

Wachira G (2014) *Consolidating the African governance architecture: Policy Briefing Paper* No. 96. South African Institute of International Affairs. Accessed 6 December 2024, https://saiia.org.za/wp-content/uploads/2014/07/Policy-Briefing-96.pdf

2 The resurgence of coups d'état in West Africa and the Sahel

Collin Olebogeng Mongale and Keaobaka Tsholo

Introduction

The recent wave of coups d'état and unconstitutional changes of government that have engulfed West Africa and the Sahel are not new phenomena. Since the onset of independence, military coups have been a common occurrence in African states. Between the 1960s and 2012, Africa has experienced over 200 military coups – both successful and unsuccessful (Barka & Ncube 2012) Suleiman (2021) asserts that, between 1958 and 2008, the West Africa region, which has been labelled a 'coup belt', experienced the highest number of coups d'état in Africa, accounting for 44.4 per cent of coups on the continent. Often, coup plotters justified their reasons for executing a coup d'état using grievances such as corruption, mismanagement, and poverty among other factors (Tazoacha 2022). On the other hand, because of greed, rooted in aspirations to cling to state power for unlimited amounts of time, some African heads of states have amended the constitutions of their countries and extended their term of office to what amounts to 'president for life'. In addition, the handing over of state control from the old regime to the new government has often been met with chaos and violence.

In the early months of 2021, four African leaders, who had each been in power for about three decades, started additional terms in office as head of state. These are Denis Sassou Nguesso in the Republic of Congo (7th term), Idriss Itno Deby in Chad (6th term), Yoweri Museveni in Uganda (6th term), and Ismail Omar Guelleh in Djibouti (5th term). All these presidents have evaded the prescribed two-term limits as established in their country's constitutions. These tendencies reflect democratic backsliding in Africa, as constitutionalism has slowly been replaced by 'strong-man rule' in which power resonates around the elite-executive. Such strong-man rule is often characterised by suppression of human rights, limited opposition (due to fears of persecution), media censorship, weak institutional checks and balances, and a biased electoral commission. Since 2019, a third of all African elections are alleged to have been tainted by the circumvention of presidential term limits (Siegle & Cook 2021), which leads to a democratic deficit on the continent.

In West Africa and the Sahel coups d'état increased between 2020 and 2022. Guinea Bissau, Guinea, Mali, Chad, Sudan, and Burkina Faso have suffered a series of attempted military takeovers and also a few that were successful (Amoateng 2022). The 2022 Ibrahim Index of African Governance (Mo Ibrahim Foundation 2022) records 11 coup attempts in the preceding three years (2020–2022), with seven of them (mainly from West Africa and the Sahel) being successful. The year 2021 saw yet another fall of democracy in West Africa and the Sahel as successful military takeovers were staged in Chad, Mali, and Sudan, the latter being considered the coup capital of the world (Garang 2022). In February 2022, Col. Paul Henri Damiba seized power in a successful coup d'état in Burkina Faso, toppling the civilian government of President Marc Roch Christian Kabore. In the same year in Guinea-Bissau an attempt was made to overthrow President Umaro Sissoco Embalo. United Nations (UN) chief Antonio Gutters labelled the resurgence of coups d'état in West Africa and the Sahel as an 'epidemic of coups' that may spill over to neighbouring countries and other regions in Africa (BBC News 2023). The influence of external forces at different times but especially in the 20th century is of grave concern because it has played a pivotal role in perpetuating conflicts and fuelling coups in West Africa and the Sahel.

The challenges of political fragility in West Africa and the Sahel have resulted in deteriorating security conditions, which inhibit development and hinder the implementation of Aspirations (3) and (4) of Agenda 2063 – to ensure 'an Africa of good governance, democracy, respect for human rights, justice and the rule of law' and 'a peaceful and secure Africa', respectively (African Union Commission 2015). So, the unfolding challenges in West Africa and the Sahel raise concerns about the relevance of regional organisations, including the Economic Community of West African States (ECOWAS) and the African Union (AU), in ensuring the maintenance of good governance, peace, and security in West Africa.

The AU adopted normative frameworks such as the 2000 Lomé Declaration and the 2007 African Charter on Democracy, Elections and Governance in an attempt to ensure good governance and democratic consolidation in the African continent. These frameworks provide principles or values to which sovereign states should abide. They include:
- respect for the Constitution and the rule of law;
- separation of powers, and an independent judiciary;
- the principle of democratic change and recognition of a role for the opposition;
- the organisation of free and regular elections; and
- guarantee of freedom of expression and freedom of the press, including guaranteeing access to the media for all political stakeholders.

The commonalities between the Lomé Declaration (African Union 2000) and the African Charter on Democracy, Elections and Governance (African Union 2007) are that both these normative frameworks perceive coups d'état as a huge threat to democratic government, peace, and security. Moreover, these normative frameworks suggest actions and measures for dealing with the perpetrators of coups and unconstitutional governments, and countries that support these actions. Nevertheless, the extent to which these measures have been executed is questionable as different coups have been treated in differently by the AU and the Economic Community of West African States (ECOWAS), leaving the perception that there are 'good coups' and 'bad coups' in Africa (Ikome 2007).

This study employs a descriptive and explorative method, and a qualitative literature assessment. Theoretically, the chapter is based on greed-versus-grievances and neopatrimonial theories, which help to explain the resurgence of coups d'état in West Africa and the Sahel. The guiding assumption of this chapter is that these coups vary greatly, and include classical military coups, constitutional coups, dynastic coups – as was seen in Chad in 2021 – and soft coups. Furthermore, coups d'état do not occur in a vacuum but are triggered by various drivers, including greed on the part of presidents and soldiers and genuine grievances such as threats of terrorism, political fragility, and corrupt and failed democratic governments, among others. Some coups have been exacerbated by influence from Russia, China, the United States of America, and/ or some European countries like France and Britain, who have used Africa as a battleground to fight their proxy wars.

Theoretical framework

Greed versus grievances theory

Contemporary asymmetric conflicts in Africa have been explained in terms of greed versus grievances (Collier, Hoeffler & Rohner 2009). Grievances refer to group interests such as socioeconomic benefits and political inclusion (Hoeffler 2011) that can be accommodated through collective action, while greed is a private incentive driving individuals who gain private rewards from participating in a rebellion or a civil war. Against this backdrop, this chapter employs the greed versus grievances theory to explain the causes of coups d'état in West Africa and the Sahel. This phenomenon is compounded by neopatrimonialism – the systemised corrupt and clandestine activities within official political institutes in which greed occurs and how these ultimately leads to grievances.

Greed theory

The theory of greed reflects competition over natural resources. Atanasiu (2024) argues that economic factors are believed to be the main cause for the outbreak of civil wars, as evidenced by the 'greedy behaviour' of rebels who organise themselves as insurgents. In this context, Hirshleifer (2001) states that 'no profitable opportunity for violence would go unused', suggesting that conflict is inevitable if rebellion is materially feasible (Mongale 2022).

The theory of greed versus grievances further explains that, in a civil war, the rebel groups may challenge the government, which does not deliver any public good to constituents, as rebellion can be perceived as producing a public good (Ives & Breslawski 2022). However, the notion of 'public good' is often exploited by rebel groups who topple their governments under the pretext of striving for the public good, only to create a 'private club good' of elites once they assume power. Moreover, because competition for resources is a known feature of modern-day conflict, these new wars that play out in one country can be categorised as resource wars (Shaw 2000) in which resources serve as an end to justify the means of civil war (Hoeffler 2011). Atanasiu (2024) argues that resource wars usually occur where there is already political instability caused by war, and that they are usually aimed at personal economic gains. As such, resource wars are fought with the sole intention of the exploitation of resources by one section of the population at the expense of the other (Hirshleifer 2001).

Resources such as oil and diamonds are easily exploited, so, if they are not properly managed, there may be violent disputes over access to, and ownership of, these resources. Funding from the diaspora or – mostly during the Cold War – aid from a superpower can increase the probability of victory for rebel groups, and access to military supplies and weapons can perpetuate and prolong the duration of civil conflicts.

Greed theory indicates that combatants' incentives for self-enrichment, including opportunities for mobilisation for rebellion, are created by access to natural and financial resources (Ballentine & Nitzschke 2003). In this sense, competition for control over these resources results in separatist conflicts and serve as a challenge to peace and security because the losers may be denied their human rights by the winners.

Grievances theory

The grievances theory suggests that the reasons behind internal conflicts are best defined as 'justice-seeking' (Collier & Hoeffler 2002). This theory comprises sub-themes such as relative deprivation and horizontal inequality as triggers of rebellions against the state.

Relative deprivation theory is often listed as the reason for the emergence of social movements, resulting from political grievances. Such grievances may breed terrorism, riots, civil wars, coups d'état and other forms of social deviation (De la Sablonnière & Tougas 2008). Relative deprivation is defined as the difference between what an individual or a group believes they deserve and what they actually have or receive in reality – the difference between ambition and achievement. For example, the achievement of an educational certificate raises the hopes and aspirations of young people, but unemployment causes disappointment and might result in conflict (Murshed & Tadjoeddin 2007).

The theory of relative deprivation has been used to explain how civil war is linked to discontent stemming from the denial of political, economic or social rights (Atanasiu 2024). Relative deprivation is a subjective dissatisfaction that seems to trouble many people (Janse 2020). This dissatisfaction is caused by comparing one person's situation with another's. Usually, individuals exposed to relative social deprivation feel that they deserve to have or receive the same as others (Gurr 1970). So, the theory of relative deprivation has formed the basis for using grievance as a justification for civil war, and civil war is linked to discontent stemming from the denial of political, economic, or social rights (Atanasiu 2024).

Horizontal inequalities between groups may be based on ethnicity, religion, language, or tribal affiliations (Siroky et al. 2020). These are known to be important causes of contemporary civil war and sectarian strife but they do not usually cause routine violence. Inequality and poverty serve as important drivers of social exclusion, while conflict, social unrest and instability are its manifestation.

The contribution of greed versus grievances in the explanation of civil war is important because both theories help to explain why groups or people rebel. For instance, anti-government rebellions by civil society groups in Sudan, Burkina Faso, and Guinea were caused by failure to provide basic services including developmental projects. There have also been rebellions in Mali, Niger, Burkina Faso, and Guinea, where military juntas executed coups d'état under the guise of battling growing insurgency and terrorism, claiming that the democratically elected states had not provided sufficient resources for the security forces. The greed versus grievances theory remains key for studying civil wars because it is vital to understand the reasons behind people's grievances to prevent future hostilities, which might hold back human security and human development. However, as the above narrative implies, the existence of grievances might result in greed among relatively deprived people. As such, rebellion employed under the cause of justice seeking might result in loot seeking by bandits who use grievances as an excuse to exert their own interests.

Neopatrimonialism theory

The greed versus grievance theory leads directly to the broader relevance of neopatrimonialism. Neopatrimonialism refers to the clandestine network(s) of informal political institutions that undermine the legitimacy of the formal political institutions of democratic constitutions (Tsholo 2021). This informal patronage is a consequence of greed, which has inspired many coups as explained above. The greed versus grievance theory is important because it explains how dysfunctional entities and tyrannical political systems lead to grievances that can ultimately result in military takeovers, thereby perpetuating the cycle of violence and deprivation.

Historical background of democratic reversals leading to military coups

From the late 1950s in the aftermath of the Second World War, many former colonies in Africa gained political independence and – in theory – democratically elected governments. However, internal power struggles and military coups have become a commonplace means of taking power, leading to the reversal of democracy and its values. Letki (2016) describes democratic reversals as incomplete levels of democratic values in political institutions and procedures when compared with the theoretical ideal of a democratic government. Kali and Moeketsi (2019) describe democratic reversals as the inability of states to move from instability, uncertainty, and vulnerability. These three factors are highlighted because this chapter postulates that military coups are, to a certain extent, responsible for political instability, which leaves states insecure (or uncertain) and vulnerable to socioeconomic challenges. Many post-colonial states in Africa are characterised by greed and neopatrimonialism with their leaders denying accountability for the declining socioeconomic conditions of their constituents. This has led to mass dissatisfaction and disgruntled populations who are unhappy with the sociopolitical and economic dichotomy between leaders and constituents. The leaders' greed and constituencies' grievances tend towards a trend of democratic reversals in many African states.

McGowan (2003) posits that, over a period of 45 years (January 1956–December 2001), 48 independent sub-Saharan African states experienced a total of 80 successful coups, 108 coup attempts, and 139 coup plots. This trend indicates that sub-Saharan African countries do not respect their post-WWII commitment to adhere to democratic principles despite the fact that all African states committed to democratic values at their independence. Hilal Khashan (2012) cautions that, although the Arab Spring was meant to usher in democratic systems in the Middle East North Africa region, genuine democratic values are 'misunderstood' by many Arab people who – along with some scholars – reject the concept of advancing the principles of democracy in Africa. Thompson (2016) argues that many African post-colonial states have failed to reach their full potential in terms of development and economic growth as a result of political instability partially caused by undemocratic military coups, which are largely due to democratic deficits. In most cases this is because there is a lack of effort by African incumbents in enforcing practices that elevate levels of democracy in political institutions, which ultimately leads to democratic backslide and deficit. These democratic backslides and deficits then leave Africans disgruntled. Military coups often take advantage of such sociopolitical situations through their ability to control access to state violence. In that some military coups justified as 'corrective action' or restoring democracy, they end up benefiting only the generals and further defeating democracy instead of restoring its process and practices. Dersso (2021) further argues that 'after all, in almost all cases, the military and other security services are the primary means of enforcement of authoritarian and repressive regimes'.

This dissatisfaction has often led to military coups to remove the disgruntling political authority and replace it with another one for better governance and standard of living. However, this has not always been the case in Africa. Most of the coups have not redistributed political power by removing political authorities as Olafsson (2020) suggests. Inter alia, we argue that, after overthrowing an 'undemocratic' administration and assuming political authority, military rule furthers the democratic reversals – often due to greed. This is because a military coup is not democratic but authoritative by nature. Hence, governments that assume power through military coups, tend to consolidate their power through coercion and suppression of any form of opposition. Moreover, in some states where coups have taken place, military rule has paved the way for tyranny instead of continuing the decolonisation process through strengthening democratic institutions. This form of political fragility, and its accompanying insecurity, is characteristic of West Africa and the Sahel, and often serves as a breeding ground for the resurgence of unconstitutional changes of government.

Political fragility and insecurity in West Africa and the Sahel

West Africa and the Sahel regions, like any other regions on the African continent, have faced the challenge of political fragility and insecurity since independence in the early 1960s. The countries that make up the Sahel and Lake Chad Basin regions are critical to the stability of West Africa, because they represent half of the sub-continent, and most have been battling with insecurity for years (Gatto 2022). ECOWAS is the regional body responsible for preserving peace and security, including the promotion of democracy, in West Africa. West Africa and the Sahelian states are battling multifaceted challenges and vulnerabilities, including political fragility, orchestrated conflicts, climate change, violent extremism, organised crime, political instability (weak and declining institutions), and poverty (Clarke 2021).

One of the drivers of state fragility in West Africa and the Sahel is the lack of good governance (Ayendele & Ilunga 2022). These assertions are supported by Sampaio (2022) who argues that there is a lack of effective economic policies, most governments are authoritarian, democracy is declining, opposition parties are beleaguered, the media is censored, and identity politics is rife in these regions. Consequently, these challenges reflect the absence of good governance, exorbitant levels of poverty, and an inability to root out despotism. This can be inferred from Sudan, where Omar al-Bashir has reigned for 30 years. He is accused of violating human rights and committing war crimes in Darfur, and is constantly avoiding the International Criminal Court (Mumbere 2019). As a result of growing discontent against his authoritarian government, al-Bashir was deposed through a military takeover in 2019 (Osman & Bearak 2019). Following his removal from power, civilians took to the streets their collective joy to celebrate his removal from power, thus glorifying the military – not for taking power but for removing al-Bashir's oppressive regime.

As postulated by Dersso (2021), the celebrations were more about the end of the previous regime than the military intervening in politics and occupying – more accurately, controlling – the democratic institutions of government. These celebrations of military interventions are understandable because of how oppressive and undemocratic the previous dictatorial regimes were. However, such celebrations must not be confused with welcoming the military as a legitimate incumbent. This is because military occupations, being authoritative in nature, also negate the concept of democracy based on their resources.

In Burkina Faso, the government of Blaise Compaoré was characterised by numerous challenges that worsened the crisis of political fragility and insecurity in the country. Compaoré served as the President of Burkina Faso for 27 years. During his administration, he had looted state resources for personal benefit, which led to a deepened crisis of poverty, unemployment, and deteriorating security for both civilians and the military. The military, allegedly, had insufficient ammunition and other military equipment to battle the growing jihadist insurgency (Nebo 2020). It was these challenges that led to the 2014 mass protests that ended the twenty-seventh regime of Blaise Compaoré. Like the Arab Spring, in which mass protests had succeeded in removing authoritarian regimes, Burkina Faso too had shown the 'power of the brick' which can serve as an alternative mechanism for changing regimes – especially if the ballot process has been circumvented and manipulated to avoid smooth transition of power (Taoko, Cowell & Callimachi 2014). These protests came after Compaoré, and his party, Congress for Democracy and Progress, attempted to amend Article 37 of the constitution, which prevented them from seeking yet another term in the 2015 elections.

A military coup brought an abrupt halt to democracy in Mali, which had enjoyed a stable democracy for 20 years (Alozieuwa 2013). Fornof and Cole (2020) posit that terrorists used the leadership vacuum to extend their operations by attempting to take control of the whole country, after having already occupied the towns of Timbuktu, Kidal, and Gao. France and neighbouring Chad supplied military aid until January 2013, when the conflict escalated, leading to a humanitarian crisis, security challenges, disruption of supply routes, and food shortages (Thompson 2016).

Although almost two thirds of West African state members are perceived to be partially democratic (Tejpar and De Albuquerque 2015) poor governance and exorbitant levels of corruption remain key causes of political fragility. In recent years, Burkina Faso, Côte d'Ivoire, Guinea-Bissau, Mali, Niger, Sudan, and Chad have been subject to unconstitutional changes of governments or military takeovers.

In her thesis on old and new wars, Kaldor (2013) highlights that the modern-day international system is characterised by asymmetric warfare (new wars), in which combatants actively challenges their governments due to growing discontent. In this sense, violent intra-state conflicts, usually involving non-state actors such as jihadists, political rebels, bandits, and self-proclaimed vigilante groups, are steadily increasing in West Africa and the Sahel regions (Abington 2019).

The crisis of terrorism is influenced by weak institutions, porous borders, historical grievances, and bad governance. Amongst the countries that have been vulnerable to growing militia operations and attacks are Niger, Mali, Burkina Faso, and Nigeria. According to data collected by the African Centre for the Study and Research on Terrorism (2022), there was a rapid increase in the number of terror attacks in 2018 and 2019. Attacks in Nigeria and Niger were perpetrated by Boko Haram and its breakaway group, the Islamic State of West Africa Province (ISWAP), Mali remains an epicentre of Al-Qaeda and ISWAP, and Jama'a Nusrat al-Islam wal Muslim (JNIM) and the Islamic State in the Greater Sahara were responsible for attacks in Burkina Faso and Niger (Apau & Ziblim 2019).

In total, between January 2019 and December 2021, West Africa and the Sahel recorded the highest number of terrorist attacks in Africa. As of April 2022, West Africa had recorded 2 602 attacks which led to 10 899 deaths (African Centre for the Study and Research on Terrorism 2022). Burkina Faso has been continuously faced with terrorist attacks since the successful popular movement that ousted former President Blaise Compaoré in 2015 (Onukwue 2022). These attacks have resulted in numerous deaths and population displacement of an estimated 1.5 million in West Africa and the Sahel. Incidents of terrorist attacks had increased drastically, from 69 attacks in 2016 to 339 attacks in 2019 (Abington 2019).

In Nigeria, Boko Haram has challenged the state's monopoly on the legal use of force as they have launched terror attacks against civilians and military personnel. The group's ideology of refusing to subscribe to the norms of democracy and advocating for strict adherence to Sharia Law has created instability in Nigeria (Onuoha & George 2015). This was evident in the mass abduction of more than 260 schoolgirls in Chibok, Borno State, in 2014. This abduction validated the group's mission of weaponising women and girls as part of their terror agenda (Sempijja & Mongale 2021). Iyi (2018) asserted that women weaponised by Boko Haram were made to act as spies, arms smugglers, recruiters, reconnoiterers, and suicide bombers. Pearson (2018) indicates that Boko Haram first deployed a female suicide bomber in June 2014, in an attack against a military barracks in Nigeria's Gombe State. Four years later, in February 2018, Boko Haram had deployed a recorded number of 469 female suicide bombers, of which 240 had been arrested before executing these acts.

In other parts of West Africa and the Sahel, JNIM has expanded its influence by instigating feuds between rival communities and offering to protect the victims. One of the services that governments in both regions have failed to provide to civilians is security (Sempijja & Mongale 2022). The deteriorating social contract between governments and their people has resulted in a wide gap between what the people need and what their governments offer them. So, if governments cannot provide public goods, terrorist groups fill this vacuum by offering the very same basic services to the people. In this way, the process of radicalisation begins with the state's failure to offer basic services to its constituents. This is evident in cases in which terrorist groups offer employment opportunities to the youth of both the Sahel and West African region, which both suffer high levels of non-literacy, youth unemployment, poverty, and other related socioeconomic challenges. In essence, violent extremism thrives in areas where the state fails to deal adequately with people's grievances, and in places where sovereignty is contested (Çonkar 2020).

Considering the demographics in the Sahel region for instance, although young people constitute the largest segment of the population in all Sahel countries, the sad reality is that their social status and economic opportunities are limited, thus lowering their prospects of acquiring decent employment. Dersso (2021) writes that 60 per cent of the Sahelian population is under 25, they lack education, they are unemployed, and they face endemic poverty and exclusion, all of which are fertile ground for disenfranchisement, grievances, and youth radicalisation. Because of frustration over lack of opportunities, including the perception of neglect, many youths had been drawn to joining the insurgence groups in the region. In Nigeria, 10.5 million children are not at school, and 70 per cent of rural children experience poverty and are severely exposed to violent extremism (Gonzalez-Perez 2011).

In a nutshell, it is these demographic challenges that enable jihadist groups to fill existing vacuums by proposing alternative public good and security to vulnerable communities, who accepted them just to survive (Pearson 2018). To a larger extent, these challenges of political fragility and security are often used to justify the resurgence of coups d'état in West Africa and the Sahel.

Findings and analysis

Traditionally, the primary function of the military is to protect state borders and ensure the safety and security of citizens against external threats. However, what has become apparent in West Africa and the Sahel is that those who have sworn in to protect their countries' constitutions have now turned their guns against their own governments (Tazoacha 2022). As a result of deteriorating governance and security, military juntas have used the leadership vacuum to seize power under the pretext of battling security crises such as terrorism and intra-communal conflicts, and use constituents' genuine grievances to advance their power and ambitions to take over state control. According to Akinola and Makumbe (2022), African military leaders, who are the legitimate custodians of weapons and munitions, have been more liable to utilise these weapons and arms illegitimately, driven by greed. This gives rise to questions around the extent to which these unconstitutional changes of government will affect or improve the security apparatus in the affected countries. Countries in

West Africa and the Sahel that have experienced coups d'état are those that have been battling with peace and security threats such as terrorism, intra-community conflicts (especially farmer–herder conflicts), poverty, unemployment, and corruption (Pearson 2018). The drivers of coups d'état in West Africa and the Sahel are greed and grievances, which will be explored in that order.

Greed as a driver of coups d'état in West Africa and the Sahel

As shown, many of the military takeovers in West Africa and the Sahel region have mainly been caused by greed, which reflects the competition over natural resources. Africa is the most naturally resourced continent, with West Africa and the Sahel producing oil, diamonds, gold, limestone, iron ore, and bauxite, among others. Many heads of state, such as the Sudanese Omar al-Bashir, have acted against their constitutional obligations to be democratic by extending their terms in office due to greed, so they can retain control and leverage over these natural resources and other aspects of the economy for individual financial benefit. To execute this greed, there needs to be a clandestine network of informal political institutes (El-Gizouli 2019). Sudan has one of the largest expanses of arable land in North Africa and the Sahel due to its strategic geographical location along the Nile River (Lowings 2019). Despite this, Sudanese people have had little to no access to these lands because they have been sold to foreign companies and individuals, due to neopatrimonialism.

Naturally, such socioeconomic inequity and the high cost of living is seen by most Sudanese as being due to greed on the part of al-Bashir. As overall Sudanese government expenditure fell between 2015 and 2017, military expenditure increased. Lowings (2019) suggests that this indicates that the government is prioritising the military despite the decline of public funds. Essentially, while the Sudanese economy was declining mainly due to rampant corruption by al-Bashir, the military (under his control) was still funded to protect him from grievances that might emerge. Eventually, as the Cameroonian Bayart (1993) describes, greed compounded by patronage in these instances inspires 'politics of the belly' and leaves many West African and Sahel states burdened by socioeconomic atrocities caused by the people who were meant to lead them into development. Ultimately, greed and patronage lead to grievances, which give rise to military takeovers.

Despite military coups being justified as actions that are in the interests of the people, they have repeatedly proven not to be the case. As Olafsson (2020) describes, coups that are executed in the interest of society redistribute power once attained, use popular support to act in the interests of the state, do not focus on retribution in attaining power, and make sure that no one is hurt in the process. However, it is evident that most states in West Africa and the Sahel are led by individuals who abuse this notion of 'public good' because of greed compounded by patronage.

Chad is a case in point where the notion of public good has been exploited by the military. In April 2021, the former President of Chad, Idriss Deby, was killed by

Libya-based rebels during an incursion. He had been head of state for just over 30 years. This could have been the moment for democracy to thrive, but Idriss Deby's son, Mahamat Deby, headed a 15-member military council and took over the state by suspending the constitution and pronouncing that transitional elections would take place after 18 months (Lacher 2022). According to the AU's Commission's Chairperson, Moussa Faki, this was not a classical military takeover (Djilo 2021). Faki pointed out that this would not be a problem for Chad as long as the interim overseers (the military) would stick to their promise that in 18 months there would be free and fair transitional elections. French President Emmanuel Macron said that France supported this notion only as a transitional process, and not as a dynastic succession, which would be viewed as greed.

However, after 18 months had passed, no elections had taken place. Mahamat Deby was said to be the interim President of Chad amidst conflicting ideologies and disagreements over which political system Chad should deploy – a unitary or a federal system (Lacher 2022). The interim presidency of Mahamat Deby threatened the possibilities of democratic practices in Chad and came to be considered dynastic. This section has negated Olafsson's (2020) assertions that military takeovers redistribute power in the interest of the state and the people, and Mahamat in Chad further proves that greed perverted by entitlement makes this impossible. Despite the takeover by the military not being violent, the aftermath of events still maintain the relics of typical militant behaviours in government that are motivated by greed. Notwithstanding its nature as a 'soft coup', this military takeover remains unconstitutional, and thus hinders the achievement of aspiration (3) and (4) of the AU's agenda 2063, while trampling upon the enshrined values of the 2000 Lomé declaration and the African Charter on Democracy, Elections and Governance of 2007.

Case studies like Sudan show how grievances can result in greed among people who were previously relatively deprived. The same liberators who take up arms to overthrow an authoritarian regime can easily be as authoritative, having used grievances as a decoy to benefit themselves and promote their self-interest.

Grievances as a driver of coups d'état in West Africa and the Sahel

Democratic governments are required to produce a conducive environment for human security and sustainable development. The concept of human security in this context refers to freedom from the fear of physical threats and freedom from want (Alkire 2003). The former entails freedom from fears of physical violence deriving from conflict and civil war, whereas the latter involves basic human needs like shelter, food, and education. Usually, democracy is closely linked to good governance, which can be defined as the transparent, efficient, and inclusive allocation of resources. Sadly, countries where democracy is disrupted and governance is questionable are prone to coups d'état because of growing discontent.

In Burkina Faso, for example, electoral integrity and human security declined and freedom of expression and digital rights were suppressed during the Blaise Compaoré regime (Schultes 2022). In 2014, Compaoré tried to amend the constitution so he could run for presidency again. This led to popular uprisings against his regime, and subsequently to his removal as the President of Burkina Faso after ruling the country for 27 years. After Compaorés fall, the civilian-led government of President Roch Marc Christian Kabore came into power in November 2015 through an electoral processes. This regime, in turn, was toppled in a military takeover led by Lieutenant-Colonel Paul Henri Damiba (Ochieng 2022). Like Compaoré, Kabore's removal was driven by grievances among state security forces, who claimed that he had failed to support the security force in their battles both the Islamic State (IS) and al-Qaeda. As of 2015, the country has been burdened with an intensifying wave of violence attributed to jihadist militants of both these groups, which has resulted into the killing of thousands and the displacement of more than two million people (Aljazeera 2022).

The prevalence of terrorist groups in Burkina Faso have led analysts to dub the country the epicentre of conflict in the Sahel. In June 2021, more than 100 people were killed in the northern village of Solhan in an attack supposedly executed by rebel militants who had crossed from neighbouring Mali, and 50 members of the state security forces were killed in attacks on the northern Inata military base in November 2021. These security threats gave Damiba a pretext to overthrow the civilian government of Kabore, thereby using citizens' genuine grievances to acquire power and gain control of the state. However, Damiba was, in turn, ousted by captain Ibrahim Traore in a military coup in 2022. Traore supposedly overthrew Damiba because he failed to handle the intensifying grievances of insecurity perpetuated by jihadist groups. Hence, in his ascendance to power, Traore emphasised a need to strengthen military operations and cooperation, and considered contracting the Russian mercenary organisation The Wagner Group to help combat the growing insurgency in the country (Aljazeera 2023).

The resurgence of coups d'état in West Africa and the Sahel has been closely tied to particular local grievances implicating the incumbent governments. In the context of Mali, these emanated from frustration over former president Ibrahim Boubacar Keita's inability to deal with the security crisis in the country because Mali, too, had experienced a growing number of insurgent attacks (Faulkner et al. 2020). Groups such as Al-Qaeda and ISWAP had carried out successful attacks against both civilians and state security forces, but issues of insecurity were not the only factor that led to Keita's removal. In 2020, public discontent and resentment pertaining to corruption and misappropriation of public funds began to manifest and, in March of that year, Keita was accused of manipulating parliamentary election results to consolidate his executive powers (Apau & Ziblim (2019).

In June of the same year, mass protests broke out in the capital of Bamako and other parts of Mali led by the June 5 movement and the Rally of Patriotic Forces (together known as M5-RFP), who demanded the resignation of the president. Likewise, Gurr (1970) in his theory of relative deprivation asserted that in situations where people believe they are deprived of public goods or material gains – especially those to which they feel entitled – they will most likely embark on a rebellion, especially if they have been exposed to these grievances and frustrations for a long time. Following public protests in Mali, the military took advantage of intensifying discontent against Keita, which created a leadership vacuum in the country. So, in August 2020, Ibrahim Keita was detained by Malian soldiers led by colonel Assimi Goïta, who was installed as interim leader (Aubyn, Ziblim & Apau 2022). In September 2020, Bah N'Daw was appointed by the coup leader Assimi Goïta as civilian interim president. In May 2021, President Bah N'Daw was ousted by a military coup led by Assimi Goïta, who was again installed as interim president, until the return to civilian government (Lacher 2022).

Guinea, which had been ruled by Alpha Conde since 2010, was not spared from the recent wave of military takeovers in West Africa. On 5 September 2021 President Alpha Conde's regime was toppled by the Special Forces Group led by Mamady Doumbouya, who justified the coup as responding to existing grievances throughout the country, saying,

> the socio-political and economic situations of the country, the dysfunction of republican institutions, the instrumentalisation of justice, the trampling of citizen's rights, the financial mismanagement … have led the republican army to live up to its responsibilities towards the people of Guinea. (Afrique 2021)

The response to the coup d'état in Guinea was international outrage and condemnation. The UN Secretary-General Antonio Guterres was quoted as saying 'I am personally following the situation in Guinea very closely. I strongly condemn any takeover of the government by force of the gun and call for the immediate release of President Alpha Conde' (Diallo 2021). In the same vein, Felix Tshisekedi, who served as the president of the AU and Moussa Faki Mahamat, who served as the president of the Commission of the AU, also reacted by condemning 'the overthrowing of the government and demanding that president Alpha Conde is released without delay' (Faulkner et al. 2020).

These incidents of unconstitutional changes of government are in violation of both the Lomé Declaration (African Union 2000) and the African Charter on Democracy, Elections and Governance (African Union 2007), including the ECOWAS protocol on good governance. It is in this context that ECOWAS has denounced all the coups discussed above, and imposed heavy sanctions against member states committing such violations. Sanctions imposed against Mali came after the military rule postponed elections that were scheduled to take place in February 2022 (Reuters 2022). However, double standards were applied to the coup in Chad by both ECOWAS and the AU. This was perhaps due to Chad's leading role in military intervention in the Sahel region where it is considered to be a key role player within the Multinational-Joint Task Force that was established to fight the growing insecurity in both regions. To prevent coups d'état, the AU and ECOWAS need to adopt a holistic approach and avoid being biased towards particular member states because such precedents encourage imitation: there is a perception that if one head of state can get away with it, others could too.

However, ECOWAS and the AU have been quick to respond to coups d'état, even if they have failed to react to the failures of governance throughout the region. So, it can be argued that the manner in which ECOWAS administers the region seems to promote corrupt governance and ignore democratic principles by not paying close attention to the implications of bad governance as one of the main triggers of military takeovers in the region.

The influence of global hegemons on military takeovers in West Africa and the Sahel

Many external players – mainly global hegemons from the West (United States of America) and the East (particularly Russia and China) – are using Africa as a power-play for their own interests. The Eastern global hegemons do not subscribe to the traditional democratic values advocated by the West and the US, so they have started to form significant military ties with African states and juntas to restrict the West's infiltration on the African continent. This is exactly how the capitalist US and the communist Soviet Union marked their spheres of ideological influence during the Cold War just before the end of the 20th century.

Russia has been a key player in the military rule in Mali in 2020, and – it is suspected – trained Malian military personnel in Moscow a year before the coup occurred. These military takeovers are not democratic just as the Eastern global hegemons do not subscribe to the liberal democratic order (Palmer, Bermudez & Jun 2024). This is key because it supports notions about what (and who) has externally and indirectly advanced the democratic deficit in which Africa finds itself. The penetration of global hegemons in Africa is only possible through a philosophical failure by Africans to advance their own affairs because of greed. For instance, Araoye (2021) stipulates that

> the relentless failure of Africa can be located in the thorough defeat of Pan-Africanism as a philosophy and ideology of political action and its associated drive to consolidate Africa's inherited colonial and post-colonial weaknesses into a continental unity, with the capacity to effectively leverage its interests as a legitimate global player. (Araoye 2021)

The implication is that Pan-Africanism is a philosophical aspiration to engage in action that calls for unity compounded by African progression. The lack thereof sees global hegemons increase their interests in former colonies in West Africa and the Sahel (Afrique 2021). This ultimately gives the global hegemons an opportunity to use African states as proxies and sponsor military takeovers to further their own interests in specific regions. In his book entitled *Neo-Colonialism: The Last Stage of Imperialism*, Kwame Nkrumah (1965) noted that this sense of interference from global hegemons (both West and East) 'seeks to fragment Africa, weaken African state institutions, prevent African unity and sovereignty, and thereby insert its power to subordinate the aspirations of the continent for pan-African consolidation'.

In the case of Africa, a fragmented and weakened continent sets the scene for more interference than unity for African states. The interference from global hegemons has gone beyond the establishment of military bases on the continent. Dossier no. 42, a publication by Tricontinental (2021), stipulates that, in the aftermath of the Northern Atlantic Treaty Organization's war on Libya in 2011, the Sahel region experienced more conflict caused by piracy, smuggling and, as this chapter has been arguing, military takeovers. This has led to France setting up the G-5 Sahel military arrangement, and the US setting drone bases that can conduct aerial surveillance in the Sahel and the Sahara Desert.

Conclusion

All coups are different, and they are carried out for different reasons and justifications, but some have similar motivating factors such as dissatisfaction based on corruption, mismanagement, and poverty. The Sahel region has been called 'the coup belt' because there have been so many coups there, not only recently, but historically too. Coups in Mali, Chad, and Sudan have made headlines globally. What they have in common is that the coups are inspired by the grievances of societies fed up with greed that leads to unconstitutional changes. The greed versus grievances theory explains why these waves of military takeovers occur, supported by neopatrimonialism that paves the way from greed to grievances. This chapter has illustrated how militias have abused and taken advantage of genuine grievances to propel military officials into illegitimate government positions that advance their interests at the expense of ordinary citizens.

A trend is noted that African states do not subscribe to the supranational AU's legislative frameworks such as the Lomé Declaration (African Union 2000) and the African Charter on Democracy, Elections and Governance (African Union 2007) that were put in place to curb these undemocratic behaviours that undermine the prospect of entrenching Africa in democratic practices and undo colonial legacies. Instead, the only penalties for these democratic deficits and backsliding come from the global superpowers of the West through sanctions. Nevertheless, interference in African affairs such as military coups by global hegemons from both East and West are not for the sake of the African country in question, but are, rather, a means of furthering their own interests in those specific states.

This is evidenced by France's involvement in, and comments on, the military takeovers in Chad and Mali. The mere fact that the French President chose to comment on those cases shows that, in fact, the comments are directed towards protecting France's interests in those states. The AU has proven to be less effective than the hegemons have in disciplining states that do not subscribe to the continental goals – for example, Agenda 2063, part of which is 'silencing the guns'. Wrong as these military takeovers are, they have revealed the lack of sovereignty of African states.

This study has revealed a clear pattern of authoritative leadership from (mostly democratically elected) African leaders since the dawn of their independence. Independence did not necessarily mean that African states had overcome the relics of colonialism. In fact, independence meant that economic sovereignty through democratisation was merely the next step after political sovereignty. However, this study has illustrated that the first step (political sovereignty) has been compromised by global hegemons, which raises the question of whether it had ever been achieved at all. As Tsholo (2021) argues, the problem with the process of democratisation in Africa is that it was not African in idea and execution. The unconstitutional extended terms in office by African leaders are a critical example of how greed and neopatrimonialism compromise democracy and thus create opportunities for people in the military to use weapons to consolidate power.

References & bibliography

Abington T (2019) Armies of women: The Syria crisis and the new war thesis. *E-international Relations Students*. Accessed 14 December 2024, https://www.e-ir.info/2019/03/27/armies-of-women-the-syria-crisis-and-the-new-war-thesis/

African Centre for the Study and Research on Terrorism (2022). Implications of coups d'état and political instability on terrorism and violent extremism in the Sahel. *African Journal on Terrorism*, Special Edition (October). Accessed 14 December 2024, https://au.int/sites/default/files/documents/42553-doc-African_Journal_on_Terrorism_Special_Edition_Oct.2022.pdf

African Union (2000) *The Lomé Declaration*. Accessed 14 December 2024, https://archives.au.int/handle/123456789/571

African Union (2007) *African Charter On Democracy, Elections and Governance*. Accessed 14 December 2024, https://au.int/en/treaties/african-charter-democracy-elections-and-governance

African Union Commission (2015) *Agenda 2063: The Africa we want; Framework document*. Accessed 6 December 2024, https://au.int/sites/default/files/documents/33126-doc-framework_document_book.pdf

Afrique J (2021) Guinea: International uproar after coup d'état against Alpha Conde. *The African Report* 6 September. Accessed 14 December 2024, https://www.theafricareport.com/124891/guinea-international-uproar-after-coup-detat-against-alpha-conde/

Akinola AO & Makumbe RC (2022) *The resurgence of military coups and democratic reversals in Africa*. Johannesburg: Institute For Pan-African Thought and Conversation

Aljazeera (2022) Burkina Faso's coup and political situation: All you need to know. *Aljazeera* 5 October. Accessed 14 December 2024, https://www.aljazeera.com/news/2022/10/5/coup-in-burkina-faso-what-you-need-to-know

Aljazeera (2023) Burkina Faso confirms it has ended French military accord. *Aljazeera* 23 January. Accessed 14 December 2024, https://www.aljazeera.com/news/2023/1/23/burkina-faso-ends-french-military-accord-says-will-defend-itself

Alkire S (2003) *A conceptual framework for human security*. Working paper, CRISE Department of International Development, University of Oxford

Alozieuwa SH (2013) The March 22, 2012 coup in Mali: Lessons and implications for democracy in the West Africa subregion in the wave of transnational terrorism. *Democracy and Security* 9(4): 383–397

Amoateng N (2022) Military coups in Africa: A continuation of politics by other means? *ACCORD* 9 August. Accessed 14 December 2024, https://www.accord.org.za/conflict-trends/military-coups-in-africa-a-continuation-of-politics-by-other-means/

Apau R & Ziblim I (2019) *Beyond rhetoric: Addressing the terrorism situation in the Sahel*. Policy Brief 001. African Centre for the Study and Research on Terrorism. Accessed 14 December 2024, http://caert.org.dz/Policy-Briefs/POLICY BRIEF 001.pdf

Araoye A (2021) Delineating pan-Africanism from contemporary conceptual deflections. *History Compass* 19(2). Accessed 3 March 2025, https://compass.onlinelibrary.wiley.com/toc/14780542/2021/19/2

Atanasiu M (2024) Conflict in Guinea: Roots of Guinean conflict from the perspective of 'greed versus grievance' theory. In J Besenyő, L Issaev & A Korotayev (Eds) *Terrorism and political contention: New perspectives on North Africa and the Sahel region*. Switzerland: Springer Cham

Aubyn FK, Ziblim I & Apau R (2022) *Coups d'état and political instability in the western Sahel: Implications for the fight against terrorism and violent extremism*. Policy Paper, April. African Centre for the Study and Research on Terrorism. Accessed 14 December 2024, https://www.peaceau.org/uploads/final-policy-paper-coups200522.pdf

Ayendele OJ & Ilunga YY (2022) *African solutions to African problems: A pathway to the region's recovery in a post-COVID world*. Conference paper, UN Office of the Special Advisor on Africa (February). Accessed 14 December 2024, https://www.un.org/osaa/sites/www.un.org.osaa/files/6._ayandele_ilunga_unosaa_final_paper_draft_ii_osaa.pdf

Ballentine K & Nitzschke H (2003) *Beyond greed and grievance: Policy lessons from studies in the political economy of armed conflict*. Stockholm: International Peace Academy

Barka HB & Ncube M (2012) *Political fragility in Africa: Are military coups d'état a never-ending phenomenon*. Abidjan: African Development Bank. Accessed 15 December 2024, https://www.afdb.org/sites/default/files/documents/publications/economic_brief_-_political_fragility_in_africa_are_military_coups_detat_a_never_ending_phenomenon.pdf

Bayart JF (1993) *The State in Africa: The politics of the belly*. New York: Longman

BBC News (2023) *Gabon coup: The latest in a series of military takeovers on the continent*. 30 August. Accessed 14 December 2024, https://www.bbc.com/news/world-africa-46783600

Clarke G (2021) *Sahel crisis: Humanitarian needs and requirements overview*. United Nations Office for the Coordination of Humanitarian Affairs (April). Accessed 14 December 2024, https://www.unocha.org/publications/report/burkina-faso/sahel-crisis-humanitarian-needs-and-requirements-overview-april-2021

Collier P & Hoeffler A (2002) On the incidence of civil war in Africa. *Journal of Conflict Resolution* 46(1): 13–28

Collier P, Hoeffler A & Rohner D (2009) Beyond greed and grievance: Feasibility and civil war. *Oxford Economic Chapters* 61(1): 1–27

Çonkar AB (2020) *Development and security challenges in the Sahel region.* Nato Parliamentary Assembly (11 December). Accessed 14 December 2024, https://www.nato-pa.int/document/2020-development-and-security-challenges-sahel-region-conkar-042-gsm-20-e

De la Sablonnière R & Tougas F (2008) Relative deprivation and social identity in times of dramatic social change: The case of nurses. *Journal of Applied Social Psychology* 38(9): 2293–2314. Accessed 14 December 2024, https://onlinelibrary.wiley.com/doi/abs/10.1111/j.1559-1816.2008.00392.x

Dersso SA (2021) Coups are always a bad idea: Even the popular ones. *Mail & Guardian* 21 September. Accessed 14 December 2024, https://mg.co.za/africa/2021-09-21-coups-are-always-a-bad-idea-even-the-popular-ones/

Diallo F (2021) Guinea: Who is Mamady Doumbouya, the man once closest to Alpha Conde? *The African Report* 7 September. Accessed 14 December 2024, https://www.theafricareport.com/125045/guinea-who-is-mamady-doumbouya-the-man-once-closest-to-alpha-conde/

Djilo F (2021) AU balancing act on Chad's coup sets a disturbing precedent. *ISS Today* 2 June. Accessed 14 December 2024, https://issafrica.org/iss-today/au-balancing-act-on-chads-coup-sets-a-disturbing-precedent

El-Gizouli M (2019) *The fall of al-Bashir: Mapping contestation forces in Sudan.* Arab Reform Initiative. Accessed 14 December 2024, https://www.arab-reform.net/publication/the-fall-of-al-bashir-mapping-contestation-forces-in-sudan/

Faulkner CM, Johnson J, Powell J & Schlel R (2020) Behind the causes of the coup in Mali: And what happens next. *Prospect Magazine* 24 August. Accessed 14 December 2024, https://www.prospectmagazine.co.uk/world/mali-coup-keita-causes-why-what-next

Fornof E & Cole E (2020) Five things to know about Mali's coup. United States Institute of Peace. Accessed 15 December 2024, https://www.usip.org/publications/2020/08/five-things-know-about-malis-coup

Garang YJ (2022) The decline of democracy and the rise of coup d'états in sub-Saharan Africa: Reflections and lessons. *AfricLaw* 25 February. Accessed 15 December 2024, https://africlaw.com/2022/02/25/the-decline-of-democracy-and-the-rise-of-coup-detats-in-sub-saharan-africa-reflections-and-lessons/

Gatto J (2022) *Breaking the cycle: Military coups in West Africa.* Fragile States Index. Accessed 15 December, https://fragilestatesindex.org/2022/07/08/breaking-the-cycle-military-coups-in-west-africa/

Gonzalez-Perez M (2011) The false Islamization of female suicide bombers. *Gender Issues* 28(1–2): 50–65

Gurr TD (1970). *Why men rebel?* Princeton, NJ: Centre of International Studies, Princeton UP

Hirshleifer J (2001) Conflict and rent-seeking success functions: Ratio vs. difference models of relative success. In AA Lockard & G Tullock (Eds) *Efficient rent-seeking*. Boston, MA: Springer

Hoeffler A (2011) Greed versus grievances: A useful conceptual distinction in the study of civil war? *Studies in Ethnicity and Nationalism* 11(2): 274–284

Ikome FN (2007) *Good coups and bad coups: The limits of the African Union's injunction on unconstitutional changes of power in Africa.* Occasional Paper no. 5. Institute for Global Dialogue. Accessed 15 December 2024, https://igd.org.za/publication/igd-occasional-paper-55/

Ives B & Breslawski J (2022) Greed, grievance, or graduates? Why do men rebel? *Journal of Peace Research*, 59(3): 319–336. Accessed 15 December 2024, https://doi.org/10.1177/00223433211014269

Iyi JM (2018) The weaponisation of women by Boko Haram and the prospects of accountability. In JM Iyi & H Strydom (Eds) *Boko Haram and international law.* Cham, Switzerland: Springer. Accessed 15 December 2024, https://www.researchgate.net/publication/326012731_The_Weaponisation_of_Women_by_Boko_Haram_and_the_Prospects_of_Accountability

Janse B (2020) *Relative deprivation theory by Gary Runciman.* Toolshero. Accessed 15 December 2024, https://www.toolshero.com/sociology/relative-deprivation-theory/

Kaldor M (2013) *New and old wars: Organised violence in a global era.* New York: John Wiley & Sons

Kali M & Moeketsi M (2019) Democratic reversals: Examining the role of the armed forces and Southern African Development Community in Lesotho. *International Journal of Research and Scientific Innovation* 3(11): 140–145. Accessed 15 December 2024, https://ideas.repec.org/a/bjc/journl/v3y2019i11p140-145.html

Khashan H (2012) The Arab Spring and democratisation in the Middle East. *World Affairs: The Journal of International Issues* 16(4): 132–147. Accessed 15 December, https://www.jstor.org/stable/48566260

Lacher W (2022) *Chad's Crisis-prone transition: Dynastic consolidation and its risks.* Comment 67/2022. Stiftung Wissenschaft und Politik. Accessed 15 December 2024, https://www.swp-berlin.org/10.18449/2022C67/

Letki N (2016) Democratic deficit, definition. *Encyclopaedia Britannica.* Accessed 15 December 2024, https://www.britannica.com/topic/democratic-deficit

Lowings B (2019) *Sudan: Economy and military in the fall of Bashir.* Policy Brief (April). Brussels International Centre. Accessed 15 December 2024, https://bic-rhr.com/sites/default/files/inline-files/Sudan Economy and Military in Fall of Bashir.pdf

McGowan P (2003) African military coups d'état, 1956–2001: Frequency, trends and distribution. *Journal of Modern African Studies* 41(3): 339–370

Mo Ibrahim Foundation (2022) Ibrahim Index of African Governance. Accessed 13 December 2024, https://mo.ibrahim.foundation/sites/default/files/2023-01/2022-index-report.pdf

Mongale CO (2022) Social discontent or criminality? Navigating the nexus between urban riots and criminal activities in Gauteng and KwaZulu-Natal provinces, South Africa (2021). *Frontiers in Sustainable Cities.* 4: 865255. Accessed 15 December 2024, https://www.frontiersin.org/journals/sustainable-cities/articles/10.3389/frsc.2022.865255/full

Mumbere D (2019) One year later: Sudanese celebrate Bashir's fall from grace. *AfricaNews* 19 December. Accessed 15 December 2024, https://www.africanews.com/2019/12/19/one-year-later-sudanese-celebrate-bashir-s-fall-from-grace//

Murshed SM & Tadjoeddin MZ (2007) Reappraising the greed and grievance explanations for violent internal conflict. *SSRN Electronic Journal*. Accessed 15 December 2024, DOI:10.2139/ssrn.1116248

Nebo A (2020) *The implications of AU & ECOWAS conspicuous silence on third terms & endemic corruption (bad governance)*. Doctoral thesis, Atlantic International University, Honolulu, Hawaii, USA. Accessed 15 December 2024, https://www.academia.edu/44471697/THE_IMPLICATIONS_OF_AU_and_ECOWAS_CONSPICUOUS_SILENCE_ON_THIRD_TERMS_and_ENDEMIC_CORRUPTION_BAD_GOVERNANCE

Nkrumah K (1965) *Neo-colonialism, the last stage of imperialism*. London: Thomas Nelson & Sons

Ochieng B (2022) Burkina Faso coup: Why soldiers have overthrown President Kaboré. *BBC Monitoring* 25 January. Accessed 15 December 2024, https://www.bbc.com/news/world-africa-60112043

Olafsson N (2020) *When military coups d'état become acts of social justice*. E-International Relations. Accessed 15 December 2024, https://www.e-ir.info/2020/01/17/when-military-coups-detat-become-acts-of-social-justice/#google_vignette

Onukwue A (2022) What's causing recent coups in West Africa? *QUARZ Daily Brief* 26 January. Accessed 15 December 2024, https://qz.com/africa/2117845/what-has-caused-three-coups-in-two-years-in-west-africa

Onuoha FC & George TA (2015) *Boko Haram's use of female suicide bombing in Nigeria*. Al Jazeera Center for Studies. Accessed 15 December 2024, https://studies.aljazeera.net/sites/default/files/articles/reports/documents/20153189319985734Boko-Harams-Female.pdf

Osman M & Bearak M (2019) Sudan's Omar Hassan al-Bashir is ousted by the military after 30 years in power. *The Washington Post* 11 April. Accessed 15 December 2024, https://www.washingtonpost.com/world/africa/sudans-military-expected-to-announce-overthrow-of-president-following-months-of-popular-protests/2019/04/11/bedcc28e-5c2b-11e9-842d-7d3ed7eb3957_story.html

Palmer A, Bermudez JS Jr & Jun J (2024) *Base development in Mali indicates continued Russian involvement*. Center for Strategic & International Studies. Accessed 1 Jan 2025, https://www.csis.org/analysis/base-development-mali-indicates-continued-russian-involvement

Pearson E (2018) Wilayat Shahidat: Boko Haram, the Islamic State, and the question of the female suicide bomber. In J Zenn (Ed.) *Boko Haram beyond the headlines: Analyses of Africa's enduring insurgency*. USA: Combatting Terrorism Center at West Point

Reuters (2022) *Mali proposes five-year election delay to West African bloc*. 2 January. Accessed 15 December 2024, https://www.reuters.com/world/africa/mali-proposes-five-year-election-delay-west-african-bloc-2022-01-01/

Sampaio A (2022) *Conflict economies and urban systems in the Lake Chad Region*. Global Initiative Against Transnational Organized Crime (November). Accessed 15 December 2024, https://globalinitiative.net/wp-content/uploads/2022/11/Lake-Chad.9Nov-web-copy.pdf

Schultes I (2022) *West Africa's recent coups: Highlight the risk of trading off development for security, the rule of law and rights*. Mo Ibrahim Foundation. Accessed 15 December 2024, https://mo.ibrahim.foundation/sites/default/files/2022-04/western-africa-coups.pdf

Sempijja N & Mongale CO (2021) Examining the human security challenges emanating from the weaponisation of women: A case study of Boko Haram and the Islamic State 2001–2018. *Anuario Espanol de Derecho Internacional* 37: 423–451. Accessed 15 December 2024, https://revistas.unav.edu/index.php/anuario-esp-dcho-internacional/article/view/41448/35135

Sempijja N & Mongale CO (2022) *Climate change, group grievances and the quest for survival: An exploration of state fragility in the Sahel*. TRENDS Research & Advisory. Accessed 15 December 2024, https://trendsresearch.org/insight/climate-change-group-grievances-and-the-quest-for-survival-an-exploration-of-state-fragility-in-the-sahel/?srsltid=AfmBOoqmSyKZedUVYKXnJfL6yBrQLweeQZQ260uco9pfBJa0yK7iKrPg

Shaw M (2000) The contemporary mode of warfare? Mary Kaldor's theory of new wars. *Review of International Political Economy* 7(1): 171–180. Accessed 15 December 2024, http://www.jstor.org/stable/4177336

Siegle J & Cook C (2021) Presidential term limits key to democratic progress and security in Africa. *Orbis* 65(3): 467–482

Siroky D, Warner CM, Filip-Crawford G, Berlin A & Neuberg SL (2020) Grievances and rebellion: Comparing relative deprivation and horizontal inequality. *Conflict Management and Peace Science* 37(6): 694–715

Suleiman MD (2021) *Towards a better understanding of the underlying conditions of coups in Africa*. E-International Relations. Accessed 15 December 2024, https://www.e-ir.info/2021/09/24/towards-a-better-understanding-of-the-underlying-conditions-of-coups-in-africa/

Taoko H, Cowell A & Callimachi R (2014) Violent protests topple government in Burkina Faso. *The New York Times* 30 October. Accessed 15 December 2024, https://www.nytimes.com/2014/10/31/world/africa/burkina-faso-protests-blaise-compaore.html

Tazoacha F (2022) *On the resurgence of military coups d'etats in Africa*. Nkafu Policy Institute. Accessed 15 December 2024, https://nkafu.org/on-the-resurgence-of-military-coups-detats-in-africa/

Tejpar J & De Albuquerque AL (2015) *Challenges to peace and security in West Africa: The role of ECOWAS*. Studies in African Security, Memo 5382. FOI, Swedish Defence Research Agency. Accessed 15 December 2024, https://www.foi.se/download/18.7fd35d7f166c56ebe0bb38f/1542369060258/Challenges-to-Peace-and-Security-in-West-Africa_FOI-Memo-5382.pdf

Thompson A (2016) *An introduction to African politics* (4th edition). London: Routledge

Tricontinental (2021) *Dossier no. 42: Defending our sovereignty: US military bases in Africa and the future of African unity*. Tricontinental: Institute for Social Research Co-publication with The Socialist Movement of Ghana's Research Group. Accessed 19 February 2025, https://thetricontinental.org/wp-content/uploads/2023/06/20210630_Dossier-42_EN_Web.pdf

Tsholo K (2021) Do transitions from liberation movements to political parties guarantee good governance? The case of ZANU-PF and the ANC. *Strategic Review for Southern Africa* 43(2): 1–5

3 Silencing the guns in Somalia

Jacqueline Nakaiza

Introduction

This chapter examines the African Union's (AU's) efforts to silence the guns and eradicate terrorism in Somalia between 2007 and 2022 because 2007 is when the AU deployed troops in Somalia, and 2022 is when the African Union Mission in Somalia (AMISOM) was changed to the African Transition Mission in Somalia (ATMIS), which was expected to end in 2024. The chapter does not focus on the new mission as many analysts opine that this was just a change of name. Also, it has only been in place for a few months, making it too early to draw conclusions. I rely on the perspective of the Uganda People's Defence Force (UPDF) contingent of AMISOM because it took the lead in combating terrorism and Uganda remained the biggest troop-contributing country for years. I supplement the views of the UPDF with narratives and opinions from journalists, researchers and expatriates. Equally, I rely on the official documents and reports of both the AU and the UN, which I combine with documentary reviews. The results indicate that the AU troops contributed significantly to the return of some normalcy in Mogadishu and managed to sustain the Federal Government in power. Nevertheless, progress in Somalia is reversible in the absence of continued and consistent pressure and political, economic, and social reforms. Al-Shabaab has not given up its ambition to control the greater part of Somalia, and it retains the ability to retake territory, as the United Nations Security Council (UNSC) admits: 'in southern and central Somalia, the group encountered little resistance in capturing several towns and villages in areas that had previously been hostile to it'.[1] The mission also facilitated security conditions that allowed international actors, including the UN, to return to Somalia. Nevertheless, a lot still needs to be done to silence the guns and achieve lasting peace as al-Shabaab remains a potent threat to security in Somalia and the region.

The chapter proceeds in four sections. The first explores the war ecology, the non-state armed actors, and the intractable conflict in Somalia where the AU has been involved since 2007 trying to silence the guns – albeit unsuccessfully. Understanding the war ecology and the actors in the insurgency could explain why efforts to silence the guns remain futile. I revisit the international norms of the responsibility to protect (R2P). I then document the AU's military incursion – the policy choice prioritised to silence the guns, fulfil the R2P, and combat terrorism. Thereafter I reflect on the failure to silence the guns. I conclude by arguing that rather than silencing the guns and eradicating terrorism as intended, the military incursion has radicalised the insurgents further. I recommend that that time is ripe for the AU to consider working with the Federal Government of Somalia (FGS) to come up with local initiatives to resolve the insurgency, and also to explore the soft diplomacy of negotiations.

The war ecology in Somalia from 2004

To appreciate the regional intervention and the deployment of peacekeepers in Somalia, it is important to understand the ecology of the conflict. By war ecology, I mean the cultural and political dynamics in Somalia – who is fighting, the nature of the combatants, what they are fighting for, where they are fighting from, and what the source of their power and resources is. The war ecology in Somalia is intricate with a myriad actors, interests, and divergences.

Somalia remains one of the world's worst cases of severe state failure: the government can't control many areas in the capital or the countryside, and hardly provides any social services. It has international recognition allowing it juridical sovereignty without the empirical sovereignty expected of UN member states. The country has a youth bulge with 75 per cent of the population having no idea or memory of state responsibilities. The government is propped up by ATMIS/AMISOM forces without whom the state would be overthrown by the militants. The war ecology is rife with non-state armed actors – a trend that tends to be pervasive in situations of state failure. Other non-state actors include economic, political, religious, and social forces sourcing their power from private and public sources both in and outside Somalia. Several nations have frigates patrolling off the Somali coast to combat piracy, while the UN has controlled Somali airspace since 1996.

Also, private security companies employing personnel from a wide range of countries operate in parts of the territory, while in other areas, jihadists from South Asia, the Arab world, and elsewhere fight with al-Shabaab (Harper 2013). Countries including Turkey, Qatar (Josef and Maruf 2018), and the United Arab Emirates have interests and influences converging on Somalia. Besides, Somalia happens to be in a very strategic part of the world where world powers can easily play out their rivalries for geopolitical ambitions. These factors may not be obvious at first glance, but they intensify the insurgency, and complicate the regional efforts to resolve the conflict.

Non-state armed actors in Somalia

In the following section on non-state armed actors in the Somali insurgency, I rely on Menkhaus's thorough description (2011) of these actors. He noted that in around 2010 there were thousands of armed groups with no education and their guns were their jobs. In an economy where unemployment is 70 per cent (Gelle, Abshir & Ali-Salad 2021) uneducated youth become ready recruits for Islamist insurgents, clan militias, and criminal gangs who integrate them into the security sector. The security sector makes up the bulk of the government services with six brigades, all of which are linked to clans and therefore represent their clan interests.[3] They are very predatory and ruthless with the local population. They are generally unpaid, and many of them defect to al-Shabaab in search of a salary.

Al-Shabaab, which was proscribed as a terrorist group in 2008, is the strongest armed group controlling large swathes of territory in the south in a quasi-state form, deliberately compelling Somalis to collaborate with them. Al-Shabaab creates insecurity, from which they profit, and they engage in acts of terrorism to demoralise the government and its supporters. As an AMISOM official noted:

> In Somalia, almost everyone is compelled to work with al-Shabaab. Big businesses in Mogadishu pay taxes to the al-Shabaab – the banks, hotels are not there because we (AMISOM) pacified Mogadishu. No they pay money to al-Shabaab so that they are not attacked. That is how weak the Somali state is.[4]

Al-Shabaab is very skilled at penetration, even into the government, AMISOM and the aid agencies, so they know almost everything. They are also very good at collaborating with different groups in Somalia. Sometimes, even at higher levels, the government may see al-Shabaab as less threatening than a local rival and will tactically collude with them.

Other non-state armed actors are the district commissioners, each of whom controls one of the 16 districts in Mogadishu as a fiefdom. The neighbourhoods are clan-based, and even the multi-ethnic ones are dominated by one clan. The district commissioner is the head of a clan paramilitary that is, essentially, a protection racket in his fiefdom. Other actors include neighbourhood watch groups, business militias, and private security companies. There are also regional militias from self-declared regional member states that display varying degrees of professionalism (Menkhaus 2011).

These actors are reinforced by a combination of cultural and political factors. One cultural factor is the clan providing security in the absence of an effective formal security sector. Somalis have more confidence in the clan paramilitaries and clan-based warlords than in the government security forces, they are more legitimate locally than the state (Menkhaus 2011). There are also intra-regional conflicts that are shaped by history as well as domestic insurgencies.

Responsibility to protect from 1991

The idea of responsibility (R2P) to protect arises from the notion that all sovereign states have the primary responsibility of protecting their citizens. In situations in which states abdicate this responsibility, it may be picked up by the international community (Evans & Sahnoun 2002, p. 104). After the total collapse of the Somali government in 1991, due to the after effects, the international community took on collective action in a timely and decisive manner (United Nations 2005). R2P is the unanimous political commitment of UN member states to act to prevent international crimes (International Refugee Rights Initiative 2017) when states have failed to fulfil this responsibility. The international community is obliged to intervene using diplomatic, humanitarian, or other peaceful means as per Chapters VI and VIII of the UN Charter (Evans & Sahnoun 2002, p. 102).

In practice, however, with R2P, those protecting have to assess issues from the perspective of the protected, rather than that of the intervener. But the state is primarily responsible for protecting its citizens, so the international community steps in only when the state abdicates it responsibility. However, such intervention should not be against the wishes of a functioning state, save for exceptional circumstances.

For Somalia, the international community was obliged to exercise the R2P in the early 1990s, and UN Resolution 794 (UN Security Council 1992) authorised the Unified Task Force to enter Somalia to ease the humanitarian crisis in the absence of an effective state. The responsibility to protect is broad and includes the responsibility to react to a state's failure to protect its citizens, the responsibility to prevent, and the responsibility to rebuild (Evans & Sahnoun 2002, p. 101). If preventive measures fail, while pursuing R2P, coercive measures (political, economic, judicial, or – in extreme cases – military) are deployed. If a military intervention commences, the principles of just cause, right authority, right intention, last resort, proportional means and reasonable prospects must be fulfilled (Evans & Sahnoun 2002, p. 101).

Since 1991, Somalia has perpetually failed to secure its territory, protect its populace from self-destruction, and respond to disasters such as severe famine. The result has been an intractable conflict between diverse armed non-state actors and Islamist groups that easily operate within the country due to the absence of a functional state. The conflict has created an unprecedented humanitarian crisis for the Somalis, internal displacements, and a massive outflow of refugees, and terrorist attacks being exported to neighbouring countries, all of which are burdensome to those sectors of the international community that have attempted interventions to alleviate the excessive suffering.

In the 1990s, the Organisation of African Unity (OAU) was reluctant to involve itself in the internal affairs of its member states (Menkhaus & Ortmayer 2000) but prioritised defending the sovereignty, territorial integrity, and independence of its member states (International Refugee Rights Initiative 2017; Healy 2009) as enshrined in Article II (c) of its charter (OAU 1963). Thus the OAU had no legal mandate to intervene in conflicts even in situations of a failed state like Somalia. The lack of a legal mandate coupled with the newly independent status of OAU states deterred the organisation from intervening and relegated the R2P to the international community.

Similarly, the UN and the international community were hesitant to intervene as they perceived the crisis as an internal matter that did not constitute a threat to international peace and security, which would justify enforcement action under Chapter VII of the UN Charter (Evans & Sahnoun 2002). As per international norms, if the Security Council is unwilling to act in a case warranting intervention, as Somalia was, then regional or sub-regional organisations under Chapter VIII of the UN Charter should be authorised to intervene (Evans & Sahnoun 2002). This clause guided the UN Security Council (2007) to pass resolution 1744 mandating the AU to deploy troops in Somalia in 2007. However, Ansems (2007, 107) observed that 'putting aside all good intentions to provide African solutions to African problems', (Ansems 2007, p. 102) there were doubts about whether the AU had the capacity to end terrorism and silence the guns.

Having noted the lacunas in the OAU charter, the AU charter (African Union Commission 2015) addressed the gaps. Regarding interventions, Article 4(h) of the AU Constitutive Act (African Union 2000, p. 7) clearly states that 'the body has the right to intervene according to a decision of the Assembly in respect of grave circumstances, namely: war crimes, genocide and crimes against humanity'. Thus, the protection of the fundamental rights of citizens is not a purely domestic concern and sovereignty cannot shield repressive states from intervention by the AU. Therefore, Article 4(h) provides for statutory intervention by the AU to prevent or halt mass atrocities in a Member State (Kuwali & Viljoen 2014).

From the R2P perspective, the international community, in collaboration with the AU's regional bodies and member states, intervened in Somalia to provide humanitarian, peacebuilding, state building, and counter-terrorism undertakings. Key engagements include peace conferences since 1991, Ethiopia's military incursion, and the deployment of AMISOM forces.

AU/AMISOM 2007–2022

In this section, I focus on the AU's involvement under AMISOM in the Somali crisis to silence the guns and eradicate terrorism. AMISOM was authorised by the UN Security Council Resolution 1744 (2007), to prepare the ground for a UN mission; enable the gradual handing over of security responsibilities to the Somali security forces contingent on their abilities, the political situation and security progress; reduce the threat posed by al-Shabaab and other armed non-state actors; help the Somali security forces to provide security for the political process at all levels; and contribute to stabilisation, reconciliation, and peacebuilding.

Since 2007, Uganda has led the deployment of troops. Uganda's President Museveni justified the deployment of the UPDF as part of AMISOM arguing:

> An AU peacekeeping force for Somalia will succeed because Africans understand the conflict better than American forces did in a disastrous 1993 mission. Our peacekeeping is different from these Western

> Countries which do not listen carefully, are full of themselves, they think they know everything that's why they make mistakes. (Cocks 2007) [5]

However, some analysts believed right from the onset of AMISOM that UPDF could not achieve much in Somalia, given the view that Uganda had not fully examined the conflict before deploying its troops.

> The president did not ask and neither answered the critical questions like what are our objectives in Somalia? What are the key success indicators? What is the timeframe of our intervention? What is our exit strategy? Without answers to these questions, I am inclined to believe that we deployed blindly into a troubled country, a factor that was likely to vitiate against success. (Mwenda 2010) [6]

Mwenda said that the primary objective in Somalia should have been to put together a group that could exercise effective military control over the country before talking of their religious or ideological leanings, observing that

> There is no way a coterie of corrupt and opportunistic civilians without basic military know-how can establish security in Somalia even if propped by Uganda and the AU. President Museveni, more than any other African I know, understands well how foreign interventions, however well-intentioned, are incapable of establishing a stable peace, leave alone a functional state. However powerful a nation's military can be, it cannot win a war in a country, however poor, unless it does the following: understand local dynamics, have clear objectives, set a timeframe for achieving them, create an exit strategy and secure political support at home. (Mwenda 2010)

Adams (1999, p. 336) concurred:

> With the departure of UNOSOM II troops in March 1995, it was more than obvious that Somali civil conflicts will have to be resolved internally by the parties themselves rather than through external intervention. At present, clan divisions and crude military balances seem to rule out a resolution through conquest by a single armed strongman.

Mwenda (2010)[7] argued further:

> No amount of UPDF presence in Somalia will bring peace to that country. Only Somalis can. Uganda's troops can only assist in peacebuilding if there are strong internal forces with a strong vested interest in peace. Somalia needs a warlord able to mobilise resources and build a military capability to take effective control of the entire country. The crisis of the state in Somalia, though initially created by internal factors, has been worsened by international interference in its domestic politics. What Somalia needs is a military strongman with the organisational ability to marshal resources and bribe, coerce, and cajole other military and civilian groups together as Museveni did in Uganda in 1986. In the mid-2000s, the Islamic Courts

Union (ICU) grew and spread rapidly, establishing order over large parts of the country. It organised around a unifying ideology of Islam and began implementing Sharia law. However, post 9/11 America was scared of anything Islamic and thus saw the ICU as an enemy. It financed Ethiopia to dislodge them from power. From their remnants emerged the al-Shabaab with largely terrorist intentions. Even when UPDF led troop contributions for Somalia, Museveni is known to be sceptical about foreign military interventions however well-intentioned. He is quoted to have commented that, 'external actors tend to distort local politics by creating artificial winners and artificial losers. Because the winner is supported by foreign forces, he lacks incentives to seek internal political integration, hoping to rely on foreign allies to consolidate their position domestically. [8]

This argument has been corroborated by Augetti and Murphy who observed that

Peace enforcement operations do not usually succeed in creating consensus in the country of intervention. Typically, only the weaker local political movements or groups applaud external intervention. The stronger local armed groups, hoping to win power by pursuing the armed struggle, oppose foreign military intervention. They see the UN and foreign coalitions as intruders trying to deprive them of the just reward for their efforts. They remain determined to fight against the new obstacle to their ambitions if they believe they can defeat it. Having already sustained several losses in the power struggle, they are ready to accept a high level of reciprocal killing. (1995, p. 344)

This is the scenario in Somalia, where there are reservations about foreign troops – even about AMISOM. Therefore, it is not surprising that after 16 years of military incursion, they have failed to silence the guns and eradicate terrorism.

Reflections on the trajectory of the AU's failure to silence the guns

After 16 years of AU troop deployment, the guns in Somalia are still rattling and the efforts to eradicate terrorism remain futile. This can be attributed to a number of factors that anyone attempting to resolve the conflict should consider. The drivers of the insurgency in Somalia are complex but my opinion is that none of the actors attempting to resolve the insurgency have exhaustively discussed the drivers. Rather, they address the symptoms by trying to eliminate al-Shabaab and propping up the FGS. In addition, the AU has been faced with a number of challenges in their efforts to fulfil their R2P, including inadequate troops, inadequate financing, and a hostile operating environment.

Many countries were reluctant to send troops to Somalia, thus constraining the mission by the limited number of peacekeepers (Bruton & Williams 2014).The inadequate numbers could not stabilise Somalia, facilitate disarmament, mitigate the humanitarian crisis, or work towards repatriation and resettlement (Agada 2008). Thus, the UNSC adopted resolution 1964 (UNSC 2010) authorising AMISOM to increase its troops to 12 000. However, it took four years to achieve the original authorised strength of 8 000. Even with increased troops, UPDF officers under AMISOM were sceptical about succeeding where the infinitely more robust, better trained, and better armed US Unified Task Force (1992–1993) and United Nations Operation in Somalia II (1993–1995) forces, with 37 000 and 28 000 personnel respectively, had failed against an earlier and far less formidable opposition than the more recent Islamist insurgents. While comparing AMISOM troop numbers to other military deployments, I observe that the numbers were not sufficient for the task at hand. For instance, in Iraq, at the peak of the incursion between 2006 and 2007, the US committed more than 160 000 troops backed by a further 100 000 support personnel. This translates into one pair of boots on the ground for every 187 Iraqis. A retired marine who had served in Iraq informed me that, in 2005, he was commanding a light infantry unit of 85 soldiers but, in 2006, this unit was reinforced with 1 200 marines.[9] AMISOM, in contrast, was tasked with much the same job with one soldier for every 500 Somalis, if it limited its ambitions to just southern and central Somalia (Pham 2011).

Despite its shortcomings, AMISOM endeavoured to return normality to Somalia. For instance, they launched Operation Panua-Eneo (Bruton & Williams 2014) in 2011 in collaboration with the Transitional Federal Government (TFG), pushed the militants out, and brought Mogadishu under the control of the state (Williams 2018). These security gains restored confidence in the possibility of stabilising Somalia for the first time since the state collapse in 1991 (African Union 2013a; 2013b). As noted in a letter from the Chair of the UNSC (2011),

> Although the offensive entailed high casualties for AMISOM forces, TFG and affiliated militias, the area of control expanded from five districts of the capital to seven, shifted the front line further away from Villa Somalia and placed al-Shabaab forces in Bakaara market and Dayniile under pressure. [10]

With regard to governance, more gains were achieved in 2012 with a provisional constitution adopted that paved the way for the elections in September, ending the eight-year transition processes in the country. To sustain the security gains, however, AMISOM continued its support for the government (Bruton & Williams 2014) because the security context remained volatile and fragile with significant parts of the country controlled by al-Shabaab militants (African Union 2021).

The initial limited mandate was prolonged to address the challenges in Somalia. After the adoption of UNSC (2015) Resolution 2232, the AU developed a revised Concept of Operations for AMISOM authorising continued offensive operations against the militants, securing critical political processes, supporting stabilisation efforts, and ensuring security for the Somalis as part of peacebuilding and reconciliation while working on the gradual handing over of security responsibilities to the Somali National Forces (SNF). This was in tandem with Ugandan President Museveni, who stated at a conference on Somalia in London:

> Borrowing the allegory of the Holy Trinity in Christianity where we have God the Father, God the Son and God the Holy Spirit, there's a need for a peaceful trinity in Somalia bringing together the internal stakeholders, the respective regions, and the international community. Even with a government in place, al-Shabaab is not eliminated from Somalia, they still maintain rural bases from where they operate undisturbed away from the regional and Somali government forces. It's from these rural areas that they infiltrate towns and kill people. (Museveni 2017)

Museveni advised that rebuilding the Somali National Forces was key to stabilising Somalia.

> Young Somalis with advanced secondary education and beyond should be recruited, so that the soldiers have leadership, and non-commissioned officers (NCOs) who link officers with the soldiers, need to be trained. If the army does not have officers and NCOs, then it's not an army. Technical staff must be trained to handle tanks, artillery, and even aircraft and gunships, to give them a technological advantage over the terrorists. The Somali military should expand recruitment to include zonal and mobile forces to guard the liberated areas, while mobile forces hunt the terrorists, aided by the air force. Militias should be integrated into the SNF and factionalism and warlord loyalties must be terminated. If these are taken, security will be restored in the whole of Somalia. (Museveni 2017)

A former UPDF commander in Somalia concurred:

> Museveni is 100 per cent spot on but how? Unfortunately, the how is not what AMISOM did. But how do you reconcile those clan dynamics with the desire to form a national army? You have people who have their clan royalties – in the north, you have a different clan, in the south, you have another, somewhere else, and another there. Somalis have strong clan attachments, to them the clan is an issue of identity that they never compromise. So how do you bring all those clans together to form a national army? Either you get a majority clan to dominate the army, and it rules by force, or you build powerful regional armies and, from them, you select people to form the national army. But the regional armies – clan armies – can defend their regions and their clans, which is fine. But you also need to draw certain elements from those clan militias to build a stronger national army. But AMISOM did not do this, hence failing to silence the guns.[11]

Similarly, a report by the Africa Center for Strategic Studies (2022) argues that

> Central to creating a culture of military professionalism is instilling within soldiers, from the lowest rank to the most senior officer, core societal values and principles that the military aspires to represent. Values such as integrity, honour, expertise, sacrifice, and respect for citizens do not necessarily emerge naturally but must be taught and regularly refreshed. Nearly all militaries provide tactical training and exercises – establishing core competencies. However, many lack an intentional strategy to build a set of core values. Creating such shared values has a powerful unifying effect on a military, amplifying force cohesion and effectiveness.

It is not clear whether the AU in its efforts to fulfill the R2P and to silence the guns ever took cognisance of this. Considering that the mission evolved haphazardly, reconstruction of the SNF has been implemented experimentally. An expert interviewed opined that

> One of the major problems with AMISOM was its uncertain nature worsened by its six-monthly mandates that disrupted the AU's proper planning process. If I was the one authorising the mandates, I would have given much longer mandates, say a three- or five-year period to allow proper strategic planning for the mission.[12]

The AU's ability to fulfill its mandate of R2P and the efforts to eradicate terrorism in Somalia have been hampered by relying on finances from the international community. For instance, as early as 2004, The Intergovernmental Authority on Development Mission in Somalia failed to deploy as intended due to a lack of technical and financial resources, despite the willingness of member countries to contribute troops. AMISOM, too, faced similar funding challenges, which partly explains the mission's failure to adopt a long-term strategy to successfully silence the guns and eradicate terrorism.

I argue that the AU prioritised AMISOM's militarised approach to help the Federal Government of Somalia (FGS) push al-Shabaab out of Mogadishu and other major towns and cities. As a combat force, AMISOM sustained the FGS in power and created a relatively secure environment that allowed the Somali peace process to take root. Despite the gains, the insurgency is still raging and shows resilience because al-Shabaab remains strong, especially in the countryside. The FGS with AU troops are mainly in major towns, but the rural areas are controlled by al-Shabaab.[13] By 2021, when an initial drawdown of the AMISOM troops had been proposed, an assessment of the situation in Somalia indicated that

> Al-Shabaab continued to mount pressure on the Somali security forces and conducts hit-and-run attacks targeting the Somali security forces and AMISOM, using improvised explosive devices (IEDs). In particular,

> the use of person-borne improvised explosive devices has continued to increase over the past year, mainly in Mogadishu. The most affected overall by al-Shabaab activities were Banaadir, Shabelle Hoose, and Shabelle Dhexe Regions. (African Union 2021, p. 3)

This is another indication that the AU has not been successful at silencing the guns and eradicating terrorists. A Somali researcher interviewed observed:

> The principal historical driver of the current Islamic insurgency in Somalia has evolved from a reaction to the external intervention, especially the United States and Ethiopia, and the only thing that all Somalis are united about is their desire to have all foreign forces out of their country. Unfortunately, AMISOM operates like an open-ended mission, after 16 years of involvement without tangible success, SNF should be allowed to take over the security of the country.[14]

Another UPDF/AMISOM commander shared his insights into why the AU cannot fully silence the guns by saying:

> Besides the clan being supreme, Somalis are very complicated people, you can't know who is al-Shabaab and who is not. For example, there was a time we (UPDF/AMISOM) rounded up a house full of explosives measuring about 40 000 kg in Janaale. And we wanted to blow up the house, destroy the explosives and arrest the people there. But when we informed the FGS and SNF, they told us to leave their people alone. But remember, in the rules of engagement, for any offensives, we plan with the SNF and don't execute without prior knowledge of the FGS.[15]

This view concurs with Mandrup (2021), who noted that

> Clan loyalties and family ties are generally more important than other loyalties. These loyalties have complicated the nurturing of the SNF for they are more interested in their clans and families than the nation. Through these loyalties, al-Shabaab obtains a very high level of infiltration enabling it to acquire timely information and equipment, and the population in Somalia favour the group and keeps its supply routes open.

In the 15 years of its deployment in Somalia, AMISOM has had substantial military gains against al-Shabaab, allowed political processes to take root, and it has supported the FGS to establish a presence in parts of central and southern Somalia. Some Somalis interviewed noted that there was no government at all before AMISOM deployed. The president, then Abdullahi Yusuf Ahmed, and his cabinet were governing the country from Nairobi. When asked why regional actors have failed to silence the guns after 15 years of involvement, a Somali diplomat indicated that it is not in the interest of regional actors to resolve the insurgency. Interestingly, evidence from the literature indicates that frontline states like Ethiopia and Kenya benefit from a weak and unstable Somalia.

On the subject of the AU's peacekeeping forces, a Somali post-doctoral researcher asked,

> Will the AU forces stay with us as long as the European Union and the United States continue to facilitate and fund them? Sadly, there haven't been any attempts by AMISOM to negotiate with the insurgents to address their grievances, drivers, and factors sustaining the insurgency. But even if the negotiations are pursued, they would not succeed as externally mediated interventions do not work in Somalia.[16]

Another Somali researcher based in Nairobi suggested that

> AMISOM played its part and there's nothing more they can do. Instead, they should withdraw all their troops from Somalia. Thereafter Hawiye, who is one of the most dominant clans, should do the fighting against Al-Shabaab without AMISOM or other nations involved. If this is done, Al-Shabaab will be defeated for they will not have any reason to fight the Hawiye. Besides, it will become more dangerous for the insurgents as Somalis will turn against them. As of now, al-Shabaab justifies their actions by saying these invaders are killing our people that's why we fight them. [17]

Commenting about the prioritised military approach in Somalia and the failure to silence the guns, Mamdani (2013) observed that

> Military victory cannot be the end of the story. That the Somali problem is more political than ... military is likely to become even more clear in the wake of a military victory. Will a military victory lead to political stabilisation or will it turn out to be but the latest round in an ongoing cycle of violence? If a military solution is achieved, is it sustainable without a political solution? Evidence from the previous experience where all attempts at a military solution only made the problem worse because they ignored the centrality of the political dimension. Is also evidenced in the insurgency in Somalia where even when there's a semblance of a Federal Government it is threatened by the prospect of renewed rebellion from already organised wartime rivals.

Conclusion and recommendation

With recourse to the international norms of responsibility to protect, the AU prioritised the militaristic approaches to silencing the guns and eradicating terrorism in Somalia. The AU, with support from international partners, has made efforts to rebuild the security apparatus of Somalia through training to enable the gradual handing over of security responsibilities to the SNF. Unfortunately, the SNF remains weak with its allegiance divided between the clans and the FGS. The government itself is weak with no functional state institutions. It hardly controls more than 10 per cent of the country, lacks empirical sovereignty, and can only survive with the backing of AU troops without whom the insurgents could overturn it easily. The insurgents on the other hand are remarkably resilient and emboldened by the precedent of the Taliban in Afghanistan following the US withdrawal (Kamal 2021). Rather than silence the guns, the AU's military incursion radicalised the Somalis who viewed the deployment as a foreign invasion that generated disastrous consequences (Malito 2015). Since 2015 actors in the insurgency have acknowledged that they are at a hurting stalemate, reiterating that al-Shabaab will not be eliminated militarily. Thus, there is a need to explore alternatives for resolving the conflict. An alternative is that the AU and the international partners should support Somalis to come up with homegrown solution to the insurgency allowing local ownership and giving Somalis the opportunity to determine the governance of their country, their destiny and their future. There should be concerted efforts to address the drivers of the insurgency because, if they are not addressed, sustainable peace will remain elusive.

Notes

1. Letter dated 15 July 2021 from the Chair of the Security Council Committee pursuant to resolutions 1267 (1999), 1989 (2011) and 2253 (2015) concerning Islamic State in Iraq and the Levant (Da'esh), Al-Qaida and associated individuals, groups, undertakings and entities addressed to the President of the Security Council
2. It has been alleged that Qatar used millions of dollars to fund the 2016–2017 election campaign of Mohamed Abdullah Mohamed (commonly known as Farmajo), who was president from 2017 to 2022. The Qatari money played a decisive role in determining the outcomes of the presidential elections of both 2012 and 2017. It is also alleged that Qatar heavily sponsored violence against opposition forces in Somalia.
3. In some instances, doing what is good for the community or clan means going into central Somalia with AMISOM to oust al-Shabaab, and then claiming the liberated areas or recovered zones in southern Somalia, such as Lower Shabelle, for yourself and your clan. The local communities then thank the security forces for liberating them from al-Shabaab but they have merely replaced one form of occupation with another.
4. Interview with an AMISOM official in Kampala, 6 January 2022.
5. Cocks T, African peace mission won't fail in Somalia: Uganda. *Reuters* 9 August 2007. Accessed 16 December 2024, https://www.reuters.com/article/world/african-peace-missionwon-t-fail-in-somalia-uganda-idUSL05760146/
6, 7, 8 Mwenda A (2010) Why Museveni Is wrong on Somalia. *The Independent* 1 August 2010. Accessed 16 December 2024, https://www.independent.co.ug/museveni-wrong-somalia/
9. Interview with a former US Marine, Wabenzi's in Muyenga, 2 July 2022.
10. Letter Dated 18 July 2011, p. 18, from the Chairman of the Security Council Committee Pursuant to Resolutions 751 (1992) and 1907 (2009) Concerning Somalia and Eritrea Addressed to the President of the Security Council. Accessed 16 December 2024, https://digitallibrary.un.org/record/708002?ln=en&v=pdf
11. Interview with a former UPDF/AMISOM Commander, Kampala, 28 August 2021.
12. Interview with an expert researcher on Somalia, Nairobi, 22 January 2022.
13. Interview with a UPDF officer, Kampala, 29 June 2022.

14 Interview with AM, a Somali Researcher based, Nairobi, 21 August 2022.
15 Interview with UPDF/AMISOM commander at the Ministry of Defence Headquarters, Mbuya, 28 June 2022.
16 Online interview with MHI, a Somali researcher based at Oxford University, 19 May 2022.
17 Interview with AM, a Somali researcher based in Nairobi, 21 August 2022.

References

Adams HM (1999) Somali civil wars. In TM Ali & RO Matthews (Eds) *Civil wars in Africa*. London: McGill-Queen's University Press. Accessed 16 December 2024, https://gsdrc.org/document-library/somali-civil-wars/

Africa Center for Strategic Studies (2022) Deepening a culture of military professionalism in Africa. Accessed 16 December 2024, https://africacenter.org/spotlight/deepening-culture-military-professionalism-africa/

African Union (2000) Constitutive Act of the African Union. Accessed 15 December 2024. https://au.int/sites/default/files/pages/34873-file-constitutiveact_en.pdf

African Union (2013a) Report of the African Union Commission on the Strategic Review of the African Union Mission in Somalia (AMISOM), 27 February. Accessed 16 December 2024, https://archives.au.int/handle/123456789/8272

African Union (2013b) Report of the Chairperson of the Commission on the Situation in Somalia, 13 June. Accessed 16 December 2024, https://au.int/en/documents/20130613/report-chairperson-commission-situation-somalia-during-peace-and-security-council

African Union Commission (2015) *Agenda 2063: The Africa we want; Framework document*. Accessed 6 December 2024, https://au.int/sites/default/files/documents/33126-doc-framework_document_book.pdf

African Union (2021) Communique of the 1037th meeting of the PSC held on 7 October 2021 on the situation in Somalia and the status of the consultations on the Independent Assessment Report on AU Mission in Somalia (AMISOM) post-2021. Accessed 16 September 2024, https://www.peaceau.org/en/article/communique-of-the-1037th-meeting-of-the-psc-held-on-7-october-2021-on-the-situation-in-somalia-and-the-status-of-the-consultations-on-the-independent-assessment-report-on-au-mission-in-somalia-amisom-post-2021

Agada S (2008) The challenges of United Nations peacekeeping in Africa: Case study of Somalia. Certificate-of-training, United Nations Peace Support Operations. Accessed 16 December 2024, https://cdn.peaceopstraining.org/theses/agada.pdf

Ansems A (2007) Somalia 2007: Starting from scratch on the long and winding road to peace and democracy? *Scientia Militaria: South African Journal of Military Studies* 36(1): 95–114. Accessed 15 December 2024, https://www.ajol.info/index.php/smsajms/article/view/42650

Augetti E & Murphy CN (1995) Lessons of Somalia for future multilateral humanitarian assistance operations. *Global Governance* 1(3): 339–365. Accessed 16 December 2024, https://digitallibrary.un.org/record/221741?ln=en

Bruton B & Williams PD (2014) *Counterinsurgency in Somalia: Lessons learned from the African Union Mission in Somalia, 2007–2013*. MacDill Air Force Base, FL: Joint Special Operations University Press

Cocks T (2007) African peace mission won't fail in Somalia: Uganda. *Reuters* 9 August. Accessed 16 December 2024, https://www.reuters.com/article/world/african-peace-mission-won-t-fail-in-somalia-uganda-idUSL05760146/

Evans G & Sahnoun M (2002) The Responsibility to Protect. *Foreign Affairs* 81(6): 99–110

Gelle LY, Abshir A & Ali-Salad MA (2021) Graduate unemployment in Somalia: Causes, socio-economic consequences and possible solutions. *Journal of Economics and Development Studies* 9(3). Accessed 16 December 2024, https://www.researchgate.net/publication/357616960_Graduate_Unemployment_in_Somalia_Causes_Socio-Economic_Consequences_and_Possible_Solutions

Harper M (2013) Somalia: Whose country is it, anyway? *The Fletcher forum of world affairs* 37(1): 161–166

Healy S (2009) Peacemaking in the midst of war: An assessment of IGAD's contribution to regional security in the Horn of Africa. Working Paper no. 59. Crisis States Research Centre, London School of Economics and Political Science. Accessed 16 December 2024, https://eprints.lse.ac.uk/28482/1/WP59.2.pdf

International Refugee Rights Initiative (2017) From non-interference to non-indifference: The African Union and the responsibility to protect. Accessed 16 December 2024, https://reliefweb.int/report/world/non-interference-non-indifference-african-union-and-responsibility-protect

Kamal O (2021). After the collapse of the Taliban: A study of the US statebuilding failure. Master's thesis. Webster University, Vienna. Accessed 2 January 2025, https://www.proquest.com/openview/ed47a16f67a22a47a978b1eba563c6a5/1?pq-origsite=gscholar&cbl=18750&diss=y

Kuwali D & Viljoen F (2014) *Africa and the responsibility to protect: Article 4(h) of the African Union Constitutive Act*. London: Routledge

Malito DV (2015) Building terror while fighting enemies: How the global war on terror deepened the crisis in Somalia. *Third World Quarterly* 36(10): 1866–1886

Mamdani M (2013) Senseless [and sensible] violence: Mourning the dead at Westgate Mall. *Aljazeera* 26 September. Accessed 16 December 2024, https://www.aljazeera.com/opinions/2013/9/26/senseless-and-sensible-violence-mourning-the-dead-at-westgate-mall

Mandrup T (2021) Security in Somalia beyond 2021: The future role of AMISOM and the international community. *ACCORD Conflict & Resilience Monitor* 24 February. Accessed 16 December 2024, https://www.accord.org.za/analysis/security-in-somalia-beyond-2021-the-future-role-of-amisom-and-the-international-community/

Menkhaus K (2011) Somalia and the Horn of Africa. World Development Report Background Case Study. World Bank. Accessed 27 February 2025, https://openknowledge.worldbank.org/server/api/core/bitstreams/9fce789f-37ae-5c9d-bdfb-dc01046275cb/content

Menkhaus K & Ortmayer L (2000) Somalia: Misread crises and missed opportunities. In BW Jentleson (Ed.) *Opportunities missed, opportunities seized: Preventive diplomacy in the post-cold war world*. Rowman & Littlefield Publishers. Accessed 16 December 2024, https://media.carnegie.org/filer_public/9e/43/9e435fc8-f8fd-4764-aabd-2c8eba103b38/ccny_book_1999_opportunities.pdf

Museveni YK (2017) Statement by President Museveni at the Somalia Conference, London 11 May 2017). Accessed 2 January 2025, https://www.yowerikmuseveni.com/statement-president-museveni-somalia-conference-london-11th-may-2017

Mwenda A (2010) Why Museveni is wrong on Somalia. *The Independent* 1 August. Accessed 16 December 2024, https://www.independent.co.ug/museveni-wrong-somalia/

Organisation of African Unity (1963) OAU Charter. Accessed 16 December 2024, https://au.int/sites/default/files/treaties/7759-file-oau_charter_1963.pdf

Pham JP (2011) Somalia: Where a state isn't a state. *The Fletcher Forum of World Affairs* 35(2): 133–151. Accessed 27 February 2025, https://www.fletcherforum.org/home/2016/9/6/somalia-where-a-state-isnt-a-state

United Nations (2005) Resolution adopted by the General Assembly on 16 September 2005: World Summit Outcome. Accessed 16 December 2024, https://www.un.org/en/development/desa/population/migration/generalassembly/docs/globalcompact/A_RES_60_1.pdf

United Nations Security Council (2010) Resolution 1964. Accessed 16 December 2024, https://www.securitycouncilreport.org/atf/cf/%7B65BFCF9B-6D27-4E9C-8CD3-CF6E4FF96FF9%7D/Somalia%20S%20RES%201964.pdf

United Nations Security Council (2011) Letter Dated 18 July 2011 from the Chairman of the Security Council Committee Pursuant to Resolutions 751 (1992) and 1907 (2009) Concerning Somalia and Eritrea Addressed to the President of the Security Council. Accessed 16 December 2024, https://digitallibrary.un.org/record/708002?ln=en&v=pdf

United Nations Security Council (2015) Resolution 2232. Accessed 16 December 2024, https://digitallibrary.un.org/record/798098?ln=en&v=pdf

Williams PD (2018) *Fighting for peace in Somalia: A history and analysis of the African Union Mission (AMISOM), 2007–2017.* Oxford: Oxford University Press

4 Measuring Nigerians' willingness to talk to police on duty

Oluwaseun Ayomipo, Babatunde Raphael Ojebuyi,
Oluwabusolami Oluwajulugbe, Oluwafunmilayo Olarewaju
Aminu and Ridwan Abiola Kolawole

Introduction

The current state of police-public relations in Nigeria is discouraging (Ike et al. 2021) and Nigerian policing styles and practices fall short of citizens' expectations. Many Nigerians perceive the police as corrupt power abusers who use excessive force, so they do not trust them (Akinlabi 2019). Scholars consider the failure of the Nigerian police force to be systemic. They list inappropriate investigation styles, inadequate information and resources, corruption, underfunding, and inadequate training as factors responsible for the failure (Akinyetun 2021; Aborisade 2018). The Nigerian police system is also believed to be politicised. Its control is centralised under the federal government, and the system is not effectively monitored (Famosaya 2020). Some studies suggest that officers of the Nigeria police use inappropriate policing styles because they do not have adequate sophisticated resources to carry out their assignments. Therefore, they resort to crude, abusive, dehumanising methods to elicit information from suspects.

Some solutions have been suggested to improve police–citizen relations in Nigeria, suggestions including reformation of the Nigeria Police Force, supply of sophisticated tools for carrying out investigations, adequate training and motivation of police officers, and deployment of campaigns to improve the public's trust and confidence in the police (Akinyetun 2021; Ike et al. 2021). The police rely greatly on citizens' support for the success of their services, while the citizens look to the police for their security. However problematic the relationship between the police and the citizens becomes, there is no legal viable alternative.

While effective policing requires good police–citizen communication, few Nigerians are willing to communicate with police on duty, and the literature rarely addresses this challenge. This study contributes to the literature on police–citizen relations in Nigeria. Specifically, it focuses on the willingness of citizens to communicate with and support the police in their work. Very few studies have been done on citizens' support for the police in Nigeria. The majority of police studies in Nigeria focus on public satisfaction with the police, confidence and trust in the police, police legitimacy, and police effectiveness (Badiora & Ntamark 2019), police corruption

(Aremu, Pakes & Johnston 2011), etc. This study fills the gap in the literature occasioned by the neglect of police–citizen intergroup communication constructs in police studies. It develops the 'willingness to communicate with police on duty' (WTCWPOD) scale, and assessed its validity and reliability. In verifying the scale's validity, the researcher evaluated the relationship between the construct (willingness to communicate with police on duty) and six of the established constructs in police studies (cooperation with the police, police effectiveness, procedural justice, moral alignment with the police, obligation to obey police, and police corruption).

Willingness to communicate is conceptualised as the readiness of an individual to interact without being forced to do so when the occasion demands. Many studies have been conducted on willingness to communicate in different communication contexts. Some studies explored how it varies among different groups of people, while some studies explored its correlates and predictors. In Nigeria, literature focusing on 'willingness to communicate' is rare, and none has been found that focuses on 'willingness to communicate with police'. Thus, this study is one of the first to explore the construct.

Willingness to communicate is context-specific and depends on several factors, including race. For example, white Americans were found to be more willing to communicate with Chinese people than with Chinese Americans (Lu & Hsu 2008). Willingness to communicate can either be in a face-to-face or virtual context. And factors that affect the construct in both contexts may differ. For example, studies have found that cell phone addiction has a negative association with willingness to communicate face-to-face, while it increases willingness to communicate with people that are distant (Allred & Atkin 2020); high levels of anxiety and uncertainty decrease one's willingness to communicate (Logan, Steel & Hunt 2016); willingness to communicate with people from other cultural backgrounds is positively associated with altruism and spiritual intelligence (Clark, Lin & Maher 2015), as does perceived competence in communication and language (Lu & Hsu 2008). A study about patient willingness to communicate with healthcare providers revealed that the more knowledgeable patients were about their health (via the information they had accessed on the internet), the more willing they were to communicate with healthcare providers (Baker & Watson 2019) and a study on how patients perceive doctors' communication skills showed that the communication competence of the health professionals best predicted patients' willingness to communicate (Mulyono et al. 2020).

James McCroskey (1992) developed the willingness to communicate scale, which has 20 items (including 8 fillers). It measures people's willingness to communicate based on the type of people they are communicating with (friend, stranger, acquaintance) and the context of the communication (in public, in a meeting, in a group, or one-on-one). The scale is valid and reliable (with a Cronbach alpha value of 0.92). Five years later, Jeffrey Kassing (1997) developed a scale for measuring willingness to communicate in an intercultural communication context. It has 12 items (consisting of 6 fillers); the exploratory factor analysis yielded 1 factor; and the reliability test showed that it has a high alpha value (0.91). The scale has been widely used and has been found to be valid and reliable in different intercultural communication contexts.

This study contributes to a larger police crime prevention effort in Nigeria. Therefore, framing the study with a police crime-prevention theory is considered appropriate. The study adopts the broken window theory, which was proposed by Wilson and Kelling in 1982 (Davis 2017). The theory posits that when there is an increase in physical and social disorders in a community, the rate of serious crime will increase over time. According to the theory, physical disorder includes abandoned buildings, piles of garbage, unemptied bins, abandoned cars, and undeveloped bushy sites, whereas social disorder includes homelessness, unemployment and substance abuse. The theory suggests that when the police pay due attention to and clamp down entirely on 'disorderly activities' in a community, there will not be breeding grounds for more serious crimes, which take much policing effort to control. This theory guided a policing strategy that has been credited with drastically reducing the crime rate in New York, although scholars are divided on how much, or even whether, it contributed (Dixon 1998). Though Wilson and Kelling did not support their broken window theory with empirical evidence, a growing number of empirical studies in different countries have been conducted to assess its propositions. Some studies (Ren, Zhao & He 2017; Hinkle 2013) support the theory's hypotheses, while others (Crichlow 2016) do not. It seems the socioeconomic and cultural contexts of researchers significantly impact how they interpret the broken windows theory.

To assess the validity of the developed WTCWPOD scale, this study proposes six hypotheses based on an assumed relationship of the construct (willingness to communicate with police on duty) with six established constructs in police studies (cooperation with the police, police effectiveness, procedural justice, moral alignment with the police, obligation to obey the police, and police corruption).

The first hypothesis is that Nigerians' willingness to communicate with police on duty would have a positive relationship with cooperation with the police. It is based on the reasoning that the more people are willing to cooperate with the police, the greater will be their willingness to communicate with them. Cooperation with the police could be defined as a favourable disposition to work with the police in preventing crime and apprehending offenders (Kochel, Parks & Mastrofski 2011; Grant & Pryce 2019; Murphy et al. 2017). The construct is widely examined in police studies.

The second hypothesis is that police effectiveness would have a positive association with willingness to communicate with police on duty. This assumption is based on the fact that the more the public perceive the police as capable of preventing crime, apprehending offenders, and appropriately punishing them, the more they would be willing to support them with information that could assist them in succeeding in their duties. Police effectiveness has been described as the public's perception of police capacity to prevent crime, apprehend offenders and punish them (Finnimore 1982). It has been widely studied in many different nations and contexts of policing, focusing on its predictors and correlates (Kochel, Parks & Mastrofski 2011).

The third hypothesis is that willingness to communicate with police on duty would have a positive relationship with procedural justice. This assumption is based on the fact that the more Nigerians perceive the police as being fair in carrying out their duties, the higher will be their willingness to support them and communicate with them while on duty. Procedural justice is a key construct in police studies. It is usually considered as potent a factor as police effectiveness in determining public perceptions and attitudes towards police in many parts of the world (Sargeant 2015; Maguire 2018; Akinlabi 2015; Peacock 2020). It is construed as a philosophy that guides the practice of policing in such a way that the laid down rules and regulations are strictly followed to ensure fairness in the task of policing (Community Oriented Policing Service n.d.). Procedural justice greatly influences police legitimacy.

The fourth and fifth hypotheses focus on the relationship between WTCWPOD and moral alignment and the obligation to obey the police respectively. Moral alignment with the police is a feeling that the police have the same set of values and ethics as oneself (Van Damme 2015), while the obligation to obey the police is a cognitive assertion that whatever the case, citizens must obey directives issued by the police (Grant & Pryce 2019; Bello & Matshaba 2021). This study hypothesises that these two constructs in police studies would have a positive relationship with citizens' willingness to communicate with police on duty. Citizens who believe that the police share their moral values will be willing to work with the police by providing information that can help them succeed in their assignments. In the same vein, citizens who believe the police must be obeyed at all costs will also be willing to communicate with them when required to do so.

The last hypothesis assumes that Nigerians' WTCWPOD will have a negative relationship with police corruption, which has diverse dimensions (Hope 2018; Bello 2020). This hypothesis is based on the reasoning that the more the citizens perceive the police as being corrupt, the less trust they will have in them, and the less willing they will be to release information to them or communicate with them while on duty.

The six hypotheses are:

Hypothesis 1: There will be a positive relationship between cooperation with the police and willingness to communicate with police on duty.

Hypothesis 2: There will be a positive relationship between police effectiveness and willingness to communicate with police on duty.

Hypothesis 3: There will be a positive relationship between procedural justice and willingness to communicate with police on duty.

Hypothesis 4: There will be a positive relationship between moral alignment with the police and willingness to communicate with police on duty.

Hypothesis 5: There will be a positive relationship between the obligation to obey police and willingness to communicate with police on duty.

Hypothesis 6: There will be a negative relationship between police corruption and willingness to communicate with police on duty.

Method

Participants and procedure

The study was a cross-sectional survey – a scale development and validation study – and was conducted in a town in southwest Nigeria in April 2021. The town was considered appropriate for the study because the aim was not to generalise the findings, but to confirm that scale is appropriate for the target population. The researcher engaged research assistants who administered pen-on-paper questionnaires in person. Residents of the town who willingly volunteered to participate in the study were recruited after giving their consent. The study adopted a convenience sampling technique. The technique was considered appropriate as the study assessed relationships among the study variables and did not generalise the findings. The demographic characteristics of the selected participants is presented in Table 4.1.

Table 4.1 *Demography of the respondents*

Variables	Characteristics	Frequency	Percentages
Gender	Female	162	51.4
	Male	149	47.3
	Did not mention	4	1.2
	Total	315	100
Age	16–35 years	284	90.2
	Above 35 years	28	8.9
	Did not mention	3	1.0
	Total	315	100
Education level	Senior Secondary School	168	53.3
	National Diploma/ National Certificate in Education	45	14.3
	First Degree/Higher National Diploma		
	Postgraduate	81	25.7
	Did not mention	11	3.5
	Total	10	3.18
		315	100
Religion	Christianity	222	70.5
	Islam	78	24.8
	Other religions	9	2.9
	Did not mention	6	1.9
	Total	315	100

Measures

All the scales used for the study were adopted from the literature, except the WTCWPOD scale, which was developed by the researcher. The scale was assessed by a high-ranking (assistant inspector-general) police officer in the Nigeria Police Force, a professor in police studies, and three communications scholars (a professor and two doctors). They all considered it appropriate. It comprises six items measured with a five-point Likert-type scale from 'very unlikely' (1) to 'very likely' (5), as shown in Table 4.2.

Table 4.2 *Study scales and Cronbach alpha values*

Willingness to communicate with police officer (α = .90)

1. I will talk with a police officer who is on a duty in my neighbourhood.
2. I will talk with a police officer over a matter that I know deserves police attention.
3. I will talk with a police officer who is on an official assignment at my community/neighbourhood meeting.
4. I will talk with a guest police officer during a 'phone-in session' of a programme on security matters on radio/TV/online.
5. I will talk with a police officer during a face-to-face meeting (workshop/seminar, etc.) on security matters.
6. I will talk with a police officer who is on patrol/stop-and-search duty on the road.

Cooperation with police (α = .86)

1. I will volunteer to attend a community meeting to discuss crime in my neighbourhood.
2. I will call the police to report a crime in my neighbourhood.
3. I will report suspicious activity in my neighbourhood to the police.

Police effectiveness (α = .89)

1. How successful do you think the police are at preventing crimes?
2. How successful do you think the police are at maintaining public order?
3. How successful do you think the police are at offering help to the public?

Procedural justice (α = .88)

1. The police treat citizens with respect.
2. The police respect citizens' rights.
3. The police take time to listen to people.
4. The police make fair and impartial decisions.
5. The police are willing to motivate (explain) their decisions when asked to do so.

Moral alignment (α = .77)

1. The police stand up for (uphold) values that are important to people like me.
2. I generally support how the police usually act.
3. I respect the police.

Obligation to obey (α = .81)

1. You have to obey police orders, even if you disagree with them.
2. Non-obedience to the police is inexcusable.
3. I accept the decisions made by the police, even if I disagree with them.

Corruption (α = .89)

1. Nigerian police take bribes.
2. Nigerian police extort money from people.
3. Nigerian police are corrupt.

The cooperation with the police scale was adapted from Hope's (2018) and Bello's (2020) studies in Kenya and South Africa respectively. It consists of three items which were measured with a five-point Likert-type scale from 1 (very unlikely) to 5 (very likely). Procedural justice, moral alignment, obligation to obey, and police effectiveness scales were adapted from Grant & Pryce's (2019) study in Jamaica. The procedural justice scale consists of five items and the moral alignment and obligation to obey scales consist of three items each. The three variables were measured with a five-point Likert-type scale from 1 (strongly disagree) to 5 (strongly agree). The police effectiveness scale consists of three items measured with a five-point Likert-type scale from 1 (very little) to 5 (very high). The police corruption scale, which was adapted from Akinlabi's 2015 study in Nigeria, consists of three items, which were measured with a five-point Likert-type scale from 1 (not at all) to 5 (very often). Table 4.2 shows the items for each study scale, with their Cronbach alpha values.

Results

Three sets of data were analysed. First, an exploratory factor analysis (EFA) and a confirmatory factor analysis (CFA) were conducted to assess the validity of the scale. Then, a correlational analysis was conducted to assess the relationships between cooperation with the police, police effectiveness, procedural justice, moral alignment with the police, an obligation to obey police, and police corruption on the one hand and willingness to communicate with police on duty on the other hand.

The exploratory factor analysis

The EFA of the six items for willingness to talk with a police officer on duty was conducted using principal factor analysis (varimax rotation). The results of the Kaiser-Meyer-Olkin measure of sampling adequacy (KMO = 0.901) and the result of the Bartlett's test of sphericity ($\chi^2(315) = 1034.27$, $p < .001$) confirmed that the study sample size was large enough for EFA and appropriate for factor analysis. All the commonalities were above 0.50. All the items were loaded on one factor (see Table 4.3), which accounted for a 66.41 per cent variation in the data. They all had loading values above 0.60, which Matsunaga (2010) affirms as a good cut-off point.

The confirmatory factor analysis

The Amos statistical package (version 20) was used to conduct a CFA to assess the fitness of the developed scale. The results in Figure 4.1 show that all six items have good loadings (greater than 0.60, $p < .001$). The model had good fit indices: the Chi-square χ^2 (9, N = 315) = 24.707, $p < .01$; the Comparative fit index (CFI) was 0.985; the Tucker-Lewis index was 0.975; the root mean square error of approximation (RMSEA) was .075; and the standardised root mean-square residual (SRMR) was .03. The model is considered good because, with CFI ≥.95 and SRMR ≤.10 or RMSEA ≤ .06 and SRMR ≤ .10, it meets one of the most conservative criteria for a good fit – that posited by Hu & Bentler (1999).

Table 4.3 *Exploratory factor analysis results*

Items	Factor 1
Willingness to talk with a police officer on duty	
B1. I will talk with a police officer who is on a duty in my neighbourhood.	.839
B2. I will talk with a police officer over a matter that I know deserves police attention.	.814
B3. I will talk with a police officer who is on an official assignment at my community/neighbourhood meeting.	.869
B4. I will talk with a guest police officer during a 'phone-in-session' of a programme on security matters on radio/TV/online.	.831
B5. I will talk with a guest police officer during a face-to-face meeting (workshop/seminar, etc.) on security matters.	.728
B6. I will talk with a police officer who is on patrol/stop-and-search duty on the road.	.802

Figure 4.1 *Confirmatory factor analysis results*

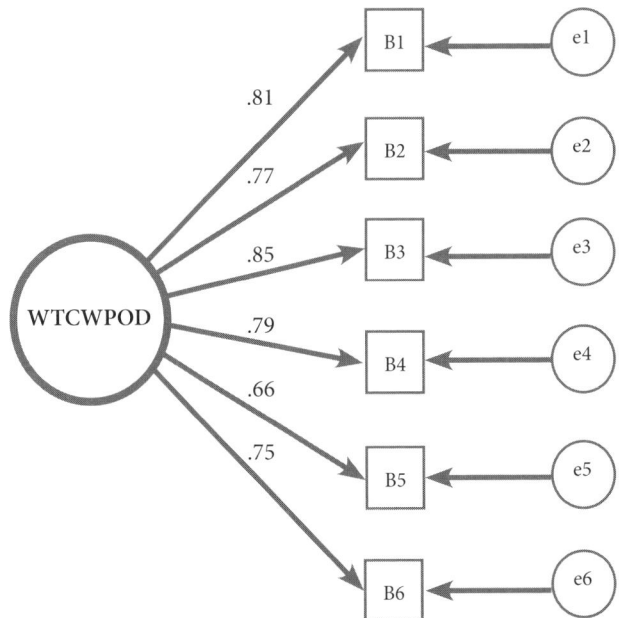

The correlational analysis

All six hypotheses were tested by calculating the Pearson product moment correlation between cooperation with the police, police effectiveness, procedural justice, moral alignment with the police, an obligation to obey police, and police corruption on the one hand and willingness to communicate with police on duty on the other hand. The first hypothesis predicted that there would be a positive relationship between WTCWPOD and cooperation with the police. The calculated Pearson product moment correlation r(313) = .77 was significant ($p < .01$). The second hypothesis predicted that there would be a positive relationship between WTCWPOD and police effectiveness. The calculated Pearson product moment correlation r(313) = .62 was significant ($p < .01$). The third hypothesis predicted that there would be a positive relationship between WTCWPOD and procedural justice. The calculated Pearson product moment correlation r(313) = .65 was significant ($p < .01$). The fourth hypothesis predicted that there would be a positive relationship between WTCWPOD and moral alignment with the police. The calculated Pearson product moment correlation r(313) = .68 was significant ($p < .01$). The fifth hypothesis predicted that there would be a positive relationship between WTCWPOD and obligation to obey the police. The calculated Pearson product moment correlation r(314) = .68, was significant ($p < .01$). The sixth hypothesis predicted that there would be a negative relationship between WTCWPOD and police corruption. The calculated Pearson product moment correlation r(314) = −.24, was significant ($p < .01$). The correlation analysis results are presented in Table 4.4.

Table 4.4 *Correlation analysis results*

	Talk with police	Cooperate with police	Police effectiveness	Procedural justice	Moral alignment with police	Obligation to obey police
Cooperate with police	.77**					
Police effectiveness	.62**	.59**				
Procedural justice	.65**	.58**	.74**			
Moral alignment with police	.68**	.56**	.69**	.85**		
Obligation to obey police	.68**	.63**	.51**	.63**	.66**	
Police corruption	−.24**	−.20**	−.38**	−.43**	−.37**	−.19**

** $p < .01$

Discussion and implications

This study developed and evaluated the willingness to communicate with police on duty (WTCWPOD) scale. The WTCWPOD is the first self-report scale to assess Nigerians' willingness to communicate with police on duty. The scale items were drawn from the literature and from the daily lived experiences of police–citizen interactions in Nigeria, which may be similar in other African countries. The study engaged exploratory factor analysis and confirmatory factor analysis to assess the validity of the scale, and also assessed the relationship of the construct with six established constructs in police studies (cooperation with the police, police effectiveness, procedural justice, moral alignment with the police, obligation to obey police, and police corruption).

The exploratory factor analysis and confirmatory factor analysis show that the WTCWPOD scale is valid. All the scale items load strongly on one factor and the model has good fit indices. The reliability test result shows that the scale is reliable (α = .90). The results of the correlational analysis also show that WTCWPOD has statistically significant, expected, and literature-supported relationships with cooperation with the police, police effectiveness, procedural justice, moral alignment with the police, obligation to obey police, and police corruption. It has strong positive relationships (Pearson product moment coefficient (r) above 0.6, $p <$ .01) with cooperation with police, police effectiveness, procedural justice, moral alignment with the police, and obligation to obey the police. Also, as expected, the WTCWPOD has a statistically significant negative relationship with police corruption.

This study contributes to knowledge in the field of police research in Nigeria. Specifically, it contributes to the literature on citizens' support for police–citizen relationship studies. Despite the recognised importance of police–citizen communication in Nigeria, there is no literature on willingness to communicate with police. Thus, the WTCWPOD scale developed and evaluated in this study will be a useful tool for police research in Nigeria, opening new prospects for research. Another advantage of this scale is that it is short. It can be incorporated into studies with other scales.

Suggestions for further studies

This study was carried out in southwest Nigeria, which is predominantly populated by Yorubas. The study can be replicated in other geopolitical zones of Nigeria that may be dominated by other ethnic groups to further assess its validity. Also, the majority of the participants in this study were young people, aged between 16 and 35, and most had post-primary school education. The study could be replicated among persons with lower levels of education, and even non-literate people, to further access its validity.

Conclusion

Nigerians' willingness to communicate with police on duty is essential to the nation's security and successful governance. That is why the Nigeria Police Force regularly engages in campaigns to persuade Nigerians to see the police as their friends with whom they can communicate freely and at any time. However, despite the recognised importance of police–citizen communication in Nigeria, there is no literature on the willingness of citizens to communicate with police. Contributing to the literature, this study developed the willingness to communicate with police on duty (WTCWPOD) scale and assessed the scale's validity and reliability. The results of the study suggest that the developed scale is valid and reliable, and that it would be a good research tool for police studies in Nigeria.

References

Aborisade RA (2018) Unsolved murders and the investigative failures of the Nigerian Police Force: Security and sociopolitical implications. *African Security Review* 27(2): 177–190. Accessed 16 December 2024, https://doi.org/10.1080/10246029.2017.1294087

Akinlabi OM (2015) Young people, procedural justice and police legitimacy in Nigeria. *Policing and Society* 27(4): 419–438. Accessed 16 December 2024, https://doi.org/10.1080/10439463.2015.1077836

Akinlabi OM (2019) Citizens' accounts of police use of force and its implication for trust in the police. *Journal of Crime and Justice* 43(2): 145–160. Accessed 16 December 2024, <https://doi.org/10.1080/0735648X.2019.1650798

Akinyetun TS (2021) Reign of terror: A review of police brutality on Nigerian youth by the Special Anti-Robbery Squad (SARS). *African Security Review* 30(3): 368–385. Accessed 16 December 2024, https://www.tandfonline.com/doi/abs/10.1080/10246029.2021.1947863

Allred RJ & Atkin D (2020) Cell phone addiction, anxiety, and willingness to communicate in face-to-face encounters. *Communication Reports* 33(3): 95–106. Accessed 16 December 2024, https://doi.org/10.1080/08934215.2020.1780456

Aremu AO, Pakes F & Johnston L (2011) The moderating effect of emotional intelligence on the reduction of corruption in the Nigerian Police. *Police Practice and Research* 12(3): 195–208. Accessed 16 December 2024, https://doi.org/10.1080/15614263.2010.536724

Badiora AI & Ntamark JJ (2019) Dynamics of public support for community policing (CP): Findings from high-crime and low-crime residential neighborhoods. *International Journal of Public Administration* 43(16): 1397–1412. Accessed 16 December 2024, https://doi.org/10.1080/01900692.2019.1669178

Baker SC & Watson BM (2019) Investigating the association between internet health information use and patient willingness to communicate with health care providers. *Health Communication* 35(6): 716–725. Accessed 16 December 2024, https://doi.org/10.1080/10410236.2019.1584778

Bello PO (2020) Do people still repose confidence in the police? Assessing the effects of public experience of police corruption in South Africa. *African Identities* 19(2): 141–159. Accessed 16 December 2024, https://doi.org/10.1080/14725843.2020.1792827

Bello PO & Matshaba TD (2021) Exploring procedural justice, obligation to obey and cooperation with the police in a sample of university students. *Contemporary Justice Review* 24(2): 262–277. Accessed 16 December 2024, https://doi.org/10.1080/10282580.2020.1870451

Clark K, Lin Y & Maher V (2015) Shall I help a stranger? Spiritual intelligence and its relation to altruism, ethnocentrism, intercultural willingness to communicate, and the intention to act. *Journal of Intercultural Communication Research* 44(4): 329–344. Accessed 16 December 2024, https://doi.org/10.1080/17475759.2015.1084590

Community Oriented Policing Service (n.d.) Procedural justice. US Department of Justice. Accessed 16 December 2024, https://portal.cops.usdoj.gov/resourcecenter/content.ashx/cops-w0795-pub.pdf

Crichlow VJ (2016) Will 'broken windows policing' work in Trinidad and Tobago? A critical perspective on zero tolerance and community policing in a multi-ethnic society. *Police Practice and Research* 17(6): 570–581. Accessed 16 December 2024, https://doi.org/10.1080/15614263.2016.1210009

Davis HE (2017) Broken and disordered: Selected critical readings on broken windows policing. *Legal Reference Services Quarterly* 36(3–4): 166–189. Accessed 16 December 2024, https://doi.org/10.1080/0270319X.2018.1405331

Dixon D (1998) Broken windows, zero tolerance, and the New York Miracle. *Current Issues in Criminal Justice* 10(1): 96–106. Accessed 16 December 2024, https://doi.org/10.1080/10345329.1998.12036118

Famosaya P (2020) Police–citizen interactions in Nigeria: The 'ordinary' aspects. *Policing and Society* 31(8): 936–949. Accessed 16 December 2024, https://doi.org/10.1080/10439463.2020.1798953

Finnimore P (1982) How should the effectiveness of the police be assessed? *Police Journal* 55(1): 56–66. Accessed 16 December 2024, https://www.ojp.gov/ncjrs/virtual-library/abstracts/how-should-effectiveness-police-be-assessed#:~:text=Traditionally%2C

Grant L & Pryce DK (2019) Procedural justice, obligation to obey, and cooperation with police in a sample of Jamaican citizens. *Police Practice and Research* 21(4): 368–382. Accessed 16 December 2024, https://doi.org/10.1080/15614263.2019.1644178

Hinkle JC (2013) The relationship between disorder, perceived risk, and collective efficacy: A look into the indirect pathways of the broken windows thesis. *Criminal Justice Studies* 26(4): 408–432. Accessed 16 December 2024, https://doi.org/10.1080/1478601X.2013.843253

Hope KR (2018) Police corruption and the security challenge in Kenya. *African Security* 11(1): 84–108. Accessed 16 December 2024, https://doi.org/10.1080/19392206.2017.1419650

Hu LT & Bentler PM (1999) Cutoff criteria for fit indexes in covariance structure analysis: Conventional criteria versus new alternatives. *Structural Equation Modeling: A Multidisciplinary Journal* 6: 1–55. Accessed 16 December 2024, http://dx.doi.org/10.1080/10705519909540118

Ike TJ, Singh D, Jidong DE, Ike LM & Ayobi EE (2021) Public perspectives of interventions aimed at building confidence in the Nigerian police: A systematic review. *Journal of Policing, Intelligence and Counter Terrorism* 17(1): 95–116. Accessed 16 December 2024, https://doi.org/10.1080/18335330.2021.1892167

Kassing JW (1997) Development of the intercultural willingness to communicate scale. *Communication Research Reports* 14(4): 399–407. Accessed 16 December 2024, https://doi.org/10.1080/08824099709388683

Kochel TR, Parks R & Mastrofski SD (2011) Examining police effectiveness as a precursor to legitimacy and cooperation with police. *Justice Quarterly* 30(5): 895–925. Accessed 16 December 2024, https://doi.org/10.1080/07418825.2011.633544

Logan S, Steel Z & Hunt C (2016) Intercultural willingness to communicate within health services: Investigating anxiety, uncertainty, ethnocentrism and help seeking behaviour.

International Journal of Intercultural Relations 54: 77–86. Accessed 16 December 2024, https://doi.org/10.1016/j.ijintrel.2016.07.007

Lu Y & Hsu CF (2008) Willingness to communicate in intercultural interactions between Chinese and Americans. *Journal of Intercultural Communication Research* 37(2): 75–88. Accessed 16 December 2024, https://doi.org/10.1080/17475750802533356

Maguire ER (2018) New frontiers in research on procedural justice and legitimacy in policing. *Police Practice and Research* 19(2): 107–110. Accessed 16 December 2024, https://doi.org/10.1080/15614263.2018.1418171

Matsunaga, M (2010) How to factor-analyze your data right. *International Journal of Psychological Research* 3(1): 97–110. Accessed 16 December 2024, DOI:10.21500/20112084.854

McCroskey JC (1992) Reliability and validity of the willingness to communicate scale. *Communication Quarterly* 40(1) 16–25. Accessed 16 December 2024, https://doi.org/10.1080/01463379209369817

Mulyono H, Saskia R, Arrummaiza VS & Suryoputro G (2020) Psychometric assessment of an instrument evaluating the effects of affective variables on students' WTC in face-to-face and digital environment. *Cogent Psychology* 7(1): 1823617. Accessed 16 December 2024, https://doi.org/10.1080/23311908.2020.1823617

Murphy K, Cramer RJ, Waymire KA & Barkworth J (2017) Police bias, social identity, and minority groups: A social psychological understanding of cooperation with police. *Justice Quarterly* 35(6): 1105–1130. Accessed 16 December 2024, https://doi.org/10.1080/07418825.2017.1357742

Peacock R (2020) Dominance analysis of police legitimacy's regressors: Disentangling the effects of procedural justice, effectiveness, and corruption. *Police Practice and Research* 22(1): 589–605. Accessed 16 December 2024, https://doi.org/10.1080/15614263.2020.1851229

Ren L, Zhao J 'Solomon' & He N 'Phil' (2017) Broken windows theory and citizen engagement in crime prevention. *Justice Quarterly* 36(1): 1–30. Accessed 16 December 2024, https://doi.org/10.1080/07418825.2017.1374434

Sargeant E (2015) Policing and collective efficacy: The relative importance of police effectiveness, procedural justice and the obligation to obey police. *Policing and Society* 27(8): 927–940. Accessed 16 December 2024, https://doi.org/10.1080/10439463.2015.1122008

Van Damme A (2015) The impact of police contact on trust and police legitimacy in Belgium. *Policing and Society* 27(2): 205–228. Accessed 16 December 2024, https://doi.org/10.1080/10439463.2015.1045510

5 Good governance remains key to Africa's sustainable development

Boikanyo C Nkwatle

Introduction

The thrust of this chapter is the impact of governance on the ability and capacity of the African continent to meet its Agenda 2063 plan. Critical to this are the progress made, the role of governance, and the challenges faced by the continent. There is no doubt that governance crises are at the core of the many problems that affect the continent. Despite the progress in countries such as South Africa, Namibia and Zambia where democratic ideals are entrenched, and which have experienced smooth power transitions and economic and infrastructural growth trajectories, the continent is being held back by the tentacles of dictatorships and autocracy. These drawbacks take the form of military coups, disputed elections marred with irregularities, violence, and with systemic corruption.

Due to the governance challenges bedevilling the continent, political conflicts, poor leadership, infrastructural collapse, and state capture are becoming the order of the day in many African countries such as Zimbabwe, Chad and Sudan. To some extent, these factors have an impact on peace, stability, and the ability of member states to provide services and sustainable growth and development. This chapter uses a theory-based evaluation to analyse the state of governance in selected member states of the African Union, and the challenges and progress made by these states to meet the Agenda 2063 goals thus far.

Background

Agenda 2063 is the blueprint and master plan for transforming Africa into a future global superpower. It is the concrete expression of the Pan-African drive for unity, self-determination, independence, progress, and collective wealth sought under Pan-Africanism and the African Renaissance. As the continent's strategic framework, it seeks to achieve its goal for inclusive and sustainable development (Ndizera & Muzee 2018). This strategic plan for the continent was prepared by the African Union Commission when celebrating the Organization of African Unity/African Union golden jubilee in 2013. As an affirmation of their commitment to support Africa's new path for attaining inclusive and sustainable economic growth and development, African heads of state signed the 50th Anniversary Solemn Declaration during the golden jubilee celebrations.

The need to envision a long-term 50-year development trajectory for Africa is critical, as Africa must revise and adapt its development agenda in response to ongoing structural transformations, increased peace, conflict reduction, renewed economic growth, social progress, the need for people-centred development, gender equality, youth empowerment, changing global contexts such as increased globalisation and the ICT revolution, and increased unity (Addaney 2018).

In addition to capturing Africa's future aspirations, Agenda 2063 also identifies significant flagship projects that include the African Continental Free Trade Area (AfCFTA) and the Grand Inga Hydropower Project, both of which have the potential to accelerate the economic development and transformation of the continent. Additionally, Agenda 2063 highlights crucial tasks to be carried out in its 10-year implementation plans to guarantee that Agenda 2063 provides the people of Africa with both quantitative and qualitative transformational outcomes (Addaney 2018).

The flagship projects of Agenda 2063 are programmes and initiatives that have been identified as key to accelerating Africa's economic growth and development as well as promoting our common identity by celebrating our history and our vibrant culture. The flagship projects include infrastructure, education, science, technology, arts, and culture, as well as initiatives to secure peace on the continent. The 15 flagship projects of Agenda 2063 are:

- an integrated high-speed train network
- an African commodities strategy
- the AfCFTA
- the African passport and free movement of people
- silencing the guns by 2020
- the Grand Inga Dam project
- a single African air-transport market
- an annual African economic forum
- the African financial institutions
- the Pan-African e-network
- Africa's outer space strategy
- an African virtual and e-university
- cyber security
- The Great African Museum
- Encyclopaedia Africana

According to the African Union (2015), the seven aspirations of Agenda 2063 are:
1. a prosperous Africa based on inclusive growth and sustainable development;
2. an integrated continent that is politically united based on the ideals of Pan-Africanism and the vision of Africa's Renaissance;
3. an Africa of good governance, democracy, respect for human rights, justice and the rule of law;
4. a peaceful and secure Africa;
5. an Africa with a strong cultural identity, common heritage, shared values and ethics;

6. an Africa whose development is people-driven, relying on the potential of African people, especially its women and youth, and caring for children; and
7. Africa as a strong, united, resilient and influential global player and partner.

These aspirations are backed up by specific goals and targets that are measurable and achievable if the African heads of state and their respective governments are intentional in their efforts and budgets. It is imperative to understand that Agenda 2063 complements the United Nations Sustainable Development Goals to make sure that countries work on both plans using the same efforts and investments (Mhangara et al. 2019).

Agenda 2063 was initiated in 2013, so enough time has passed to assess whether progress has been made. The Agenda 2063 plan is a series of five ten-year plans over its 50-year time frame. This chapter will use the first ten-year implementation plan of Agenda 2063 (2013–2023) as the basis for a critical analysis of the performance of Africa in the context of governance.

There remains a significant gap in understanding the precise impact of governance on the ability and capacity of African countries to meet the targets set out in the Agenda 2063 plan. The existing literature offers some insights into this relationship, but there is a lack of comprehensive empirical studies that systematically examine the specific governance factors that hinder or facilitate progress towards the Agenda 2063 goals. This gap in the literature presents an empirical challenge, as the existing research primarily focuses on case studies rather than the provision of concrete evidence of the impact of governance on development outcomes in Africa.

This chapter aims to address this gap by conducting a rigorous qualitative empirical analysis of the impact of governance on the ability and capacity of African countries to meet the targets outlined in the Agenda 2063 plan. Through this analysis, the chapter intends to offer valuable insights for policymakers and development practitioners in designing effective strategies to promote good governance and achieve sustainable development in African countries.

Conceptualisation of key terms

It is important to first define and conceptualise the key terms to set up a basis of understanding and decide on operational working definitions. Essential concepts are governance, sustainability and development.

Governance

Governance is defined as structures and processes that ensure accountability, transparency, responsiveness, rule of law, stability, equity and inclusiveness, empowerment, and broad-based participation (Ruhlandt 2018). Governance also refers to the norms, values, and game rules that govern how public affairs are managed in a transparent, participatory, inclusive, and responsive manner. As a result, governance can be subtle and difficult to detect. Governance, in broad terms, refers to the culture and institutional environment in which citizens and stakeholders interact with one another and participate in public affairs (Kjaer 2023).

Governance encompasses the system by which an organisation is controlled and operates and the mechanisms by which it, and its people, are held to account. Ethics, risk management, compliance, and administration are all elements of governance (Davis, Schoorman & Donaldson 2018). One could conclude that governance is the process by which rulers are given power, through which they establish rules, and through which those rules are upheld and altered. So, to comprehend governance, it is necessary to identify both the rulers and the rules, as well as the many mechanisms by which they are chosen, described, and connected to society at large (Davis, Schoorman & Donaldson 2018).

Importantly, governance is frequently confused with management, but the latter refers to the functions of planning, implementation, and monitoring to achieve predefined results (Kjaer 2023). Management refers to the processes, structures, and arrangements that are designed to mobilise and transform available physical, human, and financial resources to achieve specific goals. Individuals or groups of people who are given the authority to achieve the desired results are referred to as managers (Keping 2018). Governance systems establish the parameters within which management and administrative systems will function. Governance is concerned with how power is distributed and shared, how policies are developed, how priorities are established, and how stakeholders are held accountable (Keping 2018).

It is almost trite to state that, although there is no universally acknowledged definition of 'good governance', it may be assumed to encompass: complete respect for human rights; rule of law; effective participation; multi-actor partnerships; political pluralism; transparent and accountable processes and institutions; an effective public sector; legitimacy; access to knowledge, information, and education; political empowerment of people; equity; sustainability; and attitudes and values that foster sustainability (Doornbos 2019). Governance should therefore be 'good' to be effective in any situation, which leads to the conceptualisation of the term 'good governance' (Addink 2019). The United Nations Development Programme (UNDP n.d.) defines good governance as a system of governance that is participatory, transparent and accountable, in the same vein as being effective and equitable, with the eventual result being the promotion of the rule of law.

In conclusion, effective governance refers to the institutional and political actions and outcomes required to accomplish development objectives. The degree to which it upholds the promise of human, civil, cultural, economic, political, and social rights is the fundamental test of 'good' governance. Are the institutions of governance successfully protecting the rights to good health, safe housing, enough food, high-quality education, impartial justice, and personal security?

Sustainability

Ruggerio (2021) defines sustainability as the capacity to constantly support or maintain a process across time. Sustainability aims to stop the depletion of natural or physical resources in business and policy contexts so that they will be accessible in the future (Farley & Smith 2020). Hence, sustainable policies place a strong emphasis on how a particular policy or corporate practice will affect people, ecosystems, and the larger economy in the long run. The idea frequently corresponds to the conviction that the earth will sustain irreparable harm if significant changes are not made to the way it is managed (Farley & Smith 2020).

The three pillars of sustainability – the economy, environment, and society – are also known colloquially as profits, planet, and people. In that breakdown, the idea of 'economic sustainability' focuses on protecting natural resources – both renewable and non-renewable – that offer physical inputs for economic development (Farley & Smith 2020). The concept of environmental sustainability places more emphasis on maintaining life-sustaining ecosystems, including the soil and atmosphere, to support both economic activity and human existence. It highlights the importance of maintaining ecosystems and biodiversity. On the other hand, social sustainability focuses on how economic systems affect people, and encompasses initiatives to end hunger and poverty and fight inequality (Salas-Zapata & Ortiz-Muñoz 2019).

Sustainability in the context of development entails recognising that growth must be both inclusive and environmentally sound to reduce poverty and build shared prosperity for today's population and to continue to meet the needs of future generations. It is efficient with resources and carefully planned to deliver both immediate and long-term benefits (Salas-Zapata & Ortiz-Muñoz 2019).

Development

Growth, advancement, and positive change – or the addition of physical, economic, environmental, social, and demographic components – are all products of development. The goal of development is to raise the standard of living for the populace while protecting resources and creating or expanding employment opportunities locally and regionally. Development involves a change in the quality of something as well as the setting up of circumstances that will allow that change to continue in the future (Rogers, Jalal & Boyd 2012).

Beginning in the second part of the 20th century, development became a key topic on the global agenda. It became clear that economic progress did not always result in an improvement in the standard of living for people everywhere, and that emphasis needed to be placed on specific policies that would direct resources and promote social and economic mobility for different tiers of the population (Rogers, Jalal & Boyd 2012).

The term 'development' has undergone numerous definitions and emphases over the years from experts and academics. For instance, Amartya Sen (2000) created the 'capability approach' that described development as a tool that enables people to attain the peak of their abilities by allowing freedom of economic, social, and family action. This strategy served as the foundation for the UNDP's 1990 Human Development Index, which was created to quantify development. In the area of gender, Martha Nussbaum (2000), employing the 'capabilities approach', placed a strong emphasis on the empowerment of women as a vehicle for development (Jabareen 2008).

Professionals like Jeffrey Sachs and Paul Collier concentrated on the factors that hinder or repress progress in particular nations, causing them to remain for decades in extreme poverty (Bloom, Sachs, Collier & Udry 1998). Civil wars, a lack of natural resources, and poverty itself are some of the different poverty traps. The ability to relate to political, economic, and social realities in a nation allows for development.

Governance in Africa and the development nexus

In evaluating the state of governance in Africa over the last 10 years since the inception of Agenda 2063, it is important to note that there have been positive developments as well as regressions. While some countries have made significant strides in strengthening democratic institutions, promoting good governance, and combating corruption, others continue to face challenges such as weak institutions, political instability, and human rights abuses. The erosion of the social contract and the deterioration of the government's capacity to expand the economy in a way that benefits all citizens are significant aspects of the problem of good governance and transparency. Several critical indicators are crucial to understanding the state of governance in Africa.

Peace and security

Peace and security are critical measures of the level and state of governance in Africa. Peace and security are priority areas of Agenda 2063 because they are essential for the sustainable development of the continent. The Africa Governance Report (African Union 2019) stated that peace and security, as well as democratic governance, are necessary for social and economic progress. The imperatives of continental integration and sustainable development are intertwined, interdependent, and mutually reinforcing. So, Aspiration 4 of Agenda 2063 sees a secure and peaceful Africa as being essential to the advancement of Africa.

To effectively and critically analyse the true state of governance on the continent, one must use Agenda 2063's monitoring tools. According to the Africa Governance Report (African Union 2019), the Constitutive Act; the African Charter on Democracy, Elections, and Governance; the Declaration on Principles Governing the Conduct of Democratic Elections in Africa; the Convention on the Prevention and Combating of Terrorism; and the Protocol Relating to the Establishment of the Peace and Security Council of the African Union are among the key AU documents that are critical for assessing the peace, security, and governance aspects.

Elections

This chapter focuses mainly on the democratic aspect of elections – a thorny issue in the African context. Elections have a significant impact on governance and sustainability or development in Africa. Free and fair elections are essential for promoting good governance, as they enable citizens to choose their leaders and hold them accountable for their actions. The democratic process also plays a crucial role in promoting sustainability and development, as leaders are expected to respond to the needs of the people and prioritise policies that promote long-term prosperity.

Most of Africa's history of competitive elections shows that the process is frequently tainted by pre- and post-election turmoil. These crises typically result from a lack of trust in the electoral process, the body in charge of conducting elections, and the election results. The threat or actual boycott of elections by opposition parties, as well as violence and intimidation of political rivals, are symptomatic of these crises.

The past ten years have seen commendable progress in smooth power transitions in some of the emerging democracies. Although contested, the Democratic Republic of Congo's 2018 elections were better than the other previous elections. Zimbabwe's 2018 elections were smooth but contested, and resulted in six people losing their lives after opposition party protests about rigging. Malawi had a smooth transition of power with the opposition party taking power and the ruling party leaving power as was the case with Zambia and Lesotho as well. Although the transitions are becoming smoother, they are not perfect, so more efforts and investments are needed to strengthen democratic institutions.

The impact of free and fair elections can be felt on the economic side which is critical for sustainable development. Kenya, Ghana, Nigeria, Zimbabwe, and South Africa are just a few of the African nations that have been unable to control their soaring inflation and depreciating currencies. Zambia's inflation rate was reduced under Hichilema's administration from 24.4 per cent in August 2021 to 9.7 per cent in June 2022. To triple Zambia's growth through agriculture and increased production across all economic sectors has been the goal of President Hichilema. Leaders who are elected by the people have a greater incentive to work for the citizens than leaders who lead based on rigged elections (Resnick 2022).

Coups

The African Union has been known to be non-apologetic about refusing to recognise leadership through coups. Many countries follow a zero-tolerance approach, which has led to several coups being denounced and the military being forced to hand over power to civilian leadership. This zero tolerance to coups by the African Union has led to many coups being crushed through sustained diplomatic pressure from the Union (Avoulete 2022).

However, since the 2017 Zimbabwean election, which was basically a coup, was approved by the Southern African Development Community (SADC) and the AU, many other coups have been successful because the Zimbabwean precedent indicated that a veneer of constitutionality is sufficient for a coup to be accepted by the rest of the African Union and its community member countries.

The 2022 African Union General Assembly ended with a note from all the state leaders and the AU unequivocally denouncing coups and making their position clear that they have a zero tolerance of them. Burkina Faso, Guinea, Mali and Sudan were all suspended from the AU in 2022 due to coups in their countries. The wave of unconstitutional power transitions through coups has been rather worrying and does not inspire confidence going forward (Mohammed 2022). Bankole Adeoye, head of the AU's Peace and Security Council, told the media that, for the first time in the history of the African Union, four countries had been suspended in one calendar year for having coups (Baltoi 2023).

Military coups and wars in Africa have prompted displaced people to try to relocate to safer locations, increasing the number of refugees. Presently, one-third of all people who have been forcefully displaced live in Africa. Huge economic and other burdens that have resulted from the refugee crisis include falling growth rates, rising poverty rates, low median personal incomes, deteriorating infrastructure, family dissolution brought on by forced relocation, casualties, kidnapping of children, and recruitment into armed conflicts (Oxford Analytica 2023).

Military coups cause unrest and instability in the nations involved, deter investment, and promote widespread financial corruption. Nigeria, for instance, has risen to the top of the list of the most corrupt African nations because of the political unrest and coups during the recent decades that led to pillaging of the country's natural resources, especially oil (Balima 2020).

Sudan, under former President Omar al-Bashir (1989–2019), experienced serious political and security instability as well as strained relations with the international community. In consequence, the nation suffered significant economic losses that were made worse when South Sudan seceded from Sudan in 2011, and Sudan was labelled as a state supporter of terrorism. As a result, instability has affected the country's economy, disrupted economic reform plans, and led to a return of international pressures and sanctions. For example, the US Department of State suspended aid to Sudan (Balima 2020).

The price of bauxite, the world's main source of aluminium, increased by 40 per cent as a result of the military takeover in Guinea in September 2021, the largest increase since May 2011. This development occurred as the global economy was still rebounding from the COVID-19 pandemic, with rising demand in the automobile and construction sectors driving up prices. The economic repercussions of this disruption have been significant, with several industries reporting cost escalations and supply chain challenges. Analysts estimate that the ripple effects have led to a global economic impact in the billions of dollars, particularly in sectors dependent on aluminium production. The situation is expected to stabilise gradually, but full recovery could take years, contingent on geopolitical developments and the restoration of consistent supply chains (Decalo 2021).

Global economy

According to International Monetary Fund (IMF) projections, the forecast for global growth in 2029 is 3.1 per cent, one of the lowest five-year-ahead forecasts in decades. Four years after the outbreak of COVID-19, fiscal deficits and debts are higher than pre-pandemic projections and are forecast to remain higher over the medium term. Without decisive action, global public debt is projected to inch above 100 per cent of GDP by 2029 (IMF 2024).

Corruption

Central and east African nations lose over USD 4 billion annually due to illicit smuggling. Ghana, Burkina Faso, and Niger in particular lose revenue from the trafficking of unlawfully mined gold. The primary beneficiaries are smugglers and corrupt officials exploiting weak governance structures to siphon off the continent's resources for personal gain (Balima 2020). The lack of proper governance presents a cash cow for any politician or individual to pillage the country's resources for the sake of personal financial gain and political power.

Conflicts and terrorism

Conflicts – either between two or more countries or between tribal or warring parties within a country – are detrimental to the development of any community. The challenge with conflicts in Africa is that, while they are caused by socioeconomic problems, they also cause socioeconomic problems, further entrenching poverty and economic decline and hindering progress.

Many nations are experiencing internal disputes and various types of unrest, and there are also violent disruptions related to economic problems, racial tension, religious differences, political polarisation, violent extremism, terrorism, and other issues. According to the Geneva Academy of International Humanitarian Law and Human Rights, Africa comes second globally in terms of the number of armed conflicts, with over 35 non-international armed conflicts occurring in various countries across the continent (Geneva Academy 2024). The four main transnational regions experiencing conflict include the Mano River Area, the Great Lakes Region, the Horn of Africa, and the Sahel/Maghreb Region (African Union 2019).

The challenge of terrorism, which is at the heart of some conflicts, is increasing rather than being dealt with. Since the inception of Agenda 2063, countries battling with terrorism include Nigeria at the hands of Boko Haram, Kenya and the Horn of Africa region, and Mozambique where Islamic State is setting up operations in the marginalised and poverty-stricken Cabo Delgado province, which is rich in natural gas, but that does not benefit the locals (Bussotti & Coimbra 2023).

By the end of November 2020, the effect of terrorism in Cabo Delgado had included the emergence of widespread violence, insecurity, the death of over 2 400 people, and the displacement of over 500 000 civilians (Vhumbunu 2021). It has also disrupted economic activities, especially farming, thereby worsening food insecurity. The role of governance in this is evidenced by the systematic marginalisation of the province which resulted in poverty levels being high, making the province an easier target for radicalisation and terrorism to emerge (Vhumbunu 2021). The insurgency has had far-reaching implications within the social, economic, humanitarian, and political spheres. What is undeniable is the fact that Mozambique has not yet been able to contain and subdue the insurgents, as the country needs more capacity in terms of training, military intelligence, reconnaissance, and equipment.

In Côte d'Ivoire, which produces 50 per cent of the continent's cocoa supplies, The government and rebels fund military operations with cocoa exports, thereby prolonging the political tensions, civil wars, and coups that have plagued the country since 2002. The impact has been a reduction in the production of this commodity, further exacerbated by destruction of farms and shortage of machinery. But one of the most serious consequences of political instability in Cote d'Ivoire is that farmers have been forced in recent years to insist on higher prices for cocoa as a precaution against sudden security and political volatility and shifts. A concurrent huge increase in demand for cocoa from China, India and Europe helped push up the prices of the commodity on global markers (Ogunkalu & Eniayejuni 2019).

Socioeconomic development

This section looks at three critical aspects for socioeconomic development from the governance perspective, and summarises other priority areas mentioned in Agenda 2063.

Service delivery

The state and level of governance in Africa is evidenced by the state and quality of service delivery provided to citizens. African people are getting a raw deal from leadership mandated to provide basic social and economic services to citizens. South Africa quickly comes to mind, given the frequency of service delivery protests. In the first half of 2021, despite COVID-19, there were nearly 900 service delivery protests in South Africa. This clearly shows the state and nature of governance in Africa, and how the populace is fed up with aging infrastructure and the unavailability of basic services and goods such as water and electricity.

Zimbabwe's health system is another clear example of the state of governance and leadership in Africa. Zimbabwe's current system fails in three respects which are key to any healthcare system: policy, people and funding. The result is that it is unable to deliver the most basic care. There is a lack of medicines and functioning hospital equipment and the system is devoid of empathy. Zimbabweans believe that one goes to hospital to die, not to have one's health restored (Makoni 2020). Instead of fixing the healthcare system, which is in dire need of a fresh capital injection, the senior leadership of the country has been embroiled in a multi-million-dollar corruption scandal (Mutambara & Naidu 2021).

Sustainable use of resources

One of Africa's biggest challenges is exploiting its resources in a sustainable way. Key to this is the fact that the continent is abundantly endowed with resources that are needed in the modern era but they are being exploited by other countries to the detriment of Africa. China, for example, has played a dominant role in rare earth mining and mineral sourcing in sub-Saharan Africa with the value of mineral exports at about US$ 10 billion in 2019. This figure reflects China's extensive investments in Africa's mining sector, as well as its dependence on Africa's mineral resources to fuel its own industrial growth (Kohnert 2024). Zambia is so indebted to China that debts are being repaid in mineral rights on terms that are unfavourable to Zambia (Brautigam 2022). Zimbabwe is choking under mounting international debt as it begins to pay the price for borrowing heavily from China for infrastructure projects at the tail end of Robert Mugabe's rule (Manyeruke 2021). The loans saw Zimbabwe's public and publicly guaranteed external debt stock rise to US$ 13.35 billion by the end of December 2021.

The way forward

Most African countries achieved their highest socioeconomic growth just after gaining independence but it waned as on the euphoria wore off. Only a very few African countries are entrenching democratic principles and good governance through strong institutions rather than strong men, and the progress they make is eroded by other countries regressing. For example, Zambia's new leader, who came in through a popular vote, has been implementing impactful projects and programmes while neighbouring Zimbabwe is gradually entrenching autocratic systems (Gerzso, Van de Walle & Gloppen 2023).

Based on the progress of the last 10 years, it is unlikely that the targets set for 2063 will be met. Few problems have been solved, and most African leaders are not inspired to usher in pro-poor policies to change the lives of their citizens, but are more focused on power retention and self-enrichment (Crocker 2019).

Despite the African Union's efforts to ensure that the continent develops, it appears the continental mother body is too weak to deal effectively with the governance challenges that greatly and negatively impacts upon the capacity for the continent to achieve sustainable development. The AU has had a shaky two decades burdened with intertwined problems of governance, external dependence, and poor capacity (Adeyeye & Atidoga 2021). The countries that donate to the AU to support its commitments are actually part of the problem and sometimes contribute to the challenges it faces. This could undermine the capacity of the AU to operate effectively and enforce mandates for member countries to commit to meeting the targets of Agenda 2063.

The recommendations in this chapter include investing in combating corruption, entrenching democracy through elections, and entrenching the rule of law.

Investments in combating corruption

Corruption is at the heart of governance challenges in Africa. In fact, some countries are poor in governance systems for the benefit of engaging in corrupt activities. Putting in place strong institutions that are critical to fighting corruption is at the core of improving governance in Africa. From Malawi to South Africa and Zimbabwe, from Angola to Mozambique and Namibia, in countries across Africa high-ranking civil servants and their relatives, in cahoots with industry and business leaders, seem to have long been shamelessly stealing from the long-suffering masses (Sedgo 2022).

In this regard, Africa is not in short supply of the knowledge or policies required to fight corruption, but enforcement is a challenge. Many of the member countries are signatories of the African Union Convention on Preventing and Combating Corruption, and the focus should be on the enforcement and there is no better institution to enforce that than the AU. There is an urgent need to address corruption in the delivery of basic services such as housing, water, sanitation, and judicial systems, among others. Corruption in these areas affects all who rely on these public services, but especially the most vulnerable citizens such as women, children, and people living with disabilities (Hope 2020).

The AU seems especially pleased with its anti-corruption initiatives. It takes pride in the fact that its fight against corruption has greatly contributed to the ongoing transformation of economies across the continent and reinforces the determination towards attaining inclusive and sustainable development as envisaged in Africa's Agenda 2063. However, the well-publicised efforts of this institution to combat corruption have scarcely resulted in any noticeable improvements. The aforementioned instances clearly show that corruption is still widespread throughout the continent (Pring & Vrushi 2019). The only thing that has changed in recent years is that most African leaders now feel the need to declare their determination to fight corruption throughout their electoral campaigns due to a public awakening about the consequences of corruption (Pring & Vrushi 2019). These election promises, however, seldom transfer into action.

Eradicating corruption is not only essential to establishing firm adherence to the rule of law and political stability, but it is also critical to promoting economic growth and reducing poverty in countries such as Malawi, Nigeria and South Africa. It is time for the AU to assert its independence and demonstrate a strong, renewed and active commitment to mitigate the socioeconomic consequences of bad leadership in Africa.

Entrenching democracy through elections

Leaders who get into power through free and fair elections have a better chance of abiding by the mandate given by the populace than those who gained power through nefarious means. But leaders who get into power through rigging would know that the majority of the populace does not subscribe to their leadership so they would rather rely even more on rigging for the next elections because they do not have the buy-in of the populace (Oxford Analytica 2020).

The challenge with the African Union and other regional bodies is to rubber-stamp every election in Africa despite there being evidence of rigging and irregularities. A case in point is the 2020 Malawian elections which were approved by the SADC and went on to be overturned by Malawi's Supreme Court. These regional blocs such as the SADC and the Economic Community of West African States should be applying the standards of the African Union to complement the efforts of the AU (Oxford Analytica 2020). Standards of elections should be raised to ensure that irregularities and fraud opportunities are limited, and the continent's populace has the chance to elect people whom they want (Soyiyo 2021).

If the AU took a more proactive approach and invested in the elections of every country the continent will come to value adherence to ethical and effective leadership selection. Due to the fact that elections are still marred by irregularities and systematic violence against opposition parties, the opportunities for the continent to have quality leaders to choose from are removed almost completely. The AU through complementary efforts of the regional blocs should come up with strict conditions for elections to raise the bar of freedom and fairness. Africa should have issues-based elections just like the developed world rather than euphoria and sloganeering that is necessitated by toxic political arenas on the continent.

Entrenching rule of law

Africa still finds itself on the wrong side of history on the basis of blatant disregard of the rule of law. Countries such as the United States and the European Union have played a key role in the promotion of rule through sanctioning regimes that trample upon human rights and rule of law. The brotherhood approach is still a problem in African politics in the sense that leaders cover each other and do not face the consequences of their actions. The level of impunity has been so institutionalised and systematised that regional blocs just rubber-stamp the decisions due to the pressure from autocratic or dictatorial leaders.

Upon assuming office, President Mnangagwa had to say 'nice' words to former President Mugabe, indicating that as Mugabe was the AU's friend, his welfare would be taken care of. Observers such as Munoriyarwa and Chambwera (2020) viewed the speech as an attempt to pacify and buy the favour of the African Union member states, leaders who were friends with Mugabe. Applying critical analyses to this one example shows that there was nothing that was ever going to happen to President

Mugabe despite his record on human rights abuses and the absence of the rule of law during his reign. The African Union and its member states were friends and would overlook any violations.

Pan-Africanism is being used as a veneer to cover the blatant impunity and brotherhood that happens amongst African leaders at the expense of rule of law. It is important that the AU resolved to entrench the rule of law in order to raise the standards of accountability, transparency and responsibility: critical ingredients of good governance. It is high time Pan-Africanism stopped being abused to entrench impunity. The whole continent at the behest and leadership of the AU needs to begin to condemn violators of human rights. If the AU were to adopt such an approach, this would undermine the imperialist and neo-colonialist propaganda that is preached by the leaders of countries who have been sanctioned by the US and Europe. The forceful measures that countries such as the US and the European Union impose on countries such as Sudan and Zimbabwe should actually be executed by the African Union and the regional blocs.

Inspiration should be drawn from the ECOWAS decision that was taken in Gambia which led to Mammah Jameh vacating the office he was refusing to leave in 2016. The former leader had lost an election and was refusing to step down, which prompted the ECOWAS region to send its army to force him to abide by the needs of the majority of people who had voted him out of office. The best form of Pan-Africanism is one that propels each political leader to do good, and to be accountable and take responsibility if something wrong had been done. Autocratic leaders are forming alliances to support and protect each other when under pressure, while democrats are silenced within the AU.

Conclusion

This chapter looked at the performance – the good, the bad and the ugly – over the last 10 years since the inception of the Agenda 2063 in 2013. The conclusion and findings of the critical analysis shows that there has been backsliding in governance rather than improvement and growth. The few good examples of countries that are entrenching their democracies and instituting good governance systems are overshadowed by the ones who are in regression.

The lack of good governance on the African continent is the greatest impediment to the achievement of Agenda 2063's targets. There is no incentive whatsoever for political leaders to institute good governance, which benefits certain political players in many countries. Local conflicts are not being solved because they provide opportunities for self-enrichment. Examples of these include looting in the Malian army, constrained elections in Zimbabwe, and service delivery protests in South Africa. These continue because the resources needed to fix the problems have been frittered away by corrupt leaders.

In contrast, countries like Zambia, Ghana, and even Rwanda despite its autocratic nature, are registering sustainable and commendable economic growth due to instituting proper governance systems aided by smooth power transitions and the resilience of the populace to election rigging. Kenya's elections are becoming 'smoother' and more peaceful, and election rhetoric has been raised to become issue-based, and in Lesotho, the opposition party that came to power is showing promising signs of fixing the mess left by the previous regime.

To achieve the set targets, the AU needs 'teeth' but those teeth must be used without challenging the sovereignty of member states. Sovereignty and Pan-Africanist ideologies are being abused by autocratic regimes to shield their corrupt leaders from the law. It is high time the continent sees the baring of teeth – like ECOWAS did in 2016 in Gambia. Actions that are against good governance, the rule of law, and peace and security should be condemned by Africans first, before others. This is the time to pull our heads out of the sand and for Africa to confront its demons head on without fear or favour for the benefit of the over 1 billion people on the continent to relieve them of the consequences of poor service delivery from their leaders.

References

Addaney M (2018) The African Union's Agenda 2063: Education and its realization. In AC Onuaora-Oguno, WO Egbewole & TW Kleven (Eds) *Education law, strategic policy and sustainable development in Africa: Agenda 2063*. Cham: Palgrave Macmillan. Accessed 21 December 2024, https://www.researchgate.net/publication/318377776_The_African_Union's_Agenda_2063_Education_and_Its_Realization

Addink H (2019) *Good governance: Concept and context*. Oxford: Oxford University Press

Adeyeye JA & Atidoga DF (2021) African Union peacekeeping operations: Challenges and emerging issues. *Scholars International Journal of Law, Crime and Justice* 4(8): 492–511. Accessed 21 December 2024, https://www.researchgate.net/publication/354150156_African_Union_Peacekeeping_Operations_Challenges_and_Emerging_Issues

African Union (2019) The Africa Governance Report: Promoting African Union shared values. Accessed 21 December 2024, https://au.int/sites/default/files/documents/36843-doc-aga_report_-_english_-_online.pdf

African Union Commission (2015) *Agenda 2063: The Africa we want; Framework document*. Accessed 6 December 2024, https://au.int/sites/default/files/documents/33126-doc-framework_document_book.pdf

Avoulete K (2022) Should ECOWAS Rethink its approach to coups? *Foreign Policy Research Institute* (3 February). Accessed 21 December 2024, https://www.fpri.org/article/2022/02/should-ecowas-rethink-its-approach-to-coups/

Balima HW (2020) Coups d'état and the cost of debt. *Journal of Comparative Economics* 48(3): 509–528. Accessed 21 December 2024, https://www.sciencedirect.com/science/article/abs/pii/S0147596720300159

Baltoi D (2023) A deeper look into the West African coup wave. *Foreign Policy Research Institute* (9 January). Accessed 21 December 2024, https://www.fpri.org/article/2023/01/a-deeper-look-into-the-west-african-coup-wave/

Bloom J, Sachs D, Collier P & Udry C (1998) Geography, demography and economic growth in Africa. *Papers on Economic Activity* 2: 207–295

Brautigam D (2022) China and Zambia: Creating a sovereign debt crisis. *International Affairs* 98(4): 1347–1365. Accessed 21 December 2024, https://www.researchgate.net/publication/361794636_China_and_Zambia_creating_a_sovereign_debt_crisis

Bussotti L & Coimbra EJ (2023) Struggling the Islamic State in Austral Africa: The SADC military intervention in Cabo Delgado (Mozambique) and its limits. *Frontiers in Political Science* 5:1122373. Accessed 21 December 2024, https://www.frontiersin.org/journals/political-science/articles/10.3389/fpos.2023.1122373/full

Crocker CA (2019) African governance: Challenges and their implications. *Hoover Institution*. (14 January). Accessed 21 December 2024, https://www.hoover.org/research/african-governance-challenges-and-their-implications

Davis JH, Schoorman FD & Donaldson L (2018) Toward a stewardship theory of management. In AE Singer (Ed.) *Business ethics and strategy*. London: Routledge

Decalo S (2021) Military rule in Africa: Etiology and morphology. In S Baynham (Ed.) *Military power and politics in black Africa*. London: Routledge

Doornbos M (2019) 'Good governance': The rise and decline of a policy metaphor? *The Journal of Development Studies* 37(6): 93–108. Accessed 21 December 2024, https://doi.org/10.1080/713601084

Farley HM & Smith ZA (2020) *Sustainability: If it's everything, is it nothing?* London: Routledge

Geneva Academy (2024) Today's armed conflicts. Accessed 29 December 2024, https://geneva-academy.ch/galleries/today-s-armed-conflicts

Gerzso T, Van de Walle N & Gloppen S (2023) Legal strategies: Constitutional, administrative, judicial, and discursive lawfare. In LR Arriola, L Rakner & N van de Walle (Eds) *Democratic backsliding in Africa?* Oxford: Oxford University Press. Accessed 21 December 2024, https://academic.oup.com/book/45327/chapter/389220122

Hope KR (2020) Channels of corruption in Africa: Analytical review of trends in financial crimes. *Journal of Financial Crime* 27(1): 294–306

International Monetary Fund, 2024. *Annual Report: Sustaining the recovery*. Accessed 30 December 2024, https://www.imf.org/external/pubs/ft/ar/2024/in-focus/sustaining-the-recovery/

Jabareen Y (2008) A new conceptual framework for sustainable development. *Environment, Development and Sustainability* 10: 179–192. Accessed 21 December 2024, https://link.springer.com/article/10.1007/s10668-006-9058-z

Keping Y (2018) Governance and good governance: A new framework for political analysis. *Fudan Journal of the Humanities and Social Sciences* 11: 1–8. Accessed 21 December 2024, https://doi.org/10.1007/s40647-017-0197-4

Kjaer AM (2023) *Governance*. Hoboken: Wiley

Kohnert D (2024) Prospects and challenges for the export of rare earths from sub-Saharan Africa to the EU. *International Journal of African Studies* 4(1): 87–110. DOI:10.51483/IJAFRS.4.1.2024.87-110

Makoni M (2020) COVID-19 worsens Zimbabwe's health crisis. *The Lancet*, 396(10249): 457. Accessed 21 December 2024, DOI:10.1016/S0140-6736(20)31751-7

Manyeruke C (2021) Chinese economic development projects in Zimbabwe. In SO Abidde, & TA Ayoola (Eds) *China in Africa: Between imperialism and partnership in humanitarian development*. Lanham, MD: Rowman & Littlefield

Mhangara P, Lamba A, Mapurisa W & Mudau N (2019) Towards the development of Agenda 2063 geo-portal to support sustainable development in Africa. *ISPRS International Journal of Geo-Information* 8(9): 399. Accessed 21 December 2024, https://doi.org/10.3390/ijgi8090399

Mohammed H (2022) The resurgence of military coups in Africa and the role of the African Union (AU). *Socialscientia: Journal of Social Sciences and Humanities* 7(3): 82–110. Accessed 28 February 2025, https://journals.aphriapub.com/index.php/SS/article/view/1584/1506

Munoriyarwa A & Chambwera C (2020) Who are the arbiters of truth? Mainstream journalists' responses to fake news during the 2017 Zimbabwe coup. *Communicatio: South African Journal of Communication Theory and Research* 46(4): 75–95. Accessed 21 December 2024, https://hdl.handle.net/10520/ejc-commu-v46-n4-a5

Mutambara VM & Naidu M (2021) Probing the context of vulnerability: Zimbabwean migrant women's experiences of accessing public health care in South Africa. *African Human Mobility Review* 7(1): 6–26. Accessed 28 February 2025, https://epubs.ac.za/index.php/ahmr/article/view/863/647

Ndizera V & Muzee H (2018) A critical review of Agenda 2063: Business as usual? *African Journal of Political Science and International Relations* 12(8): 142–154. Accessed 21 December 2024, DOI:10.5897/AJPSIR2018.1114

Nussbaum, MC (2000. *Women and human development: The capabilities approach*. Cambridge, UK: Cambridge University Press

Ogunkalu HO & Eniayejuni A (2019) Democracy and electoral outcomes: Comparative analysis of Nigeria and Ivory Coast elections. Paper presented at the Challenges of the Knowledge Society Conference, Bucharest, 1–18 May

Oxford Analytica (2020) Malawian election ruling may not end political unrest. *Daily Brief* 30 January. Accessed 21 December 2024, https://dailybrief.oxan.com/Analysis/DB250356/Malawian-election-ruling-may-not-end-political-unrest

Oxford Analytica (2023) Sao Tome coup allegations fuel political uncertainty. *Daily Brief* 26 January. Accessed 21 December 2024, https://dailybrief.oxan.com/Analysis/DB275560/Sao-Tome-coup-allegations-fuel-political-uncertainty

Pring C & Vrushi J (2019) *Global corruption barometer: Africa 2019: Citizen's views and experiences of corruption*. Transparency International. Accessed 21 December 2024, https://images.transparencycdn.org/images/2019_GCB_Africa3.pdf

Resnick D (2022) How Zambia's opposition won. *Journal of Democracy* 33(1): 70–84. Accessed 21 December 2024,
https://www.journalofdemocracy.org/articles/how-zambias-opposition-won/

Rogers PP, Jalal KF & Boyd JA (2012) *An introduction to sustainable development*. London: Routledge

Ruggerio CA (2021) Sustainability and sustainable development: A review of principles and definitions. *Science of the Total Environment* 786: 147481. Accessed 21 December 2024,
https://www.sciencedirect.com/science/article/abs/pii/S0048969721025523

Ruhlandt RWS (2018) The governance of smart cities: A systematic literature review. *Cities* 81: 1–23. Accessed 21 December 2024,
https://www.sciencedirect.com/science/article/abs/pii/S0264275117312283

Salas-Zapata WA & Ortiz-Muñoz SM (2019) Analysis of meanings of the concept of sustainability. *Sustainable Development* 27(1): 153–161. Accessed 21 December 2024, DOI:10.1002/sd.1885

Sedgo H (2022) Corruption in Africa: Effects on resource allocation and the role of leadership. Doctoral dissertation, Université de Nanterre-Paris X. Accessed 21 December 2024,
https://theses.hal.science/tel-03987952

Sen, AK (2000) What is development about? In G Meier & JE Stiglitz (Eds) *Frontiers of Development Economics: The future in perspective*. Oxford: Oxford University Press and Washington: World Bank

Soyiyo S (2021) Electorates' perceptions towards women leadership and the effects of the perceptions on performance of women candidates in Malawi. *Journal of Public Administration* 56(2): 323–338. Accessed 21 December 2024,
https://journals.co.za/doi/epdf/10.10520/ejc-jpad-v56-n2-a12

United Nations Development Program (UNDP) (n.d.) *Governance*. Accessed 21 December 2024,
https://www.undp.org/eurasia/our-focus/governance

United Nations Development Program (UNDP) (1990) *Human development index*. Accessed 21 December 2024,
https://hdr.undp.org/data-center/human-development-index#/indicies/HDI

Vhumbunu, CH (2020) Insurgency in Mozambique: The role of the Southern African Development Community. *ACCORD* 20 February. Accessed 21 December 2024,
https://www.accord.org.za/conflict-trends/insurgency-in-mozambique-the-role-of-the-southern-african-development-community/

PART 2

AFRICA'S SUSTAINABLE DEVELOPMENT AND REGIONAL INTEGRATION

6 Attributes of community leaders for sustainable development

Awelani J Nemathithi, Joseph Francis, Lufuno R Kone and Phellecy Lavhelani

Introduction

In African communities, leadership is regarded as a means to promote oneness, truth, freedom, peace, reconciliation, justice and right relations (Marumo 2019). Since 1994, South Africa has been practicing a new form of local governance that emphasises public participation in policymaking. The introduction of ward committees through the Local Government Municipal Structures Act 117 of 1998 was intended to translate the fundamental political commitment of 'The people shall govern' into practical action by addressing pressing national challenges such as underdevelopment, unemployment, stagnation, inequality, and poverty (Idasa & Afesis-corplan 2005). This chapter aims to identify the attributes of ideal grassroots community leaders for sustainable development, focusing on the case of ward committees in Ha-Mashau village of Vhembe District in Limpopo, South Africa

Background

Overall, ward committees serve as essential participatory structures within local government, ensuring direct community participation and representation in decision-making processes. Their roles encompass communication, consultation, advocacy and mobilisation, which are all aimed at promoting community engagement and fostering effective governance. By actively involving the community in the planning and decision-making processes, ward committees contribute to the sustainable development and well-being of their respective wards.

Ward committees play a crucial role in ensuring direct voter participation and involvement in the decision-making processes of councils. They are integral parts of the structures and processes that impact the lives of ordinary citizens. The primary responsibilities of ward committees include communicating and consulting with their respective communities regarding development and service plans (Diedericks & Seitlholo 2018). Most importantly, they act as a direct and unique link between municipal councils and residents. This is important because it enhances community participation in municipal decision-making

(Attah, Obera & Isaac 2017). In 2005, in what was the Department of Provincial and Local Government (DPLG), and is now the Department of Cooperative Governance and Traditional Affairs, outlined the specific roles and powers of ward committees as:

- serving as an official specialised participatory structure within the municipality;
- establishing formal and impartial communication channels and fostering cooperative partnerships between the community and the council;
- assisting the ward councillor in identifying the challenges and needs of the residents;
- acting as a mobilising agent for community action within the ward;
- addressing all matters that impact and benefit the community;
- acting in the best interest of the community; and
- ensuring active community participation in the integrated development planning process, municipal budgeting, and decision-making regarding the provision of municipal services and formulation of by-laws.

The roles and powers articulated above are vital for effective functioning of ward committees in local governance. By actively engaging with their communities and facilitating active participation in decision-making processes, ward committees contribute to inclusive and democratic governance at the local level. In the process, they serve as intermediaries between the municipal council and grassroots organisations, advocating for the interests and needs of the communities they represent.

As stipulated in the Municipal Systems Act 32 of 2000, ward committees are expected to play a crucial role in engaging communities and grassroots organisations during integrated development planning within their respective municipal wards. This facilitates community deliberations and enables the compilation of community needs and priorities. In turn, this informs municipal planning and budgeting processes. The integrated development plan, created through a consultative process, serves as a strategic growth and development roadmap for a five-year period and seeks to identify the most effective solutions for sustainable improvement in quality of life for communities.

Ward committees are representative structures that are responsible for conveying the aspirations, potentials and problems of the community to their respective municipalities (Naidoo & Ramphal 2018). For example, the 2007 Breede Valley Municipality policy for ward committee elections in South Africa was adopted to ensure that any citizen is qualified to stand and serve in the committee. It sought to entrench gender equality and the inclusion of previously disadvantaged individuals, including the youth and differently abled persons.

Despite the commitment to practice participatory democracy within the government and grassroots organisations since the introduction of new governance systems in South Africa, community members often lack the capacity and empowerment to drive their development effectively (Dean 2017). These problems are not exclusive to Ha-Mashau Village but it was chosen because it experiences continuous protests due to socioeconomic challenges and a lack of effective engagement between service providers and communities. The change agents responsible for public mobilisation and community engagement lack sufficient knowledge and skills (Siphuma 2016) so the municipality makes decisions on behalf of residents without consulting them. This shows that, even though there are systems, acts, and bylaws to guide the operation and conduct of ward committees, practical application is challenging.

This gap demands that the attributes that community members perceive as ideal in individuals who serve on ward committee be explored and clarified. By understanding the qualities that make local representatives productive and effective in driving and mobilising sustainable rural development, this study seeks to contribute to the understanding of effective community leadership within the context of ward committees.

By identifying the attributes of ideal grassroots community leaders, this study aims to shed light on the qualities that potentially enhance the capacity and empowerment of ward committee members, ultimately fostering more effective community-driven development. The study findings are expected to inform policies and practices that promote sustainable rural development and empower communities and grassroots organisations to participate actively in determining the direction and pace of their own progress.

Theoretical framework

Contemporary research on charismatic, transactional, transformational, and servant leadership emphasises the significance of personality traits. These concepts are recognised as implicit leadership qualities that explain the underlying factors contributing to the success or failure of leaders (Lord et al. 2020). Servant leadership is a practical philosophy that prioritises serving others rather than 'leading' them (Gandolfi & Stone 2018). This expands service to individuals and institutions. Hankins (2019) expands this understanding by defining a servant leader as an individual who prioritises the needs of others above their own and strives to improve the well-being of individuals, particularly the vulnerable and underprivileged in society. Becoming a servant leader requires something beyond human knowledge and choice (Frantz 2018).

This study uses an adapted version of the Greenleaf (2002) servant leadership theory that was first devised in 1977. It explains that servant leaders consciously decide to prioritise serving others and place their aspirations, needs and interests above their own. Their primary objective is to serve and fulfil the needs of others. Greenleaf identifies encouragement, collaboration, trust, foresight, listening, ethical use of power, and empowerment as essential qualities of a servant leader. It is worth noting that servant leadership is regarded as both effective and ethical due to its emphasis on values and attributes such as altruism, responsible morality, accountability, empowerment, integrity, trust, service, modelling, appreciation of others, vision, and transformative influence. All these attributes of servant leadership make the Greenleaf theory suitable for the context of the current study. Servant leaders focus on others rather than themselves, understanding their role as providers and facilitators.

This study aims to identify the attributes of ideal grassroots community leaders for sustainable development, specifically focusing on ward committees in the Ha-Mashau village of Collins Chabane Local Municipality in the Vhembe District of Limpopo province, South Africa. The Greenleaf servant leadership theory was chosen to identify the ideal attributes of effective leaders for sustainable rural development because of its potential to provide a deeper understanding of leadership values for institutional transformation and their contribution to sustainable development.

Problem statement

Some scholars have reported that ward committees are 'captured' and utilised to further the material and political ambitions of some individuals and therefore do not represent the aspirations, interests and demands of grassroots communities (Mbhele 2017; Mngxali 2008). It is noted that, for most poor people in South Africa, participatory development remains an unattainable aspiration (Modise 2017). The results of Sekgala's study on public participation in integrated development planning concluded that change agents lack the necessary knowledge of how to engage communities effectively, resulting in ineffective ward committees (Sekgala 2016).

As mentioned, the Ha-Mashau area, where this study was conducted has experienced continuous protests due to socioeconomic challenges and lack of effective engagement between service providers and communities. It was argued that municipal councillors deliberately chose ward committee members based on their political affiliations. Consequently, the ward committees served primarily as extensions of political party structures and rarely represented the full spectrum of community interests. The area was characterised by various challenges, namely limited access to basic services, high unemployment rates, poverty, and inadequate infrastructure. Addressing these issues and promoting sustainable development requires effective grassroots community leaders in ward committees. Therefore, it is essential for community members to elect leaders who possess attributes that align with the visions of the community. This study aims to determine the community-perceived ideal attributes of community leaders for leading sustainable development in a rural community.

Rationale

Leadership plays a vital role in many aspects of society, so it is crucial to have effective ward committees that can facilitate processes leading to improved well-being for local residents. The outcomes of this study are intended to help ward committee members to recognise the special set of skills required to lead sustainable rural development initiatives. Previous studies have highlighted the significance of ward committees as mechanisms for public participation (Modise 2017; Masuku & Jili 2019; Siphuma 2009) but there has been little or no research that specifically focuses on the attributes of ideal grassroots community leaders within the context of ward committees. Understanding the attributes that contribute to effective grassroots community leadership is essential for empowering local communities and fostering sustainable development practices. By identifying these attributes, policymakers, development practitioners, and community members can enhance leadership capacity and promote inclusive decision-making processes.

Objective

The aim of this study was to determine the community-perceived attributes or preferred qualities of people who serve in ward committees.

Methodology

The study targeted youth and adult residents of Ha-Mashau, located in Limpopo province in South Africa. Ha-Mashau falls under Ward 8 of the Collins Chabane Local Municipality within Vhembe District Municipality. Like many other South African rural communities, Ha-Mashau faces many socioeconomic and environmental challenges. Livelihood opportunities are limited so most people in the community keep livestock, harvest wood, and/or practise subsistence agriculture.

A qualitative research approach underpinned by an exploratory design was adopted. The exploratory research design was chosen mainly due to limited studies on community-perceived attributes of individuals eligible to effectively serve in ward committees. This design allows for a comprehensive exploration and understanding of the research problem (Cabrera 2011).

The study respondents were youth and adults residing in Ha-Mashau village. A total of 57 people voluntarily participated in a community workshop specifically held to collect data on the study question. This was facilitated at the royal family premises in Ha-Mashau Doli, which was accessible to the participants. For data collection, the 57 participants were divided into two groups – youth and adults – and then into male and female to ensure better coverage of the population and unbiased perspectives on the study question. Each of these sub-groups was divided into two, giving eight focus groups, each one consisting of between six and nine participants. The frequency distribution of the participants from different age groups and genders is presented in Table 6.1.

A semi-structured interview guide was used to facilitate the discussions. The respondents were asked to identify and discuss the qualities they believed were important for individuals eligible to serve in the ward committee. Focus group discussions were chosen because they allow for the collection of a large amount of data from diverse participants simultaneously. In addition, the use of semi-structured interviews made it possible to probe further, and thereby gain a deeper understanding of the identified phenomena.

Data were analysed following the thematic content analysis approach, which involved identifying recurring themes and patterns within the data and grouping them based on similarity (Braun & Clarke 2019). This approach allowed for the identification of key attributes and qualities perceived by the community as important for effective leadership within the ward committee.

Results

Biographical details of participants

Most participants resided in the Guvhungwa and Doli villages in the Ha-Mashau area. Slightly more than half of the participants who participated in focus group discussions (53 per cent) were female. More adults participated in the study than youths, and most of the respondents had attained secondary schooling.

Community-perceived ideal attributes of ward committee members

Table 6.1 summarises the themes and subthemes of community perceptions of the ideal attributes that ward committee members should exhibit. The community-perceived ideal attributes of ward committee members were grouped into five sub-themes, namely personality, education, communication skills, accessibility, and interest in local governance and community building. Education was the most common theme, followed by personality and interest in local governance and community building, with communication skills and accessibility being considered less important. Emphasising the importance of education, some community members said:

> Educated people have the ability to handle different situations calmly and can differentiate between wrong and right. [Women's group: Doli village]

> An educated leader will help community members in getting a sense of self dependence and confidence. This way people may make their own decisions, and express their views and opinions. [Female youth: Guvhungwa village]

At least someone who went to school will be able to read, write and interpret communications. [Men's group: Doli village]

Table 6.1 *Community-perceived ideal attributes of ward committee members*

Perceived attributes	Youth				Adults				Tally
	Group 1	Group 2	Group 3	Group 4	Group 5	Group 6	Group 7	Group 8	
Gender	Female	Female	Male	Male	Female	Female	Male	Male	
Frequency (n)	6	7	6	6	8	9	8	7	57
Educational background: Basic – at least matriculation certificate	✓	✓		✓		✓	✓	✓	6
Personality									
Honest, accountable, trustworthy		✓	✓		✓	✓		✓	5
Empathetic, approachable	✓		✓	✓	✓			✓	5
Good personality	✓	✓				✓	✓		4
Passionate about development	✓		✓			✓			3
Patient	✓			✓		✓			3
Helpful			✓	✓					2
Intelligent							✓		1
Youthful	✓								1
Interest in local governance and community building									
Dedicated to community work	✓	✓	✓			✓			4
Understands social challenges			✓						1
Communication skills									
A good communicator		✓				✓			2
A good listener								✓	1
Multilingual					✓				1
Accessibility									
A local resident						✓		✓	2
Active participant in civic gatherings							✓		1

The results of the study as shown in Table 6.1 provide interesting insights into the perceived attributes of ideal grassroots community leaders for sustainable rural development, with a particular focus on comparing and contrasting perspectives based on age and gender.

Regarding the perceived attributes of ideal community leaders, youth and adult participants shared similar perspectives on the importance of leaders having a good personality, especially being transparent, accountable, trustworthy, approachable, and empathetic. These attributes were perceived to be essential for building effective relationships with community members and fostering collaboration.

Some differences in perspectives were observed between youth and adults. For example, youth emphasised the importance of leaders being passionate about development and having a heart for helping others. This suggests that the youth prioritise leaders who are driven by a genuine desire to bring about positive change, and are actively engaged in community development initiatives. In contrast, adults highlighted the significance of leaders displaying intelligence and patience. These attributes may be associated with the wisdom and experience that come with age, suggesting that the adults value leaders who can provide guidance and maintain composure when faced with challenging situations.

Both youth and adults expressed similar perspectives with respect to interest in local governance and community building. For both age groups, ideal leaders were those who were helpful, dedicated to community work and understood social challenges within the community. This reflects a shared expectation for leaders who are genuinely committed to addressing the needs and concerns of their communities.

Both youth and adults recognised the importance of leaders who exhibited good communication and listening skills but adults placed a greater emphasis on leaders' being multilingual. The diverse cultural and linguistic landscape of the Ha-Mashau area might have influenced their views. This implies that the ability to communicate effectively and understand the perspectives of community members in their own language is a valuable attribute for building trust and fostering inclusivity.

In terms of accessibility, youth and adults agreed on the importance of having leaders who live in the village. This shared expectation for leaders may have been influenced by the need for leaders who have a deep understanding of the local context and are familiar with the specific challenges and needs of their communities. The youth also emphasised the importance of leaders who actively participated in civic gatherings. It was clear that the youth valued leaders who actively engaged with their communities, participated in local meetings and events and involved themselves in local decision-making processes.

In summary, there were inter-age group similarities and differences in the perceived attributes of ideal grassroots community leaders. Youth prioritised qualities such as passion, having heart for helping others and active community engagement. On the other hand, adults highlighted intelligence, patience and multilingualism as crucial attributes that leaders should exhibit. The latter differences may emanate from the unique perspectives and experiences of each age group. Similarly, male and female respondents in the study shared similar perspectives with respect to perceptions on many attributes. The slight difference in participation rates observed in the study may suggest a more balanced representation of both genders in grassroots leadership discussions. In conclusion, the findings of this study highlight the diverse perspectives within the Ha-Mashau community. These results provide valuable insights for understanding the expectations and preferences of different age and gender groups with respect to grassroots leadership for sustainable rural development.

Discussion

The aim of the study was to explore the attributes of ideal grassroots community leaders for sustainable rural development, specifically focusing on ward committees in the Ha-Mashau area. Of the 57 participants in the current study, female community members slightly outnumbered their male counterparts. This observation challenges the common notion that most organisations remain disproportionately male-dominated (Bhatt 2017). However, in community development studies, female participation often exceeds male involvement due to women's roles as primary caregivers and their proximity to community welfare issues (Razavi 2011). This underscores the importance of acknowledging gender disparities in participatory initiatives (Uduji, Okolo-Obasi & Asongu 2019), highlighting that women's representation can indicate an emphasis on inclusive community planning. Such trends may reflect evolving societal structures that promote gender equity. More adults than youth responded, indicating a relative lack of interest among the youth in attending social gatherings and contributing to community development (Francis et al. 2011; Chitongo et al. 2019; Chauke 2020).

Most of the respondents had completed secondary education. Educational background was also the most popular attribute that people selected as important for members of a ward committee. Respondents were of the opinion that elected officials should possess a certain level of political education to be capable of addressing social and governmental challenges effectively (Modise 2017).

The residents of Ha-Mashau expressed the need for ward committee members to have strong personalities to facilitate good working relationships and effective communication with stakeholders. Personality is a significant predictor of effective leadership and plays a crucial role in enhancing performance (Judge & Bono 2000; Hogan & Sherman 2020). People with strong personalities can inspire and motivate others, build consensus, and get things done (Sifat 2019). It has been argued that performance is directly dependent on personality (Dartey-Baah 2014), and that the personality of an individual plays a significant role when that person is given a leadership responsibility (Mbandlwa 2018).

Genuine interest and commitment to local governance and community development were highlighted as essential qualities of ideal ward committee members. They should possess a deep understanding of community challenges and have a burning desire to take action for the community's benefit. Effective leaders are often people who are interested in, and committed to, addressing the needs of their communities, and can build relationships with individuals from diverse backgrounds (Shields & Hesbol 2020).

Although considered to be the least important attribute, communication skills were identified as essential attributes of ward committee members. Effective communication skills, including speaking, listening, writing, and multilingualism, are essential for effective leadership for development (Manley & Titchen 2017). Facilitation skills, in particular, play a vital role in bridging the gap between councillors and community members.

The findings of the current study also highlight the importance of ward committee members' being locally based and actively involved in local municipality affairs to ensure accessibility. This observation is supported by the argument that leaders should be able to coach, teach and instil trust in their followers (Weiskittel 1999). In this respect, accessibility is a fundamental requirement.

In conclusion, the study identified several key attributes of ideal grassroots community leaders for sustainable rural development within ward committees in Ha-Mashau. These include a strong personality, genuine interest and commitment to community development, effective communication skills, and local accessibility. The findings contribute to the existing literature on grassroots community leadership and can inform the selection and development of ward committee members, ultimately promoting sustainable rural development in Ha-Mashau and similar communities.

Conclusion and recommendations

The current study highlighted the ideal attributes of ward committee members to lead grassroots community development. The importance of ward committee members' having a strong personality, genuine interest, and commitment to community development was emphasised. Effective communication skills, local accessibility, and educational background were revealed to be crucial for effective leadership of ward committee core business. It is worth noting that the current study provides valuable insights into the selection and nurturing of ward committees, which ultimately contributes to the promotion of sustainable rural development in Ha-Mashau and similar communities. These findings can guide policymakers and community stakeholders in fostering effective grassroots leadership and driving positive change for the benefit of grassroots communities.

References

Attah E, Obera VA & Isaac S (2017) Effective leadership and change management for sustainable development in Nigeria. *International Journal of Public Administration and Management Research* 4(2): 39. Accessed 23 December 2024, https://www.researchgate.net/publication/322063567_effective_leadership_and_change_management_for_sustainable_development_in_nigeria

Bhatt A (2017) Global gender parity insights from the World Economic Forum's gender gap report. *Chicago Policy Review* 29 March. Accessed 2 January 2025, https://chicagopolicyreview.org/2017/03/29/global-gender-parity-insights-from-the-world-economic-forums-gender-gap-report/

Braun V & Clarke V (2019) Reflecting on reflexive thematic analysis. *Qualitative Research in Sport, Exercise and Health* 11(4): 589–597. Accessed 23 December 2024, https://doi.org/10.1080/2159676X.2019.1628806

Cabrera NL (2011) Using a sequential exploratory mixed-method design to examine racial hyperprivilege in higher education. *New Directions for Institutional Research* 2011 (151): 77–91. Accessed 23 December 2024, DOI:10.1002/ir.400

Chauke TA (2020). Youth apathy in an electoral democracy: A critical discourse on civil participation in South Africa. *African Journal of Gender Society and Development* 9(2): 35–51. Accessed 23 December 2024, DOI:10.31920/2634-3622/2020/9n3a2

Chitongo L, Tagarirofa J, Chazovachii B & Marango T (2019) Gendered impacts of climate change in Africa: The case of Cyclone Idai, Chimanimani, Zimbabwe, March 2019. *The Fountain: Journal of Interdisciplinary Studies* 3(1): 30–44. Accessed 23 December 2024, https://journals.cuz.ac.zw/index.php/fountain/article/view/149

Dartey-Baah K (2014) Effective leadership and sustainable development in Africa: Is there 'really' a link? *Journal of Global Responsibility* 5(2): 203–218. Accessed 23 December 2024, https://doi.org/10.1108/JGR-03-2014-0014

Dean RJ (2017) Beyond radicalism and resignation: The competing logics for public participation in policy decisions. *Policy and Politics* 45(2): 221. Accessed 23 December 2024, DOI: 10.1332/030557316X14531466517034

Department of Local Government (2005) *Having your say: A Handbook for ward committees.* Accessed 23 December 2024, https://www.gov.za/sites/default/files/gcis_document/201409/dplgwardhandbook0.pdf

Diedericks M & Seitlholo S (2018) Challenges facing the effective functioning of ward committees as a mechanism to promote local democracy in the former Tlokwe Local Municipality (TLM). *Politeia* 37(1): 12. Accessed 23 December 2024, https://doi.org/10.25159/0256-8845/4287

Francis J, Mamatsharaga P, Dube B & Chitapa T (2011) Making youth voices count in development programming in Makhado municipality, Limpopo province. *Journal of Geography and Regional Planning* 4(5): 302. Accessed 23 December 2024, https://academicjournals.org/journal/JGRP/article-full-text-pdf/A84EA8F40842.pdf

Frantz D (2018) The role and impact of local government communication strategies in participatory governance: The case of Lamberts Bay. Unpublished Master's dissertation,

University of the Western Cape. Accessed 23 December 2024, https://uwcscholar.uwc.ac.za/items/eb394ff4-4135-4b0a-a389-fb4a3e2cbbc2

Gandolfi F & Stone S (2018) Leadership, leadership styles, and servant leadership. *Journal of Management Research* 18(4): 261–269. Accessed 23 December 2024, https://www.lasnny.org/wp-content/uploads/2018/11/Leadership-Leadership-Styles-and-Servant-Leadership.pdf

Greenleaf RK (2002) *Servant leadership: A journey into the nature of legitimate power and greatness* (3rd edition) Mahwah, NJ: Paulist Press. Accessed 22 December 2024, https://www.urbanleaders.org/620Leadership/92Readings/articles/Greenleaf-Servant%20Leadership.pdf

Hankins MA (2019) *A servant-leader's approach to homelessness.* Greenleaf Center for Servant Leadership. Accessed 23 December 2024, https://medium.com/@jriverarincon/a-servant-leaders-approach-to-homelessness-8ad06772984

Hogan R & Sherman RA (2020) Personality theory and the nature of human nature. *Personality and Individual Differences* 152: 109561. Accessed 23 December 2024, DOI:10.1016/j.paid.2019.109561

Idasa & Afesis-corplan (2005) *Ward committee resource book: Best practices & lessons learnt for municipal officials, councillors and local government practitioners.* Department of Provincial and Local Government. Accessed 3 January 2025, https://d7.westerncape.gov.za/sites/www.westerncape.gov.za/files/documents/2006/2/ward_committee_resource_book.pdf

Judge TA & Bono JE (2000) Five-factor model of personality and transformational leadership. *Journal of Applied Psychology* 85(5): 751–765

Lord RG, Epitropaki O, Foti RJ & Hansbrough TK (2020) Implicit leadership theories, implicit followership theories, and dynamic processing of leadership information. *Annual Review of Organizational Psychology and Organizational Behavior* 7: 49–74. Accessed 23 December 2024, https://doi.org/10.1146/annurev-orgpsych-012119-045434

Manley K & Titchen A (2017) Facilitation skills: The catalyst for increased effectiveness in consultant practice and clinical systems leadership. *Educational Action Research* 25(2): 256–279. Accessed 23 December 2024, 10.1080/09650792.2016.1158118

Marumo PO (2019) Reconciliation in South Africa in light of the imago Dei and koinonia. *Verbum et Ecclesia* 4(40): a1905. Accessed 23 December 2024, https://verbumetecclesia.org.za/index.php/VE/article/view/1905

Masuku MM & Jili NN (2019) Public service delivery in South Africa: The political influence at local government level. *Journal of Public Affairs* 19(4): e1935. Accessed 23 December 2024, DOI:10.1002/pa.1935

Mbandlwa Z (2018) Assessing the ward councillors' leadership characteristics and their impact on service delivery in eThekwini Metropolitan Municipality. PhD thesis, Durban University of Technology. Accessed 28 December 2024, https://www.academia.edu/download/100482779/MBANDLWAZ_2018.pdf

Mbhele Z (2017) Assessing the ward committee system: The case of Greater Kokstad Municipality. Master's thesis, University of Stellenbosch. Accessed 23 December 2024, https://scholar.sun.ac.za/items/5325a53d-bf5e-4582-af64-ba178f76b043

Mngxali N (2008) Public participation at local government level in South Africa: A critical analysis of integrated development planning and ward committees. Master's thesis, University of Cape Town. Accessed 23 December 2024, http://hdl.handle.net/11427/3751

Modise LJ (2017) The notion of participatory democracy in relation to local ward committees: The distribution of power. *In die Skriflig* 51(1): a2248. Accessed 23 December 2024, https://doi.org/10.4102/ids.v51i1.2248

Naidoo C & Ramphal RR (2018) The factors that affect public participation for effective municipal service delivery: A case of ward committees. *South African Journal of Industrial Engineering* 29(4):82–93. Accessed 23 December 2024, https://doi.org/10.7166/29-4-1948

Razavi S (2011) Rethinking care in a development context: An introduction. *Development and Change* 42(4): 873–903. Accessed 3 January 2025, DOI:10.1111/J.1467-7660.2011.01722.X

Sekgala MP (2016) Ward committee challenges in South Africa's local municipalities: Functions and dysfunctions. *Journal of Public Administration and Development Alternatives* 1(1.1): 1–14. Accessed 23 December 2024, https://journals.co.za/doi/pdf/10.10520/EJC-934032071

Shields CM & Hesbol KA (2020) Transformative leadership approaches to inclusion, equity, and social justice. *Journal of School Leadership* 30(1): 3–22

Sifat RI (2019) Role of leadership for achieving sustainable development goals. *GIS Business* 14(3): 5–14. Accessed 23 December 2024, https://ssrn.com/abstract=3693538

Siphuma TF (2016) The role of ward committee in enhancing public participation: A case study of Thulamela Municipality. Unpublished Doctoral Dissertation, University of Venda. Accessed 23 December 2024, http://hdl.handle.net/11602/367

Siphuma ZR (2009) An assessment of the role of public participation in IDP: The Thulamela Municipality. Doctoral dissertation, University of Stellenbosch. Accessed 23 December 2024, https://scholar.sun.ac.za/items/2b4b378f-e234-4973-a74a-ac7053f61e72

Uduji JI, Okolo-Obasi EN & Asongu SA (2019) The impact of corporate social responsibility interventions on female education development in the rural Niger Delta region of Nigeria. *Progress in Development Studies* 20(1): 45–64. https://doi.org/10.1177/1464993420902593

Weiskittel P (1999) Assessing your potential to become a leader. *ANNA Journal* 26(6): 559–560. Accessed 23 December 2024, link.gale.com/apps/doc/A58431324/AONE?u=anon~9684cd2f&sid=sitemap&xid=6e782c71

7 African continental free trade potential for South Africa's renewable energy

Phemelo Michelle Mashamaite

Introduction

Because the link between the use of non-renewable fossil fuels and climate change is irrefutable, governments, academia, and civil society recognise that the transition to renewable energy is urgent. However, while it is widely acknowledged that reducing CO_2 emissions is essential to mitigate against climate change, there is a strong correlation between economic growth and the use of fossil fuels for residential, industrial and commercial energy consumption (Bhuiyan et al. 2022).

The African Continental Free Trade Area (AfCFTA), which has been in effect since 2021, can be utilised by African governments as a de-risking strategic investment framework to inform their innovative systematic approach to establishing a regional solar alliance. This alliance can be conceptualised as an intergovernmental treaty that provides African mining organisations with a platform to trade raw, unrefined minerals and processed mineral products with member states that have signed the AfCFTA agreement.

Historically, fossil fuels, notably coal, have formed the foundational energy source underpinning industrialisation and economic expansion, providing reliable energy. However, this dependence on fossil fuels poses substantial challenges to sustainable development. While these energy sources have historically driven economic progress, they are simultaneously the predominant contributors to greenhouse gas emissions, exacerbating climate change and causing environmental degradation.

Governments, academia, and civil society recognise the urgent need for a transition to renewable energy. Although reducing CO_2 emissions is widely acknowledged as critical for sustainable development, a challenge is that Africa's population is expected to grow rapidly (International Renewable Energy Agency (IRENA) 2021), further intensifying the energy demand. Meeting this energy requirement is important for fostering economic development, creating employment, and alleviating poverty. However, continued reliance on coal and other fossil fuels jeopardises long-term sustainable development, and undermines international climate objectives, such as the Paris Agreement's mandate to achieve net-zero carbon emissions by 2050. This contradiction accentuates the pressing need for energy transition policies that balance economic growth and environmental sustainability.

To effectively decouple economic growth from environmental degradation, renewable energy sources, particularly solar energy, must be gradually adopted to supplement coal as the primary energy generating source. AfCFTA presents a strategic opportunity for governments and mining organisations to secure the critical minerals essential for renewable energy infrastructure. This could facilitate the establishment of a sustainable regional solar alliance and inclusive energy framework. The alliance can be conceptualised as an intergovernmental treaty that provides African governments with opportunities to procure the essential minerals for manufacturing solar panels while offering mining organisations a platform on which to trade raw, unrefined and processed mineral products with member states. This approach can ease Africa's transition to renewable energy and promote an affordable, sustainable and equitable energy transition (Bojek 2022).

The Renewable Energy Independent Power Producer Procurement Programme (REIPPPP) is an energy sector reform to address the national service delivery crisis of electricity insecurity (Eberhard 2001) and secure sufficient renewable energy to mitigate the shortfall of on-grid demand power supply (Montmasson-Clair et al. 2017) thereby supporting South Africa's voluntary pledge to combat climate change, made at the 2009 UN climate change conference, known as COP 15. The REIPPPP is a reactive hybrid system that has enabled the South African energy sector to envision diversifying energy production to provide a flexible power supply grid. It is the first large-scale competitive tender process to decentralise Eskom's generation capacity and to reduce the state's dependence on coal (Republic of South Africa 2019).

It is crucial to emphasise that the transition to clean, renewable rooftop solar photovoltaic (PV) energy technologies relies on essential minerals such as copper, lithium, nickel, cobalt, and rare earth elements. These minerals are integral components used in manufacturing solar panels and batteries for energy storage. By leveraging the AfCFTA agreement, the South African government can effectively procure these critical minerals to implement a cost-competitive renewable energy manufacturing sector. This underscores the South African government's commitment to advancing its energy transition goals.

However, the supply of these essential minerals is vulnerable to factors such as exchange rate fluctuations and price increases. These challenges directly impact the economic viability of clean energy technologies and influence the ability of governments to foster a thriving clean technology manufacturing industry. As African nations strive for net zero carbon emissions, addressing these vulnerabilities becomes increasingly critical to achieving sustainable energy transitions and fostering economic growth. The current generation mix of the Southern African

Power Pool (SAPP) energy supply comprises coal, hydro, nuclear, diesel, and gas, with coal being a predominant source of electricity generation and air pollution. Solar photovoltaic renewable energy is not included in the SAPP's energy-generating options. This may be because the primary challenge for member states in the SAPP and Southern African Development Community (SADC) is improving energy security and reliability through generation, transmission, and distribution to cater to the energy demand within the African continent (Economic Consulting Associates 2009).

The South African government initiated REIPPPP – a premier large-scale competitive tender for renewable energy projects valued at $8.5 billion. This initiative aims to engage private entities in diversifying power generation capacity by procuring alternative renewable sources. The REIPPPP underscores South Africa's proactive measures in fulfilling its voluntary commitment to reduce carbon dioxide emissions by 42 per cent in 2025, as pledged at the 2009 COP 15 in Copenhagen. The transition to renewable energy, particularly solar PV energy, necessitates critical mineral security. However, a significant oversight that persists in South Africa's Just Energy Transition strategy is neglecting to capitalise on the AfCFTA as an intra-regional trade instrument for acquiring critical minerals essential for manufacturing solar panels. This oversight has the potential to impede Gauteng's ability to transform the West Rand into a special economic and solar Renewable Energy Development Zone (REDZ), hindering the country's exports, and holding back the creation of green economic opportunities.

This chapter explores how South Africa can utilise the AfCFTA to secure critical minerals for manufacturing solar panels. The West Rand is used as an exploratory case study to showcase the potential benefits of successfully implementing solar-focused REDZs and highlight how solar renewable energy initiatives within REDZs can stimulate economic growth, create job opportunities, and improve access to clean and affordable energy in township communities.

Background

South Africa's power utility, Eskom, is committed to producing, transferring, and distributing enough electricity to satisfy the demands of South African citizens informed by the Reconstruction and Development Programme (RDP) policy. The RDP aimed to address the imbalance and legacy of colonial sovereignty by connecting areas that were previously excluded from accessing the basic service of electricity to the power grid, thereby fulfilling Eskom's mandate as a national government functionary (Bekker et al. 2008; Theron 2017). Equally important was the promotion of good governance and adequate service delivery (Parliamentary Monitoring Group 2000). In 1999, the Inter-Ministerial Cabinet Committee on Restructuring State Assets hosted an Electricity Supply Industry

Lekgotla, aimed at crafting a policy framework to guide the structural reform process (Darmani et al. 2014).

In 2008, the South African Network Infrastructure Review confirmed the need to reform the South African energy sector due to the adverse environmental effects of using coal to generate electricity (Newbery & Eberhard 2008; Zeng et al. 2017), acknowledging the need to accelerate the innovation of alternative energy resources to produce clean and affordable power (Eberhard 2001) to achieve the 7th Sustainable Development Goal.

At COP 15 the South African government voluntarily pledged to decrease carbon dioxide emissions by 42 per cent by 2025, demonstrating its political commitment through proactive measures such as renewable energy programmes to combat climate change United Nations Framework Convention on Climate Change (UNFCCC 2010). The transition to renewable energy in the South African energy sector was primarily motivated by eliminating coal-fired power generation to secure a sufficient renewable energy supply and achieving a zero per cent carbon emission target by 2050 (Montmasson-Clair et al. 2017).

The environmental costs of using coal to generate electricity (Friedlingstein et al. 2011) are increasingly an issue, and Eskom's dysfunction, which has resulted in loadshedding, infringes citizens' fundamental rights as outlined in section 5(1) of the National Energy Act 34 of 2008, which states that citizens should receive reliable and affordable electricity.

The Portfolio Committee on Public Enterprises Inquiry into Eskom's governance, procurement, and financial sustainability revealed that the vertically integrated power parastatal's organisational performance began deteriorating in 2000 with the introduction of rotational power cuts for mines (Khan, Thopil & Lalk 2016). This decline can be attributed to pervasive organisational pathologies (Caiden 1991), including administrative corruption arising from unauthorised, fruitless, and wasteful public procurement practices and other financial mismanagement. These issues severely hampered the operational efficiency of the power parastatal and exacerbated mediocre governance (Kessides 2020). To mitigate the shortfall in on-grid demand power supply, the South African government proposed the adoption of the REIPPPP in 2011 (Republic of South Africa 2019).

Methodology

The REIPPPP can be conceptualised as an energy sector reform to address the national service delivery crisis of electricity insecurity (Eberhard 2001) using renewable energy supply (Montmasson-Clair et al. 2017), and thereby supporting the mandate of the COP 15 voluntary pledge to combat climate change (United Nations Framework Convention on Climate Change (UNFCCC) 2010). The REIPPPP is a reactive hybrid system that has enabled the South African energy sector to envision diversifying energy production to provide a flexible grid power supply. It is the first large-scale competitive tender process to decentralise Eskom's generation market to reduce the state's dependence on coal (Republic of South Africa 2019).

This chapter explores the potential impact of the AfCFTA on accelerating energy reform and mineral security in South Africa and facilitating a just energy transition. A comprehensive documentary review and a qualitative mode of inquiry were conducted. The study focused on a purposive sample criterion that included African countries that signed and agreed to participate in the AfCFTA. These countries were Cameroon, the Democratic Republic of the Congo (DRC), Ghana, Guinea, Mali, Mozambique, Namibia, Nigeria, South Africa, and Zimbabwe. The sample selection criteria were based on the production of essential minerals such as copper, cobalt, nickel, lithium, rare earth elements, chromium, zinc, platinum-group minerals, and aluminium, which are required for manufacturing solar panels and batteries. The case study that was designed focused on townships in South Africa's West Rand District Municipality. Originally established as African mining compounds in 1959, these townships traditionally relied on gold and uranium mining activities. The area was chosen because it could readily transform into a REDZ. This selection provides insights into the implications and opportunities for integrating renewable energy initiatives into regions historically dependent on mining (Peberdy, Harrison & Dinath 2017).

The regional notion for renewable energy in African developmental states

A nation's economic growth is driven by its ability to mobilise and secure resources effectively. As a result, a prosperous economy relies on technological advancements, optimal utilisation of human capital, and other outcomes of deliberate and ongoing strategic planning and development. However, relying heavily on fossil fuels for energy generation can have significant environmental consequences, contributing to a substantial increase in the country's carbon footprint. Additionally, many developing countries still require fossil fuels to meet the energy needs of their local communities. These countries must adopt an integrated government intervention approach that emphasises the importance of green energy generation to promote sustainable development. This approach can help create the necessary conditions for sustainable development while raising awareness about the benefits of utilising renewable energy sources (Adhikari 2021).

Harnessing the abundant opportunities that renewable energy presents can transform SADC, AfCFTA, and SAPP member states by establishing policy guidelines and regulatory frameworks that support systematic innovation to achieve universal energy access in Africa by 2030. Advocating for a fair and inclusive transition to renewable energy is vital in developing tailored plans for transforming the power sector, facilitating access to renewable energy, mitigating risks, and fostering public–private partnerships. Ultimately, these endeavours will enhance and modernise the existing power grid.

Establishing new partnerships among African governments and utilising the AfCFTA as a tool for inter-regional trade is essential for limiting regional temperature increases to 1.5 degrees Celsius above pre-industrial levels, as pledged at COP 15 (UNFCCC 2010).

Leveraging the AfCFTA as an instrument of inter-regional trade will help governments overcome grid instabilities caused by insufficient on-grid generation capacity that disrupts businesses and negatively impacts the growth of the African economy (Höhne et al. 2016).

One of the factors driving the African continent's energy transition is that more than half of the global population growth between 2020 and 2050 is expected to take place in Africa. To ensure that the continent's vast population can access affordable, reliable, sustainable energy by 2030 (International Renewable Energy Agency 2021), it is imperative that
- the leaders of the developmental states within the continent utilise renewable energy sources to promote socioeconomic growth while mitigating climate change;
- power suppliers, energy service providers, and grid operators fulfil their financial obligations to renewable energy producers by sustaining and expanding their grids as demand grows;
- regulatory environments and institutions be strengthened to keep electricity production and distribution cost-reflective; and
- African governments build the requisite human capacity and skills to implement energy transitions on their own terms while simultaneously promoting economic growth and job creation across the continent.

Coal is a non-renewable resource, but it is an important contributor to South Africa's economy. It is likely to generate $240 billion in the first decade of the just energy transition but this will decrease to $175 billion by 2040 as demand increases for reduced carbon emissions (Internation Energy Agency (IEA) 2021b). However, essential energy transition minerals such as copper, lithium, nickel, cobalt, graphite, silicon, and REEs are likely to generate significant revenue.

The current and potential barriers affecting South Africa's mineral security and renewable energy initiative

The solar PV energy market is projected to surpass non-renewable coal electricity generation, with the capacity to triple to 1 500 GW, so the demand for critical minerals like silicon and copper is soaring due to the dominance of solar PV energy in renewable energy capacity additions (IEA 2021b).

Table 7.1 shows the importance of the critical minerals required to manufacture solar panels and energy storage systems (batteries).

Table 7.1 *Critical minerals required for rooftop solar photovoltaic (PV) panels*

Critical minerals required	Type of solar PV equipment	
	Solar PV system	Battery storage system
Aluminium	●	●
Chromium	○	○
Cobalt	○	●
Copper	●	●
Lithium	○	●
Nickle	○	●
Platinum-group minerals	○	○
Rare earth elements	○	●
Zinc	○	○

Key: Each circle represents the importance of the mineral, particularly for solar PV renewable energy
High ● Low ○
Source: Adapted from IEA 2021b

Table 7.2 illustrates that South Africa has most of the required minerals for manufacturing solar panels and batteries for the small-scale embedded generators required to establish the West Rand District Municipality as a REDZ to meet its REIPPPP target. However, the deficiency in lithium, cobalt, and aluminium underscores the need to procure these minerals through the AfCFTA from SAPP, SADC and AfCFTA member states.

The South African government's implementation of the REIPPPP represents a significant step towards diversifying the country's electricity supply industry capacity (Eberhard & Naude 2017). This large-scale, 8.5 billion-dollar competitive tender process, which is the first in South Africa, aims to mobilise private companies through procurement to diversify power generation using alternative renewable sources such as solar PV, on-shore wind, and hydro-electric power (Mavhunga 2023).

Table 7.2 *A snapshot of South Africa's mineral security for solar panels*

Mineral	South Africa's mineral reserves in kilograms (kg)
Chromium	200 000 000 (Two hundred million)
Coal	53 136 000 (Fifty- three million, one hundred and thirty-six thousand)
Copper	11 000 000 (Eleven million)
Nickle	3 700 000 (Three million, seven hundred thousand)
Platinum-group minerals	63 000 000 000 (Sixty-three billion)
Rare earth elements	716 675 945 (Seven hundred and sixteen million, six hundred and seventy-five thousand, nine hundred and forty-five)
Zinc	14 000 000 000 (Fourteen billion)

Source: Adapted from Mining Review Africa (2021)

The key objectives of the REIPPPP are multi-faceted, with the focus on:
- generating 17 800 MW of electricity by 2030;
- promoting sustainable development and climate action;
- fostering economic growth and attracting foreign direct investment;
- ensuring energy diversification and security;
- reducing poverty and stimulating economic development; and
- promoting good governance and service delivery (Department of Public Enterprises 2019).

In light of the critical mineral security required for solar PV and battery manufacturing, the South African government can leverage the AfCFTA to address the shortage of lithium, cobalt, and aluminium. Tables 7.1 and 7.2 indicate the significance of this strategic approach for strengthening South Africa's position in renewable energy production and promoting sustainable development. By capitalising on the AfCFTA, South Africa can procure the critical mineral resources needed to manufacture solar photovoltaic panels and battery storage. This strategic positioning can increase investment, job creation, and economic growth in the renewable energy sector, positioning South Africa as a critical player in the regional manufacturing and supply chain of solar photovoltaic systems.

South Africa's strategic positioning: Leveraging AfCFTA for critical minerals in solar PV renewable energy

Africa boasts significant reserves of most of the strategic minerals needed for various industries, including renewable energy. One of the minerals that is not abundant in South Africa is lithium, which is essential for manufacturing batteries. As significant economies worldwide strive to embrace renewable energy solutions, the demand for lithium continues to rise, driving efforts to secure stable lithium sources and providing Africa with an opportunity for international investment in lithium mining projects (Ndebele 2023). Cobalt, another essential mineral in battery manufacturing, is also experiencing a surge in demand due to the global shift towards environmental sustainability and the growing adoption of electric vehicles and renewable energy storage solutions, emphasising its strategic importance in the clean energy transition (World Bank Group 2023).

In this context, Africa's abundant reserves of lithium and cobalt present an attractive opportunity for investors. By strategically leveraging platforms like the AfCFTA, South Africa can position itself as a critical player in the regional PV and battery storage supply chain (Jaganmohan 2023).

Lithium

The combined lithium resources of Zimbabwe, the DRC, Ghana, Namibia, and Mali are 4.38 million tonnes, which illustrates that the African continent has the potential to have the highest ranking in the global lithium mining commodity market (Barich 2022). Nine lithium mining projects are being developed in Zimbabwe, Namibia, Mali, Ghana, and DRC (Bulbulia 2022).

Cobalt

The DRC produces 70 per cent of the world's cobalt as a by-product of copper. The multinational commodity trading and mining company, Glencore, produced more than 40 per cent of the DRC's cobalt in 2019, and between 10 per cent and 20 per cent is produced by artisanal and small-scale miners (Jaganmohan 2023). South Africa has access to 27 per cent of the world's cobalt mineral security via Katanga Mining Ltd, which is owned by Glencore (IEA 2021a).

Aluminium

The top aluminium-producing countries in Africa are Mozambique, Guinea, Cameroon, and South Africa. In 2021, Guinea, which produced 87.4 million metric tonnes, was the continent's top aluminium producer, followed by Mozambique. Zimbabwe's economic and financial crises decreased its production to 3 000 metric tonnes in 2016 (Sasu 2023). Mozambique's bauxite (a rock that is the main source of aluminium) exports rose by 19 per cent to about 10 547 tonnes in 2020 (Besta 2021).

By strategically leveraging the AfCFTA to partner with African countries that have plenty of lithium, cobalt, and aluminium, South Africa can procure all the necessary mineral resources for manufacturing solar panels and battery storage, which will position the country as a critical player in the solar photovoltaic supply chain (Mavhunga 2023). However, South Africa will need to create an environment that will enable it to partner with African countries by initiating partnerships for research and development; implementing bilateral trade agreements; and actively contributing to infrastructure development, technology transfer, and capacity building.

Partnership, research and development

South Africa should initiate AfCFTA solar PV renewable energy dialogue and investment forums between the respective member states and investors to inform trade policy. Such dialogue would foster collaboration for research and development activities related to mineral extraction, refinement, processing, and manufacturing, and enable public–private partnerships to achieve Africa's climate change objectives and solar renewable energy targets. They can serve as knowledge-sharing and capacity development platforms for African developmental states to identify and mitigate potential barriers and legal risks that may emerge from the partnerships (Amoasi, Kombat & Ibrahim 2022).

Bilateral trade agreements, policy harmonisation, and regulation

To make the African market accessible to the investor community, policy clarity, enhanced regulation, and transparent implementation strategies that establish Africa's energy transition roadmap are indeed paramount (African Union 2018). Policy clarity, improved regulation, and transparent implementation strategies are essential for making the African market investor-friendly and facilitating the establishment of Africa's energy transition roadmap. South Africa can lead efforts to streamline regulatory frameworks and promote transparency and good governance in extractive industries (World Bank Group 2023).

With the assistance of the AfCFTA secretariat, South Africa can initiate bilateral trade agreements with individual member states of AfCFTA and SAPP to facilitate the procurement of lithium, cobalt, and aluminium. These agreements can outline terms for exchanging resources, investment facilitation, and technology transfer (Amoasi Kombat & Ibrahim 2022).

Infrastructure development, technology transfer and capacity building

The partnership will help member states to build solar PV renewable energy project pipelines, shape joint policy and regulatory frameworks, strengthen dialogue between investors and governments, promote a single power market, facilitate infrastructure development growth, and expedite the establishment of additional pan-African green banks (Amoasi Kombat & Ibrahim 2022).

Leveraging the AfCFTA for South Africa's renewable energy initiative and mineral security

The first wave of special economic zones (SEZs) emerged in the 1980s within the global market of developed states. It became a megatrend in the early 2000s, prompting the many developing states on the African continent to join the emerging third wave. This has enabled African governments to attract industrial activities, leading to significant market growth and increased competitiveness in the global value chain. Currently, the African continent accounts for 24 per cent of the SEZs worldwide and has, over the past 20 years, progressively established 60 per cent of the world's SEZ regulatory frameworks and policies. Because SEZs are familiar in Africa, they can help to overcome the conservative challenges that have hindered progress. So, African policymakers are responsible for ensuring that their policies align with the goals of sustainable development and the Fourth Industrial Revolution, both international megatrends shaping the need for African countries to utilise SEZs as tools for economic development (United Nations Conference on Trade and Development (UNCTAD) 2021a).

Establishing SEZs on the African continent has catalysed investment. These zones have a distinct regulatory framework that differs from the rules and regulations that govern a country's local and national economies. Their purpose is to provide infrastructure support, financial incentives, and other services that benefit small and medium enterprises and their local economies within the jurisdiction of the zones. Furthermore, SEZs were created to provide relief from tariffs such as customs duties, as they function as independent customs territories. The evidence presented in the UNCTAD handbook (2021a) suggests that improvements are needed to attract more foreign direct investment and generate employment opportunities. Importantly, most African SEZs still need to be further developed, and most African manufacturing and supply value chains must increase their exports and improve their infrastructure (UNCTAD 2021a).

South African SEZs were enacted in 2000 to promote local economic development and create an enabling environment for expanding the West Rand REDZs. The SEZ programme criteria currently require SEZ-integrated development zones to be close to an international airport or seaport. However, these requirements ignore the government's failure to adopt pro-poor local economic policies to develop South African township economies. This failure can be traced back to the colonial segregation practice of situating proletariat human settlements on the outskirts and peripheries of central business districts to supply cheap labour to core economic centres within cities (UNCTAD 2021a).

These criteria were challenged by the enactment of the Special Economic Zones Act 16 of 2014, which stated that municipalities could to apply to become designated SEZs if they could demonstrate their capacity to support South Africa's industrial development goals, such as manufacturing goods, or providing services, creating employment opportunities, and attracting both domestic and foreign investment to help upgrade existing infrastructure. Most South African township economies continue to suffer from persistent socioeconomic challenges, such as concentrated poverty and the absence of economic transformation, which contribute to widening inequality gaps despite the country's progressive and equitable constitution. These informal economies struggle to take advantage of economic opportunities and require greater access to entrepreneurial networks (Turok, Scheba & Visagie 2020).

The South African National Department of Trade, Industry and Competition and South Africa's Industrial Policy Action define an SEZ as a geographically designated area for strategic industrialisation and regional and economic development (South African Business 2023).

Benefits and opportunities of leveraging the AfCFTA

The Gauteng provincial government has identified the West Rand as suitable for a SEZ for urban agriculture, green hydrogen, and solar power. The region has a mining-centric economy that is in dire need of being diversified. Identifying a sustainable local economic trajectory beyond mining can boost the country's manufacturing capacity, increase exports, and create green economic opportunities to accelerate turning the Gauteng City-Region into a single, multitier integrated SEZ (Hartley & Morrow 2021).

The study elucidated in this chapter explored the West Rand District Municipality as a potential REDZ to grant township economies access to the restricted formal market value chain by leveraging the AfCFTA for REIPPPP mineral security. This would address the effect of low investment in socioeconomic welfare drives, which contributes to high unemployment, poverty, and inequality rates in South African township economies. The West Rand District Municipality meets the critical solar PV and REDZ requirements (World Bank Group 2021), so it could expand into the Western Electricity Grid Infrastructure power corridor (Laurie, Van Zyl & Barbour 2019).

Transforming the West Rand District Municipality into a REDZ would involve establishing a new network of industries, economies, and cities. It is adjacent to the Lanseria Airport and Maropeng World Heritage Sites (Gauteng City-Region 2019). The West Rand REDZ will play a significant role in helping South Africa unlock technological innovation and industry potential in solar renewable energy, and promote and contribute to developing a resilient manufacturing and supply chain.

Leveraging the AfCFTA for renewable energy mineral security can transform the West Rand into a socioeconomic production centre, solar PV farm, and industrial hub that may contribute to increased foreign and domestic investment, value-added exports, sustainable job creation in the emerging green economy, and help to reduce the district's overreliance on the mining industry, which is on the brink of collapse (West Rand District Municipality 2023).

The West Rand REDZ will not only support South Africa's national energy transition in promoting technological innovation and industry potential in solar renewable energy, it can also provide local manufacturing employment (Cobenefits 2019). Other employment opportunities from this transformation include procurement, transport, solar panel installation, grid connection, and operation and maintenance (GreenCape 2020). The manufacturing and supply market of battery energy storage and solar system components could benefit South Africa's economy by reducing the costs of material imports and improving material availability. The manufactured rooftop solar PV panels, lithium battery components, and systems can be traded with SADC and SAPP member states on the AfCFTA (World Bank Group 2020; UNCTAD 2021b).

The West Rand SEZ and REDZ could help reduce trade barriers, integrate African mining economies, address infrastructure gaps, improve the manufacturing and supply chain for solar PV and battery components and systems, and promote intra-African trade, which would help AfCFTA and SAPP member states to reform and diversify their economies to take advantage of secure renewable energy market access by harvesting the abundant solar irradiation (Subban 2023; Gauteng City-Region 2019).

The AfCFTA will create a larger market for renewable energy projects, attracting more investors and fostering competition. This can reduce renewable energy generation costs and enhance investment and financing opportunities for South Africa's REIPPPP and SAPP member states. It will also serve as a consistent regulatory and harmonised investment framework to increase investment inflows to support the development and expansion of renewable energy infrastructure in South Africa, thus overcoming informal, illegal mining sectors, poor road infrastructure, and chaotic violence (Barich 2022). This example could inspire other SAPP member states such as Mozambique, Namibia, and Zimbabwe to follow suit.

The AfCFTA can help secure critical solar renewable energy mineral resources and help South Africa to successfully implement its REIPPPP, by establishing a REDZ in the West Rand District Municipality. This could rehabilitate West Rand township economies that have been struggling to diversify beyond the historically overused mining economy, simultaneously helping to promote a just energy transition. Establishing REDZs can create an enabling environment for pro-poor, community-based renewable energy initiatives operationalising the REIPPPP and utilising the AfCFTA to promote an inter-regional green economy value chain. It can improve South Africa's socioeconomic development, thus promoting sustainable economic growth through education, skills development, and job creation.

The AfCFTA can play a significant role in South Africa's REIPPPP and the SAPP, offering various benefits and opportunities in the SADC region. It can be used as a consistent policy prescript and legislative framework to overhaul outdated regulations governing trade, cross-border initiatives, investment, and capital flows while integrating solar photovoltaic energy in the SAPP. It can help the South African government influence potential investors to reconsider the organisational performance status of the largest SAPP state-owned enterprise – Eskom – as a possible barrier to mineral security and South Africa's renewable energy initiative.

Although conflict-related risks in critical minerals required for just energy transition are currently low, governance issues within South Africa's energy sector remain a challenge. The advancement of South Africa's SEZs is hindered by red tape, and ANC government policies often deter local investment opportunities due to their pro-market-based approach (Visser 2023). As a result, the emerging REDZs risk becoming an opportunity for exploitation, discouraging potential investors and undermining AfCFTA's potential to advance renewable energy initiatives in Africa.

However, leveraging the AfCFTA as a framework to harmonise renewable energy policies, regulations, and standards among AfCFTA, SAPP and SADC member states can mitigate these challenges. The AfCFTA agreement can play a crucial role in supporting African renewable energy initiatives including South Africa's REIPPPP, and strengthening the SAPP by promoting investment, encouraging fair competition, and enhancing market access. The AfCFTA agreement can help foster regional cooperation and support renewable energy infrastructure development, contributing to sustainable economic growth, improved energy security, and the mitigation of climate change impacts in the SADC region (Caiden 1991; Republic of South Africa 2018). Through its framework for harmonising energy policies, regulations, and standards, the AfCFTA agreement enables resource sharing, facilitates electricity exchange among the SAPP countries, and improves energy security and access for South Africa and other participating countries within the SAPP.

Potential barriers to leveraging AfCFTA

The dysfunction of South Africa's primary power utility, Eskom, has been exacerbated by procurement irregularities, organisational pathologies and administrative corruption such as maladministration, unauthorised fruitless and wasteful expenditure, and mismanagement of funds (Caiden 1991). The 2018 inquiry into governance, procurement and the financial sustainability of Eskom (Republic of South Africa 2018) highlights specific problems contributing to Eskom's dysfunction, including:
- the state capture scandal, which involved authorising excessive amounts to entities such as Trillian and McKinsey, and indicates a lack of oversight in decision-making processes within Eskom;
- inadequate procurement practices leading to controversial contracts with coal providers such as Tegeta Optimum Coal Mine and The New Age;
- non-adherence to contracts resulting in undue renegotiation;

- mismanagement of, and failure to maintain, significant infrastructure projects, particularly the Medupi and Kusile power plants; and
- governance shortcomings resulting in inefficiencies and operational failures.

Eskom's inability to fulfil its function of providing reliable and affordable electricity, unprincipled procurement practices, corruption, and profligate spending of state resources demonstrate weak institutional capacity and mediocre governance. The government struggles to manage internal organisational risks, which can be perceived by prospective stakeholders as an institutional gap (Republic of South Africa 2018; Institute of Directors Southern Africa 2016). Consequently, these procurement irregularities and organisational pathologies can pose significant investment and trade risks that could hinder South Africa's ability to leverage the AfCFTA for bilateral trade agreements to secure critical minerals for manufacturing rooftop solar systems.

Many AfCFTA members have substantial lithium, cobalt, and aluminium reserves, which South Africa does not have, and that are essential for manufacturing solar panels to facilitate the country's green energy transition (Mokhele 2019). South Africa's green energy transition may face challenges due to unregulated and informal mining, unsafe working conditions, the use of child labour, poor road infrastructure, violence, lack of accountability, and environmental and social effects (Barich 2022; IEA 2021b).

The environment, society, and governance (ESG) of mining enterprises are at risk due to the significant energy consumption and greenhouse gas emissions associated with producing and processing critical minerals such as copper, lithium, nickel, cobalt, and rare earth elements. As the demand for these minerals rises with the accelerated adoption of renewable solar energy, there is a pressing need for a substantial increase in their supply from various new sources. This heightened production activity poses a serious threat to the ESG factors of mining enterprises (IEA 2021b).

Conclusion

Overall, South Africa has the potential to play a crucial role in fostering collaboration and partnership among member states of the AfCFTA and the SAPP. By leveraging its economic strength, industrial expertise, and regional influence, South Africa can contribute to the sustainable procurement and utilisation of critical minerals, namely lithium, cobalt, and aluminium, from AfCFTA member states that have substantial amounts of these resources. This will create an enabling environment for the West Rand District Municipality, a special economic and renewable development zone. It meets the solar PV technical criteria because it comprises mining townships, which signifies the existence of mine land, and it is an ideal location for solar farm development with a high level of direct average radiation. Transforming the region into a SEZ and REDZ could unlock technological innovation and industry potential while fostering resilient manufacturing and supply chain development, thus advancing South Africa's industrial needs and contributing to the socioeconomic development and integration of the continent. While the AfCFTA offers immense opportunities for South Africa's renewable energy and mineral security objectives, there are some challenges, such as governance shortcomings, institutional capacity constraints, and environmental concerns associated with mining activities. These may hinder the leveraging of the AfCFTA for its renewable energy initiatives and mineral security. Addressing these challenges through regional cooperation, investment promotion, and the resolution of governance and environmental concerns is crucial. South Africa can maximise the benefits of the AfCFTA and lead the way in sustainable development within the African continent.

References

Adhikari M (2021) An economically sustainable approach to the energy transition in developing countries. *National Bureau of Asian Research*. Accessed 24 December 2024, https://www.nbr.org/wp-content/uploads/pdfs/publications/adhikari_apr21.pdf

African Union (2018) *AUC programme on harmonised continental regulatory framework for the energy sector in Africa: The case of the electricity sector*. Accessed 25 December 2024, https://www.tralac.org/images/docs/12842/auc-programme-on-harmonised-continental-regulatory-framework-for-the-energy-sector-in-africa-electricity-au-stc-ttiet-sub-committee-on-energy-march-2018.pdf

Amoasi N, Kombat E & Ibrahim A (2022) *The roles AfCFTA can play in Africa's energy transition agenda with the Institute for Energy Security (IES) Ghana*. Accessed 25 December 2024, https://www.linkedin.com/pulse/roles-afcfta-can-play-africas-energy-transition-agenda-omono-okonkwo/

Barich A (2022) *Globally significant discoveries position Africa as potential major lithium hub*. S&P Global Market Intelligence 5 September. Accessed 25 December 2024, https://www.spglobal.com/marketintelligence/en/news-insights/latest-news-headlines/globally-significant-discoveries-position-africa-as-potential-major-lithium-hub-71819527

Bekker B, Eberhard A, Gaunt T & Marquard A (2008) South Africa's rapid electrification programme: Policy, institutional, planning, financing and technical innovations. *Energy Policy* 36(8): 3125–3137. Accessed 13 January 2025, https://doi.org/10.1016/j.enpol.2008.04.014

Besta S (2021) Profiling the top four bauxite exporting countries in Africa. *NS Energy* 5 February. Accessed 25 December 2024, https://www.nsenergybusiness.com/analysis/bauxite-exporting-countries-africa/?cf-view

Bhuiyan MA, Zhang Q, Khare V, Mikhaylov V, Pinter G & Huang X (2022) Renewable energy consumption and economic growth nexus: A systematic literature review. *Frontiers in Environmental Science* 10. Accessed 24 December 2024, https://www.frontiersin.org/articles/10.3389/fenvs.2022.878394

Bojek P (2022) *Solar PV: Technology deep dive*. September 2022. International Energy Agency September. Accessed 13 January 2025, https://www.iea.org/energy-system/renewables/solar-pv

Bulbulia T (2022) Lithium projects in Africa increasing, but Americas will still dominate – Fitch Solutions. *Mining Weekly* 8 August. Accessed 25 December 2024, https://www.miningweekly.com/article/lithium-projects-in-africa-increasing-but-americas-will-still-dominate-fitch-solutions-2022-08-08

Caiden GE (1991) What really is public maladministration? *Public Administration Review* 51(6): 486–493. Accessed 24 December 2024, https://doi.org/10.2307/976599

Cobenefits (2019) Future skills and job creation through renewable energy in South Africa: Assessing the co-benefits of decarbonising the power sector. Accessed 25 December 2024, https://www.cobenefits.info/wp-content/uploads/2019/03/COBENEFITS-Study-South-Africa-Employment.pdf

Darmani A, Arvidsson N, Hidalgo A & Albors J (2014) What drives the development of renewable energy technologies? Toward a typology for the systemic drivers. *Renewable and Sustainable Energy Reviews* 38: 834–847. Accessed 24 December 2024, https://doi.org/10.1016/j.rser.2014.07.023

Department of Public Enterprises (2019) *The roadmap for Eskom in a reformed electricity supply industry*. Department of Public Enterprises, Government of South Africa. Accessed 25 December 2024, https://www.gov.za/sites/default/files/gcis_document/201910/roadmap-eskom.pdf

Eberhard A (2001) Competition and regulation in the electricity supply industry in South Africa. Trade and Industrial Policy Strategies. Accessed 24 December 2024, https://www.tips.org.za/files/Competition_and_Regulation_in_the_Electricity_Supply_Industry_in_South_Africa.pdf

Eberhard A & Naude R (2017) *The South African renewable energy IPP procurement programme: Review, lessons learned and proposals to reduce transaction costs*. Cape Town: Graduate School of Business. Accessed 25 December 2024, https://www.gsb.uct.ac.za/files/EberhardNaude_REIPPPPReview_2017_1_1.pdf

Economic Consulting Associates (2009) The potential of regional power sector integration: South African power pool transmission and trading case study. Working Paper, Energy Sector Management Assistance Program, World Bank, October. Accessed 23 December 2024, http://hdl.handle.net/10986/17509

Friedlingstein P, Solomon S, Plattner G-K, Knutti R, Ciais P & Raupach MR (2011) Long-term climate implications of twenty-first century options for carbon dioxide emission mitigation. *Nature Climate Change* 1: 457–461. Accessed 24 December 2024, https://doi.org/10.1038/nclimate1302

GreenCape (2020). Utility-scale renewable energy 2020: Market intelligence report. Accessed 25 December 2024, https://green-cape.co.za/assets/RENEWABLE_ENERGY_MIR_20200330_WEB.pdf

Hartley R & Morrow R (2021) *A special economic zone masterplan for Gauteng*. The Brenthurst Foundation. Accessed 25 December 2025, https://www.thebrenthurstfoundation.org/downloads/sez-30-.pdf

Höhne N, Hagemann M, Kuramochi T, Gonzales S, Sterl S, Day T, Hsu A, Rosengarten C, Weinfurter A, Xu K & Yan C (2017) *Renewable energy and energy efficiency in developing countries: Contributions to reducing global emissions, Second report*. United Nations

Environment Programme, The 1 Gigaton Coalition. Accessed 24 December 2024, https://newclimate.org/sites/default/files/2016/11/onegigatonreport_2016.pdf

International Energy Agency (2021a) *The Role of critical minerals in clean energy transitions: World energy outlook special report.* Accessed 25 December 2024, https://iea.blob.core.windows.net/assets/ffd2a83b-8c30-4e9d-980a-52b6d9a86fdc/TheRoleofCriticalMineralsinCleanEnergyTransitions.pdf

International Energy Agency (2021b) World energy outlook 2021, IEA Paris. Accessed 23 December 2024, https://www.iea.org/reports/world-energy-outlook-2021

International Renewable Energy Agency (2021) The renewable energy transition in Africa: Powering access, resilience and prosperity. Accessed 23 December 2024, https://www.irena.org/-/media/Files/IRENA/Agency/Publication/2021/March/Renewable_Energy_Transition_Africa_2021.pdf

Jaganmohan M (2023) *Cobalt mine production in South Africa 2013–2020*. Statistica 3 May. Accessed 25 December 2024, https://www.statista.com/statistics/974894/cobalt-mine-production-in-south-africa/

Institute of Directors Southern Africa (2016) *King IV: Report on corporate governance for South Africa.* Accessed 25 December 2025, https://www.iodsa.co.za/page/king-iv

Kessides IN (2020) *The decline and fall of Eskom: A South African tragedy.* Report 45, The Global Warming Policy Foundation. Accessed 24 December 2024, https://www.thegwpf.org/content/uploads/2020/06/Decline-Fall-Eskom.pdf

Khan MT, Thopil GA & Lalk J (2016) Review of proposals for practical power sector restructuring and reforms in a dynamic electricity supply industry. *Renewable and Sustainable Energy Reviews* 62(C): 326–335. Accessed 24 December 2024, https://ideas.repec.org/a/eee/rensus/v62y2016icp326-335.html

Laurie S, Van Zyl H & Barbour T (2019) *Strategic environmental assessment for the expansion of electricity grid infrastructure in South Africa: Economic assessment specialist report.* Council for Scientific and Industrial Research. Accessed 25 December 2024, https://gasnetwork.csir.co.za/wp-content/uploads/2020/03/01_EGI-Expansion-SEA_Summary-to-Part-5_Binder.pdf

Mavhunga CC (2023) Africa's move from raw material exports toward mineral value addition: Historical background and implications. *MRS Bulletin* 48: 395–406. Accessed 25 December 2024, https://doi.org/10.1557/s43577-023-00534-3

Mining Review Africa (2021) *Facts and figures 2021: Changing mines – changing lives.* Accessed 23 December 2024, https://www.miningreview.com/gold/facts-and-figures-2021-changing-minds-changing-lives/

Mokhele K (2019) Political risk analysis of the renewable energy sector in South Africa and the effect on foreign direct investment. MEng ME thesis, University of Cape Town. Accessed 25 December 2024, http://hdl.handle.net/11427/30868

Montmasson-Clair G, Kritzinger K, Scholtz L & Gulati M (2017) *New roles for South African municipalities in renewable energy: A review of business models.* Discussion paper, South African–German Energy Partnership. Accessed 24 December 2024, https://www.crses.sun.ac.za/files/research/publications/technical-reports/New roles for SA municipalities in RE - Discussion Paper - June 2017_final.pdf

Ndebele L (2023) Africa could rescue the US as lithium demand projected to surge 42 times. *News24* 8 February. Accessed 25 December 2024, https://www.news24.com/news24/africa/news/africa-could-rescue-us-as-lithium-demand-projected-to-surge-42-times-20230208

Newbery D & Eberhard A (2008) *South African network infrastructure review: Electricity.* National Treasury and the Department of Public Enterprises, Government of South Africa. Accessed 24 December 2024, https://www.gsb.uct.ac.za/files/saelectricitypaper08.pdf

Parliamentary Monitoring Group (2000) Restructuring of state-owned enterprises: Briefing 15 February 2000. Accessed 24 December 2024, https://pmg.org.za/committee-meeting/3977/

Peberdy S, Harrison P & Dinath Y (2017) *Uneven spaces: Core and periphery in the Gauteng city-region.* Gauteng City-Region Observatory, 1 September. Accessed 24 December 2024, https://doi.org/10.36634/DTLV3720

Republic of South Africa (2018) *Report of The Portfolio Committee on Public Enterprises on the inquiry into governance, procurement and the financial sustainability of Eskom*, 28 November. Accessed 25 December 2024, https://www.parliament.gov.za/storage/app/media/Links/2018/November 2018/28-11-2018/Final Report - Eskom Inquiry 28 NOV.pdf

Republic of South Africa (2019) Integrated resource plan, Government Gazette No. 42784. Accessed 23 December 2024, https://www.gov.za/sites/default/files/gcis_document/201912/42784gon1360.pdf

Sasu D (2023) *Africa: Bauxite production in Africa 2010–2021.* Statista 26 October. Accessed 25 December 2024, https://www.statista.com/statistics/1038455/african-bauxite-production/

South African Business (2023) *Gauteng's special economic zones are multiplying,* 10 November. Accessed 25 December 2024, https://www.southafricanbusiness.co.za/11/2023/construction-and-engineering/gautengs-special-economic-zones-are-multiplying/

Subban V (2023) Africa: The impact of the African Continental Free Trade Area on the continent's mining sector. *Global Compliance News* 27 January. Accessed 25 December 2024, https://www.globalcompliancenews.com/2023/01/27/https-insightplus-bakermckenzie-com-bm-international-commercial-trade-africa-the-impact-of-the-african-continental-free-trade-area-on-the-continents-mining-sector_01252023/

Theron A (2017) Eskom's electrification programme improves quality of life. *ESI Africa*, 24 May. Accessed 13 January 2025, https://www.esi-africa.com/features-analysis/eskoms-electrification-programme-improves-quality-of-life/

Turok I, Scheba A & Visagie J (2020) Strengthening township economies in South Africa: The case for better regulation and policy innovation. *Environment and Urbanization* 35(2): 297–309. Accessed 25 December 2024, DOI:10.1177/09562478231193829

United Nations Conference on Trade and Development (UNCTAD) (2021a) *Handbook on special economic zones in Africa: Towards economic diversification across the continent.* Accessed 25 December 2024, https://unctad.org/system/files/official-document/diaeia2021d3_en.pdf

United Nations Conference on Trade and Development (UNCTAD) (2021b) *Implications of the African Continental Free Trade Area for trade and biodiversity: Policy and regulatory recommendations.* Accessed 25 December 2024, https://unctad.org/system/files/official-document/ditctedinf2021d3_en.pdf

United Nations Framework Convention on Climate Change (UNFCCC) (2010) *Report of the Conference of the Parties on its fifteenth session, held in Copenhagen from 7 to 19 December 2009 Addendum Part Two: Action taken by the Conference of the Parties at its fifteenth session.* Accessed 23 December 2024, https://unfccc.int/documents/6103#beg

Visser A (2023) *Requests for compensation due to shifting of SEZ requirements.* Moneyweb, 12 January. Accessed 25 December 2024, https://www.moneyweb.co.za/mymoney/moneyweb-tax/requests-for-compensation-due-to-shifting-of-sez-requirements/

West Rand District Municipality (2023) *State of the District address by the West Rand district municipality executive mayor.* Accessed 25 December 2024, https://www.wrdm.gov.za/wp-content/uploads/documents/reports/SODA-Speech-15-March-2023.pdf

World Bank Group (2020) *The African Continental Free Trade Area: Economic and distributional effects.* Accessed 25 December 2024, https://openknowledge.worldbank.org/server/api/core/bitstreams/ef1aa41f-60de-5bd2-a63e-75f2c3ff0f43/content

World Bank Group (2021) *Global solar atlas.* Accessed 25 December 2024, https://apps.solargis.com/prospect/map?show-registration=1&c=-28.95946,22.412109,5&s=-26.24565,27.55538

World Bank Group (2023) *Battery storage market and value chain assessment in South Africa: Synthesis report.* Accessed 25 December 2024, https://documents.worldbank.org/en/publication/documents-reports/documentdetail/099155502102332395/p17268201ebc89050b1960f40c8377523a

Zeng S, Yuchen L, Lui& Xin N (2017) A review of renewable energy investment in the BRICS countries: History, models, problems and solutions. *Renewable and Sustainable Energy Reviews* 74: 860–872. Accessed 24 December 2024, https://doi.org/10.1016/j.rser.2017.03.016

8 Sustainable food systems transformation in South Africa

Lavhelesani R Managa

Introduction

In South Africa, the urgency for an inclusive transformation of food systems that leaves no one behind has never been more critical. This transformation is essential for several reasons. Firstly, it is crucial for achieving food security and improving nutrition across the country, where a significant proportion of the population continues to suffer from hunger and malnutrition (Simelane et al. 2024). According to Statistics SA (2023), approximately 11 per cent of South Africans experienced food insecurity in 2021, highlighting the dire need for systemic change.

Secondly, transforming food systems can drive economic growth and reduce poverty, inequality, and unemployment. Agriculture remains a key sector in many African economies, including South Africa, contributing significantly to GDP and employment. South Africa's agricultural sector accounted for 2.4 per cent of the national GDP in 2022 (Department of Land Reform and Rural Development (DALRRD) 2022b). Furthermore, the sector is a major source of employment, providing jobs for about 5.3 per cent of the country's labour force. The importance of agriculture is underscored by its role in food security, rural development, and export earnings. For instance, South Africa is a leading exporter of citrus fruits, wine, and maize, with agricultural exports valued at over $10 billion in 2019 (Sihlobo 2020). These figures highlight the sector's critical role in the nation's economic and social fabric. Therefore, transforming South Africa's agricultural systems and making them more inclusive can create more job opportunities, enhance productivity, and stimulate economic development. This is particularly important in rural areas, where agriculture is often the primary source of livelihood.

Thirdly, transforming South Africa's food systems is essential for addressing critical issues such as food waste, sustainable management of natural resources, and climate change mitigation. The current agricultural practices in South Africa often contribute significantly to environmental degradation, including deforestation, water scarcity, and greenhouse gas emissions. Adopting innovative and eco-friendly agricultural practices to mitigate these negative impacts and promote environmental sustainability is imperative. Precision farming, which utilises advanced technologies such as GPS and data analytics, can optimise resource use and enhance crop yields while minimising environmental footprints (Soto et al. 2019; Javaid et al. 2022; Hedley

2015). Agroforestry, the integration of trees and shrubs into agricultural landscapes, can improve soil fertility, sequester carbon, and provide additional income streams for farmers (Zaca et al. 2023; Wilson & Lovell 2016). Organic agriculture, which emphasises the use of natural inputs and biodiversity, can enhance soil health, reduce pollution, and promote resilience to climate change.

Lastly, the transformation of food systems is a matter of social justice and equity. Inclusive transformation can help to empower smallholder farmers, women, and youth, all of whom are often marginalised in current food systems due to historical disparities, including those stemming from apartheid. By providing these groups with access to resources (for example land), education, and markets, we can promote greater equity and ensure that the benefits of agricultural development are shared more broadly.

This chapter reflects on the state of South Africa's food systems, highlighting disparities and inefficiencies; explores the impact of the non-functioning food system on the country's population, particularly marginalised and vulnerable groups; and discusses and underscores the importance of supporting policy reforms by addressing environmental challenges and food waste, leveraging technology and innovations, and promoting urban agriculture as potential strategies to transform sustainable food systems in South Africa.

Methodology

A scoping literature review was the first step in exploring the transformation towards a sustainable and equitable food system in South Africa. The goal was to map the existing research, identify key concepts, and uncover gaps in the literature. The scoping review followed a systematic approach, adhering to the framework proposed by Arksey and O'Malley (2005) and further refined by Levac, Colquhoun and O'Brien (2010). In addition, the generative artificial intelligence tool Chat GPT 4.0 was used to supplement the literature search strategy and improve the manuscript's readability.

Literature search strategy

A comprehensive search strategy was developed to capture a wide range of relevant literature. The electronic databases searched included PubMed, Scopus, Web of Science, and Google Scholar. Additionally, grey literature sources such as government reports, policy documents, and non-governmental organisation publications were included to ensure a holistic understanding of the topic. The search terms used included combinations of the following keywords: sustainable food systems; equitable food systems; transformation; South Africa; agriculture; agro-processing; food security; policy reform; nutrition; resilience; technology and innovation; urban food systems and inclusive growth. Boolean operators (AND, OR) were employed to refine the search results.

Inclusion and exclusion criteria

Only articles written in English and published between 1994 and 2024 were considered. This study proposes 1994 as the base year because that is the year of South Africa's first universal-franchise election. The democratic dispensation that began with the end of apartheid, brought about significant changes in various sectors, including agriculture. Since then, the country has implemented land reform policies aimed at addressing historical injustices and promoting equitable access to land for previously disadvantaged groups; shifted towards sustainable agricultural practices and the promotion of small-scale farming initiatives to improve food security and reduce poverty; and invested in infrastructure development, research and development, and skills training programmes to support the growth of the agricultural sector – hence its significance to this study. Only research focused on South Africa, or with significant relevance to the South African context, and papers addressing sustainable and equitable aspects of food systems, including policy, governance, agriculture, nutrition, and socioeconomic factors, were included. Figure 8.1 summarises the selection procedure followed.

Figure 8.1 *Selection procedure used for the literature review*

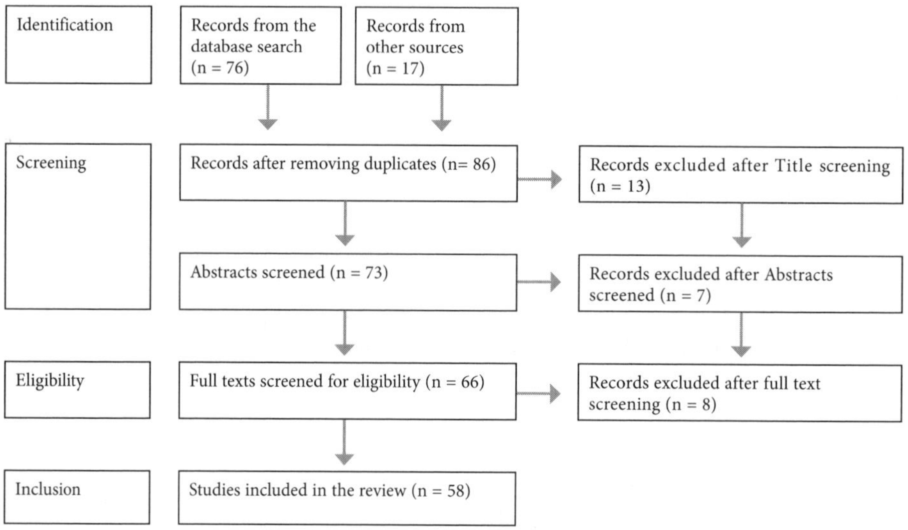

Stage	Process	Exclusions
Identification	Records from the database search (n = 76); Records from other sources (n = 17)	
Screening	Records after removing duplicates (n = 86)	Records excluded after Title screening (n = 13)
	Abstracts screened (n = 73)	Records excluded after Abstracts screened (n = 7)
Eligibility	Full texts screened for eligibility (n = 66)	Records excluded after full text screening (n = 8)
Inclusion	Studies included in the review (n = 58)	

Data analysis

The data were analysed and synthesised using pre-determined thematic areas of importance, while also articulating some of the emerging national food systems transformation pathways and best practices for sustainability, equality and resilience building. Both qualitative and quantitative analytic approaches were used. Special attention was placed on identifying and documenting necessities and key drivers for food systems transformation in South Africa, in line with the objectives outlined in the United Nations Agenda 2030 and the African Union's 2014 Malabo declaration that renewed its commitment to the Comprehensive African Agricultural Development Programme (African Union 2024).

Need for food systems transformation in South Africa

Food systems transformation in South Africa is crucial due to various factors such as climate change, population growth, and economic disparities. The country faces challenges in terms of food security, sustainability, and access to nutritious food for all its citizens. There is a growing awareness of the need to shift towards more sustainable and resilient food systems that can address these issues effectively. Initiatives such as promoting agroecology, supporting small-scale farmers, and reducing food waste are being implemented to drive this transformation. At the national level, the transformation of the food system seeks to achieve multiple goals aligned with the National Development Plan (NDP) 2030 (National Planning Commission 2012), the United Nations Sustainable Development Goals Commission 2030 (United Nations 2015), and the African Union's Agenda 2063 (African Union Commission 2015).

Experiences of food insecurity

Despite being classified as a middle-income country, South Africa grapples with significant levels of food insecurity and malnutrition. According to Statistics SA (2023), in 2021, 15 per cent (2.6 million) and 6 per cent (1.1 million) of the nearly 17.9 million households in South Africa reported inadequate and severely inadequate access to food, respectively. These findings are corroborated by the National Food and Nutrition Security Survey, which indicated that 79.2 per cent of households experienced little to no hunger, while 15.3 per cent and 5.6 per cent of households faced moderate to severe hunger (Simelane et al. 2024). Although these statistics might suggest that food insecurity in South Africa is not at a crisis level, the survey further revealed that 18.6 per cent of households consumed poor diets, and 23.3 per cent consumed borderline diets. This indicates that a significant portion of the population survives on nutrient-poor food groups.

The UN Food and Agriculture Organization (FAO), European Union, Centre de coopération internationale en recherche agronomique pour le développement, and Centre of Excellence for Food Security (FAO 2022) have highlighted that South Africa faces a triple burden of malnutrition: undernutrition, micronutrient deficiencies, and overweight/obesity. These conditions underscore the profound inadequacies within the current food system, which fails to provide affordable, nutritious, and culturally appropriate food for all citizens.

Rural areas are particularly affected, facing challenges such as limited access to resources and infrastructure, which contribute to higher levels of household food insecurity. Factors such as unemployment, poverty, and the adverse effects of climate change disproportionately impact these regions, exacerbating existing disparities. The COVID-19 pandemic further intensified the situation, with lockdowns and the ensuing economic crisis leading to job losses and increased food prices. This scenario presents a paradox, given the country's existing food security and agricultural policies, which ostensibly aim to ensure food availability and accessibility for all.

In light of these challenges, it is imperative to re-evaluate and strengthen South Africa's food security strategies, focusing on creating resilient food systems that can withstand economic and environmental shocks while ensuring equitable access to nutritious food for all population segments.

Ensuring equitable share of the agricultural sector

The legacy of apartheid has left deep socioeconomic divides in South Africa, which are starkly reflected in the country's food system. Smallholder farmers, who are predominantly black, often face significant barriers such as limited access to land, credit, and markets, while large agribusinesses, which are predominantly owned by white South Africans, dominate the sector (FAO 2022; Sihlobo & Qobo 2021). According to a 2017 land audit report, white South Africans, who make up just over 7 per cent of the population, own 26 663 144 hectares or 72 per cent of the total 37 031 283 hectares of farms. In contrast, coloured people own 5 371 383 hectares (15 per cent), Indians own 2 031 790 hectares (5 per cent), and black people own a mere 1 314 873 hectares (4 per cent) (DALRRD 2017). Consequently, black farmers contribute only between 5 per cent and 10 per cent of the agricultural output in the country. In 2019, black farmers' contributions to maize, wheat, potato, and poultry outputs were only 4.7 per cent, 1.3 per cent, 1.0 per cent, and 4.2 per cent, respectively (Table 8.1). However, there has been a notable shift in cattle farming, with black farmers accounting for 34 per cent of the cattle share (DALRRD 2017).

This racial disparity is deeply rooted in the country's apartheid history, particularly due to the enactment of the Native Land Act of 1913. This legislation prohibited black people from buying or renting land outside designated reserves, which constituted only about 7 per cent of the country's land area. The enduring effects of such policies continue to shape contemporary society, manifesting in ongoing segregation and significant income disparities between white and black individuals. This inequality not only undermines the livelihoods of smallholder farmers but also limits the diversity and resilience of the food system.

Addressing these disparities is crucial for accelerating economic transformation and agricultural reform in South Africa. It is not merely a matter of policy but a necessity for creating a more equitable, sustainable, and prosperous society. Achieving this requires a holistic approach that addresses historical injustices, promotes inclusive growth, and ensures the sustainable use of resources. By doing so, South Africa can build a food system that is not only more just and equitable but also more resilient and capable of meeting the needs of all its citizens.

Table 8.1 *Black farmers' share of agricultural outputs in South Africa: 2015 to 2019*

Commodities	Average: 2015–2019		
	Employment	Production value R000	Black farmer share in output: 2019
Maize	29 289	27 038 097	4.7%
Soybeans	7 654	5 698 270	3.1%
Wheat	2 912	5 805 830	1.3%
Cotton	3 876	1 967 187	2.4%
Citrus	128 219	15 046 134	12%
Deciduous fruit	79 443	15 660 627	10%
Viticulture	163 441	7 057 260	1.6%
Potatoes	42 158	6 972 320	1.0%
Tomatoes	9 764	2 364 149	8.6%
Wool	23 976	3 397 506	11.0%
Mohair	6 765	554 582	12.8%
Cattle	89 752	31 992 265	34.0%
Poultry	52 836	47 863 345	4.2%

Source: National Agricultural Marketing Council 2019

Addressing the post-harvest food waste

Like many countries in Africa, South Africa is grappling with a significant and pressing challenge of food waste. The country loses between 9 and 10 million tonnes of food annually, with a per capita waste of 177 kg annually (Department of Environment, Forestry and Fisheries & Council for Scientific and Industrial Research (CSIR) 2021). This amounts to 30 per cent of agricultural production wasted, resulting in a loss of R61.5 billion from the economy, representing 2.1 per cent of GDP lost each year. The implications of this are far-reaching, exacerbating the already critical issue of food insecurity. This paradox of abundance and scarcity highlights the inefficiencies within our food supply chain, from production and distribution to consumption. The processing, packaging, and consumption stages are collectively responsible for a staggering 67 per cent of food loss (AgriSA 2024). This includes mishandling during transportation, inadequate storage facilities, and inefficient processing techniques that lead to substantial wastage. As indicated in Table 8.2, the discarded food includes a wide range of items, from fresh produce and dairy products to grains and meat, all of which could have been utilised to feed the millions of South Africans who go to bed hungry every night.

Table 8.2 *Proportion of post-harvest losses in South Africa*

Segment	Category	Range of percentage loss
Food	Roots and tubers	10–40%
	Milk	8–16%
	Fruits and vegetables	15–44%
	Cereals, oil seeds and pulses	15–30%
	Fish and seafood	10–40%
	Meat	6–8%

Source: Council for Scientific and Industrial Research (2021)

Fruits and vegetables make up a significant portion of this waste, with an astonishing two million tonnes discarded annually due to superficial reasons such as blemishes, irregular shapes, or minor imperfections (Fourie et al. 2023). Shockingly, one in five imperfect fruits and vegetables, which remain nutritionally intact and perfectly edible, end up in landfills, contributing to the growing environmental crisis because decomposing food in landfills generates methane, a potent greenhouse gas that contributes to climate change (Parameshwari 2017). The resources used to produce this wasted food – water, energy, and labour – are also squandered, further straining the environment.

Addressing this issue requires a multifaceted approach. Initiatives such as improving food storage and transportation infrastructure, promoting food recovery and redistribution programmes, and raising public awareness about the importance of reducing food waste are crucial. By tackling food waste head-on, South Africa can make significant strides towards a more sustainable and equitable food system, ensuring that the bounty of our land benefits all its people.

Making food systems more resilient to environmental challenges

South Africa's food system is grappling with significant environmental challenges, which render production systems increasingly unstable. Agriculture, a cornerstone of the nation's economy, is a major contributor to greenhouse gas emissions, water scarcity, and soil degradation. The heavy reliance on monoculture and industrial farming practices has precipitated a troubling loss of biodiversity, and heightened agricultural sector vulnerability to climate change's impacts. For instance, periodic droughts, which are becoming more frequent and severe due to climate change, devastate crop yields and livestock production. These droughts reduce food availability and strain water resources, further exacerbating the challenges faced by farmers and communities (Pereira & Drimie 2016).

Current agricultural practices, which are aimed at maximising short-term yields, are proving to be unsustainable in the long run. Soil degradation, driven by overuse of chemical fertilizers and pesticides, is diminishing the land's fertility, making it harder to grow crops year after year. Water scarcity, exacerbated by inefficient irrigation methods and climate variability, threatens the very foundation of agricultural productivity.

Therefore, adopting more sustainable farming and food production practices is desirable and essential for ensuring long-term food security and environmental health. This transformation could include a shift towards agroecological practices emphasising biodiversity, soil health, and water conservation. It could also involve the adoption of climate-smart agriculture techniques that enhance resilience to climate impacts while reducing greenhouse gas emissions. By entirely embracing sustainable agricultural practices, South Africa has the potential to cultivate a more resilient and robust food system. This system not only nurtures the environment by preserving biodiversity, reducing carbon footprints, and conserving precious water resources but also significantly enhances the well-being of its people. It ensures food security, promotes healthier lifestyles and fosters economic stability for farmers and communities. In doing so, South Africa can pave the way for future generations to thrive in a harmonious relationship with nature, where the delicate balance between human needs and environmental stewardship is maintained and celebrated.

Strategies for sustainable and inclusive food systems

Supporting food systems policy reform and implementation

The concept of transformation has been extensively discussed in South Africa, yet the tangible progress in food security and nutrition does not necessarily reflect this rhetoric. Therefore, the country must rethink its food systems strategy to create a more resilient, inclusive, and sustainable framework that aligns with both the 2030 Agenda for Sustainable Development and the African Union's Agenda 2063. This necessitates meaningful policy reforms, sustained investment, and resource allocation to ensure that existing policies and programmes effectively contribute to transforming food systems.

To this end, implementing the Agriculture and Agro-Processing Master Plan (AAMP) is pivotal. The AAMP stands as a testament to South Africa's commitment to inclusivity and resilience in its journey towards a transformed food system. The strategic objectives of the AAMP aim to address the multifaceted challenges faced by the agriculture and agro-processing sectors to promote inclusive growth, competitiveness, and sustainability (DALRRD 2022a). These objectives encompass various critical aspects such as food security, market access, innovation, farmer support, employment, safety, governance, and environmental sustainability. The country can make significant progress towards overall economic recovery and development by achieving these objectives.

However, South Africa's policy landscape is often fragmented and lacks coherence. Integrated approaches that address the multiple dimensions of food systems

– including agriculture, health, environment, and social equity – are urgently needed. Strengthening institutions and fostering multi-stakeholder collaboration are key to creating a more inclusive and resilient food system. The lack of policy coherence and coordination, inadequate data and information systems, and weak governance and enforcement of regulations hinder effective decision-making and the implementation of programmes designed to transform food systems. Therefore, the governance of the policy space needs to be strengthened.

Managing food systems remains an ongoing challenge. Developing tailored programmes or solutions for different groups is crucial, as each faces distinct challenges. Addressing these unique needs through targeted interventions can significantly enhance the effective transformation of food systems. By fostering a holistic and integrated approach, South Africa can pave the way for a more sustainable and equitable food system that benefits all segments of society.

Reimagining the imperatives of land reform programmes

Despite initiatives like the Comprehensive Agricultural Support Programme and the Land Redistribution for Agricultural Development (DALRRD 2022c; Ministry for Agriculture and Land Affairs (2001), the current systems often fail emerging or smallholder farmers in South Africa. One of the key objectives of land reforms in South Africa was for the process to lead to the emergence of a cohort of black small-scale commercial farmers who would realise substantive agricultural production levels using irrigation and actively contribute to the local and national agricultural value chains. The available evidence suggests that this and other key objectives of the reforms have been difficult to attain, and the contribution of land reform to the livelihoods of the beneficiaries has been negligible in many parts of the country (Chikozho, Managa & Dabata 2020; Chikozho & Managa 2018).

One of the disturbing features of the main academic and policy-oriented discourses on the success or failure of the land reform programme is that, right from the beginning, land reform was primarily understood and evaluated according to the absolute volumes of land transferred from the predominantly white commercial farmers to the previously disadvantaged black emerging farmers. Achievement of targets set in this regard was given prime importance and continues to pervade most assessments of progress in this domain. Much less attention has been paid to the actual use of the land for productive purposes by the beneficiaries of the land redistribution programme once the land transfers are in place.

This narrow focus on volumetric land transfers has overshadowed the critical need to evaluate the effectiveness of land use and the real impact on the beneficiaries' agricultural productivity and economic empowerment. The current approach has led to land reform being seen as a quantitative exercise rather than a qualitative transformation. There is an urgent need to go beyond the assessment of land transfers from white people to black people in volumetric terms and to begin to articulate the significance of the main challenges and opportunities emerging farmers face in using the land for productive purposes.

Emerging farmers encounter numerous obstacles, including limited access to capital, inadequate infrastructure, insufficient technical support, and market access issues (Chikozho & Managa 2018; Simelane et al. 2024; Sihlobo & Qobo 2021). These challenges hinder their ability to utilise the land effectively and achieve the intended outcomes of the land reform programme. By shifting the focus towards understanding and addressing these barriers, policymakers can better support the emerging farmers in realising their potential.

A re-evaluation of the land reform programme is necessary to ensure that it meets the quantitative targets of land redistribution and fosters the qualitative growth and empowerment of black small-scale commercial farmers. This will help analysts identify the potency or limitations of existing land reform policies and support systems for emerging farmers. A more comprehensive approach that includes capacity building, access to resources, and market integration is crucial for the success of land reform and the sustainable development of South Africa's agricultural sector. This will ultimately contribute to the broader goals of economic development, food security, and social equity in South Africa.

Women and youth in agriculture

Women are central to agriculture and food systems due to their extensive involvement throughout the value chain, from production and processing to preparing, selling, and marketing food. According to the UN Food and Agriculture Organization, women constitute nearly 50 per cent of Africa's agricultural labour force. Despite their significant contributions, women remain underrepresented and less empowered than their male counterparts in key areas of food production. For instance, a land audit conducted by the Department of Rural Development and Land Affairs in 2015 revealed that of the 39 per cent of land owned by individuals in South Africa, only 17 per cent is owned by women, compared to 47 per cent owned by men (National Planning Commission 2021). The remaining land is co-owned by both men and women.

Empowering women in agriculture is crucial for enhancing economic participation and extending benefits beyond the farm gate. Access to essential resources such as infrastructure, electricity, water, education, and innovation, along with fair wages for female farm workers, significantly impact their ability to perform unpaid care work at home and in their communities. Without these resources, the livelihoods of children and families are jeopardised. Therefore, deliberate efforts should be made to mainstream gender policies, such as achieving the 50 per cent target for women in the Beneficiary Selection and Land Allocation Policy (Republic of South Africa 2020), coupled with the necessary support to make the land productive, can transform agriculture and food systems in South Africa and across the continent.

Attracting youth to agriculture is equally vital for transforming Africa's food systems. The agricultural sector in Africa is currently dominated by an ageing population, necessitating the engagement and empowerment of young people to ensure the sector's sustainability and productivity. By involving youth in agriculture, we can introduce fresh ideas, innovation, and technological advancements that enhance productivity, efficiency, and profitability. Additionally, youth involvement in agriculture addresses the issue of unemployment among young people in Africa, providing them with opportunities for income generation and economic empowerment.

In line with the aspirations of the NDP (National Planning Commission 2012) in South Africa, technology has emerged as a catalyst for attracting young entrants into the agricultural value chain. Technological advancements enable young people to manage farms, even on a small scale, using their smartphones to monitor weather conditions, pesticide usage, water levels, nutrient levels, and other critical factors. Numerous youth-owned South African agritech solutions have successfully disrupted the agricultural sector, attracting multi-million-dollar investments globally (ADAMA 2024). These innovations enhance agricultural productivity and position the sector as a viable and attractive career option for the younger generation.

Promoting smart urban agriculture

It has traditionally been the norm for food production to take place in rural areas, where ample land and agricultural practices have supported local food systems for generations. However, with the rapid growth of urban populations and the increasing challenge of food insecurity, there is a pressing need to reimagine and promote urban and peri-urban food systems. South Africa is experiencing rapid urbanisation, with over 68 per cent of the population living in urban areas and cities (O'Neill 2024). Urban agriculture – cultivating, processing, and distributing food within and around cities – offers a sustainable solution for providing food, income, and employment opportunities, especially for disadvantaged urban residents facing challenges like competition for land and insecure land tenure arrangements (Ritchie, Rosado & Roser 2022). By integrating food production into urban planning, cities can enhance food security, reduce the carbon footprint associated with long-distance food transportation, and create green spaces that improve the quality of urban life.

In South Africa, urban agriculture plays a big role in addressing food security issues by providing urban residents with access to fresh and nutritious produce (Thom & Conradie 2013). According to Statistics SA (2023), urban areas, particularly the biggest metros like Johannesburg and Cape Town, are associated with high proportions of households that reported inadequate and severely inadequate access to food. The projections by the UN and other organisations indicate that these two metros are among the fastest-growing cities in South Africa, partly because they are receiving large volumes of people seeking employment and better living conditions. Thus, more urban households should be encouraged to participate in agricultural activities or produce their own food as a strategy for increasing household food security, creating employment, and promoting sustainable development (Kanosvamhira 2024).

The dimensions of sustainability in urban agriculture encompass environmental, economic, and social aspects and include factors such as economic activities, location, areas, scale, products, destination, economic viability, social equity, environmental responsibility, cultural relevance, food security, resource efficiency, biodiversity conservation, climate resilience, community empowerment, health and well-being, waste reduction, water conservation, energy efficiency, land use optimisation, knowledge sharing, innovation, inclusivity, and policy coherence. These dimensions provide a comprehensive framework for evaluating the sustainability of urban agriculture initiatives, considering the environmental, economic, and social impacts of such practices in urban settings (Bisaga, Parikh & Loggia 2019).

However, despite promotion by authorities, urban agriculture in South Africa faces several challenges that require urgent attention. In low-income settlements, residents face the challenges of limited resources such as land and water, precarious living conditions, lack of land tenure, access to services, environmental risks, lack of policy support, and other socioeconomic factors (Bisaga, Parikh & Loggia 2019; Bennedetti et al. 2023). For instance, the challenging environment on the Cape Flats, including sandy soils and water shortages, makes vegetable production difficult. Over 6 000 small-scale and micro-farmers, predominantly elderly women, operate on the Cape Flats, but with insecure land tenure (Olivier 2016.) In addition, urban agriculture may not significantly impact food security or livelihoods due to low production and limited market access. Therefore, urban farming should utilise innovative solutions and digital technologies to address the challenges of inefficient, unsustainable, resource-starved ecosystems that negatively affect the local economy and food production. Table 8.3 summarises the significant challenges to sustaining urban farming in South Africa and the potential solutions required.

Table 8.3 *Challenges and potential solutions for sustainable urban agriculture in South Africa*

Challenges	Scenarios	Actions needed
Limited land availability	Urban areas often have limited land resources, making it challenging for urban farmers to find suitable and affordable land for cultivation. This restricts the scale of production and limits the ability to meet market demand.	Adopt farming techniques that maximise space usage and can be implemented indoors in controlled environments (e.g., vertical farming, rooftop gardens, hydroponics and aquaponics). Promote the establishment of community gardens in available public spaces and convert underutilised spaces (e.g., agri-parks, abandoned buildings, and brownfields).
High land and property costs	The high cost of land and property in urban areas can make it financially burdensome for urban farmers to acquire or lease land for agricultural purposes. This can hinder their ability to establish or expand their operations.	Foster partnerships between government agencies, private companies, and non-profit organisations to support urban agriculture initiatives through funding, resources, and expertise.
Zoning and regulatory restrictions	Zoning regulations and land-use policies may not always be supportive of urban agriculture. Restrictions on land use, such as designating certain areas for residential or commercial purposes only, can limit the availability of land for agricultural activities.	Advocate for policies that support urban agriculture, such as zoning laws that allow for urban farming, tax incentives for green roofs, and grants for urban agriculture projects.
Limited access to water resources	Urban farmers may face challenges in accessing sufficient and affordable water resources for irrigation. Water scarcity or high water costs can impact the viability of urban agriculture ventures.	Adopt rainwater harvesting. Adopt greywater recycling. Utilise drought-tolerant crops. Adopt smart irrigation technologies. Adopt water-efficient landscaping.
Lack of infrastructure and resources	Urban agriculture requires adequate infrastructure such as storage facilities, transportation networks, and processing facilities, to effectively bring products to market. Limited access to these resources can hinder market access for urban farmers.	Improving infrastructure such as water supply systems, storage facilities, and transportation networks can help reduce production losses and ensure food reaches consumers efficiently.
Limited market channels	Urban farmers may face challenges in accessing established market channels such as supermarkets or restaurants due to competition from larger-scale producers or difficulties in meeting volume and quality requirements.	Develop local food markets and distribution networks. Develop community-supported agriculture programmes or direct-to-consumer sales. Encourage farmers to join formal cooperatives.

Challenges	Scenarios	Actions needed
Consumer preferences and awareness	Urban farmers may need to educate consumers about the benefits of locally grown produce and differentiate their products from those available in traditional retail markets. Building consumer awareness and demand for urban agriculture products can be a challenge.	Provide education and training programmes for urban residents on sustainable farming practices, gardening techniques, and the benefits of local food production.
Seasonality and production limitations	Urban agriculture is often limited by seasonality and the availability of suitable growing conditions. This can result in fluctuations in supply and challenges in meeting consistent market demand throughout the year.	Leveraging technologies such as greenhouses, vertical farming, and hydroponics can help mitigate the effects of seasonality by providing controlled environments where crops can be grown year-round. Promote crop diversity.
Limited access to financial resources	Access to capital and financing options can be a challenge for urban farmers, particularly those from disadvantaged backgrounds or with limited credit history. Lack of financial resources can hinder investment in infrastructure, equipment, and marketing efforts.	Establish microfinance institutions or programmes that provide small loans to urban farmers. Establish more grants, subsidies, and incentives. Leverage public-private partnerships.
Quality and safety regulations	Urban farmers must comply with quality and safety regulations to ensure the integrity of their products. Meeting these standards can require additional resources and expertise, which may pose challenges for small-scale urban farmers.	Providing education and training for urban farmers on best practices for food safety and quality can help ensure that they are aware of potential risks and how to mitigate them. Regular inspections and audits of urban agriculture sites can help ensure compliance with safety standards.

Source: Author

Leveraging agricultural technologies and innovation

Leveraging technology and innovation is crucial for creating equitable and sustainable food systems. These technologies can help address various challenges such as climate change, resource scarcity, and food security, by optimising agricultural practices and making them more efficient and resilient. For instance, many African countries, including South Africa, have strategically embraced precision agriculture – a cutting-edge approach that leverages advanced technologies such as drones, artificial intelligence, and remote sensors. These innovations are employed to meticulously monitor crop conditions, enabling farmers to make data-driven decisions. The primary objectives of this approach are to significantly boost crop yields and optimise the use of resources, thereby enhancing agricultural productivity and sustainability. With the global population expected to reach 9.7 billion by 2050, the demand for food will only continue to rise, placing unprecedented pressure on our agricultural systems. By utilising advanced technologies, precision farming can help meet this escalating demand by optimising resource use, increasing crop yields, and minimising food waste.

Digitalisation of value chains can provide benefits like financial inclusion, better market access, and improved extension services for smallholder farmers, especially through the use of mobile phones and wireless technologies (Dhulipala et al. 2024). At a national level, South Africa's agricultural technology sector is rapidly developing, showcasing local ingenuity and improving agriculture production and resource utilisation. Numerous agritech tools, including precision agriculture applications, biotechnology, and mobile platforms, are being tested and deployed. These tools improve farming efficiency, reduce risks, and increase yields and profit margins (Myeni, Mokhele & Fyfield 2023; Benfica et al. 2023; Balasundram et al. 2023). Technology initiatives, including data analytics and marketplace apps, offer innovative solutions for farmers. Precision agriculture platforms in South Africa include Aerobotics, Hello Tractor, Khula, Nile, and Mezzanine. According to the South African Agricultural Business Innovation Survey 2019–2021, approximately 67.1 per cent of all agribusinesses engaged in innovative scientific, technological, organisational, financial and commercial initiatives, aimed to introduce new innovations to the market (Centre for Science, Technology and Innovation Indicators 2024).

Despite some promising advancements, smallholder farmers and small agribusiness enterprises in South Africa face multifaceted barriers to adopting new technologies. Some of the key barriers include limited access to technology and digital infrastructure in rural areas, high costs associated with implementing and maintaining technology solutions, lack of technical skills and knowledge among farmers, resistance to changing traditional farming practices, and inadequate government support and policies to promote technology adoption in agriculture (Bontsa et al. 2023; Mhlanga & Ndhlovu 2023; Dunga & Mhlanga 2023). Additionally, issues such as unreliable electricity supply and connectivity challenges further hinder the widespread adoption of technology in the agricultural sector. There is also a dearth of technical skills and extension services within the agricultural department, hampering the implementation of digital adoption programmes.

To fully leverage the transformative potential of widespread adoption of agricultural technology and innovation in South Africa's food systems, several pivotal strategies can be implemented, including:
- providing access to affordable and appropriate technology for smallholder farmers;
- offering training and capacity-building programmes to ensure farmers can effectively use the technology;
- creating supportive policies and regulations that encourage the adoption of technology in agriculture;

- establishing partnerships between government, the private sector, and research institutions to drive innovation and adoption;
- promoting knowledge sharing and collaboration among farmers to facilitate the spread of successful practices;
- improving access to affordable digital devices, reducing regulatory limits on data transfer, and providing adequate digital skills training; and
- increasing awareness of government financial support for innovation among targeted farmers.

However, while advancements in agricultural technology can lead to increased productivity and efficiency, they also pose a significant challenge to employment in the agricultural sector. The increased efficiency and productivity of automation and advanced machinery can decrease the need for manual labour. A handful of skilled operators overseeing automated systems can now perform tasks that once required a large workforce. This shift can potentially displace a significant number of agricultural workers, particularly those engaged in manual and repetitive tasks. In South Africa, where agriculture is a major source of employment, this could lead to increased unemployment and economic instability. Therefore, it is essential to recognise that, while technology can enhance productivity, its implementation must take into account the social and economic well-being of the workforce and other stakeholders.

Conclusion

The transformation of South Africa's food systems is a complex but necessary endeavour. It requires a holistic approach that addresses the interlinked issues of food security, socioeconomic inequality, and environmental sustainability. By adopting inclusive and sustainable practices, South Africa can build a food system that is resilient, equitable, and capable of meeting the needs of its population now and in the future. This perspective underscores the urgency and multifaceted nature of food systems transformation in South Africa, highlighting the need for coordinated efforts across various sectors and levels of society.

Despite several efforts, South Africa still faces significant challenges, including land reform issues, climate change impacts, and socioeconomic inequalities. Continued commitment and collaboration among stakeholders are essential to achieve the 2030 goals for food system transformation.

Such transformation requires that the underlying issues and challenges within the food systems, such as limited access to resources, inadequate infrastructure, lack of technological advancements, and vulnerability to climate change, be addressed. Investing in research and innovation, promoting sustainable agricultural practices, and empowering local communities are also key components in driving meaningful change. Hence, a holistic and multifaceted approach is necessary to transform Africa's food systems and ensure long-term sustainability and prosperity.

References

ADAMA (2024) *14 great South African agritech solutions* 1 February. Accessed 25 December 2024, https://www.adama.com/south-africa/en/innovation/south-african-agritech-solutions

African Union (2024) *African Union launches the 4th CAADP Biennial Review Report and Post-Malabo Roadmap.* Accessed 26 December 2024, https://au.int/en/pressreleases/20240320/african-union-launches-4th-caadp-biennial-review-report-and-post-malabo

African Union Commission (2015) *Agenda 2063: The Africa we want; Framework document.* Accessed 6 December 2024, https://au.int/sites/default/files/documents/33126-doc-framework_document_book.pdf

AgriSA (2024) *South Africa's food waste crisis: Inspiring collective action for a sustainable tomorrow.* 9 April. AgriSA Disaster Relief Fund. Accessed 25 December 2024, https://agrisa.org.za/agrisa-disaster-relief-foundation/south-africas-food-waste-crisis-inspiring-collective-action-for-a-sustainable-tomorrow/

Arksey H & O'Malley L (2005) Scoping studies: Towards a methodological framework. *International Journal of Social Research Methodology* 8(1): 19–32. Accessed 25 December 2024, https://doi.org/10.1080/1364557032000119616

Balasundram SK, Shamshiri RR, Sridhara S & Rizan N (2023) The role of digital agriculture in mitigating climate change and ensuring food security: An overview. *Sustainability* 15(6): 5325. https://doi.org/10.3390/su15065325

Benfica R, Chambers J, Koo J, Nin-Pratt A, Falck-Zepeda J, Stads G-J & Arndt C (2023) Food system innovations and digital technologies to foster productivity growth and rural transformation. In J von Braun, K Afsana, LO Fresco & MHA Hassan (Eds) *Science and innovations for food systems transformation.* Cham: Springer Nature. Accessed 25 December 2024, https://link.springer.com/chapter/10.1007/978-3-031-15703-5_22

Bennedetti LV, De Almeida Sinisgalli PA, Ferreira ML & Lemes de Oliveira F (2023) Challenges to promote sustainability in urban agriculture models: A review. *International Journal of Environmental Research and Public Health* 20(3): 2110

Bisaga I, Parikh P & Loggia C (2019) Challenges and opportunities for sustainable urban farming in South African low-income settlements: A case study in Durban. *Sustainability* 11(20): 5660. Accessed 25 December 2024, https://doi.org/10.3390/su11205660

Bontsa NV, Mushunje A, Ngarava S & Zhou L (2023) Utilisation of digital technologies by smallholder farmers in South Africa. *South African Journal of Agricultural Extension* 51(4): 104–146. Accessed 25 December 2024, https://sajae.co.za/article/view/15337

Centre for Science, Technology and Innovation Indicators (2024) *Modernising South Africa's agricultural sector through innovation: Results from the South African Agricultural Business Innovation Survey, 2019–2021.* Cape Town: Human Sciences Research Council. Accessed 25 December 2024, https://hsrc.ac.za/wp-content/uploads/2024/07/AgriBIS2019-21_MainReport_V5-FINAL-WEB.pdf

Chikozho C & Managa R (2018) *Can we unlock rural socio-economic transformation through land reform? Revisiting the land redistribution public policy imperatives in South Africa.*

Pretoria: HSRC Press. Accessed 25 December 2024, http://hdl.handle.net/20.500.11910/11800

Chikozho C, Managa R & Dabata T (2020). Ensuring access to water for food production by emerging farmers in South Africa: What are the missing ingredients? *Water SA* 46(2): 225–233. Accessed 25 December 2024, https://doi.org/10.17159/wsa/2020.v46.i2.8237

Council for Scientific and Industrial Research (2021) *45 per cent of available food supply in South Africa wasted, shows new CSIR study.* 10 August. Accessed 25 December 2024, https://www.csir.co.za/food-supply-south-africa-wasted-shows-new-csir-study

DALRRD (Department of Agriculture, Land Reform and Rural Development) (2017) *Land Audit Report: Phase II: Private land ownership by race, gender and nationality* November, Version 2. Accessed 25 December 2024, https://www.gov.za/sites/default/files/gcis_document/201802/landauditreport13feb2018.pdf

DALRRD (2022a). *Agriculture and agro-processing master plan.* Department of Agriculture, Land Reform and Rural Development. Accessed 25 December 2024, https://www.dalrrd.gov.za/images/News Letters/DALRRD News Letters/DALRRD Newsletter issued on 03 Jun 2022.pdf

DALRRD (2022b). *Economic review of the South African agriculture 2022.* Accessed 25 December 2024, https://www.dalrrd.gov.za/images/Branches/Economica Development Trade and Marketing/Statistc and Economic Analysis/statistical-information/economic-review-of-the-south-african-agriculture-2022.pdf

DALRRD (2022c) *Comprehensive agricultural support programme.* Accessed 3 January 2025, https://old.dalrrd.gov.za/Programme/Comprehensive-Agricultural-Support-Programme

Department of Environment, Forestry and Fisheries & Council for Scientific and Industrial Research(2021) *Food waste prevention & management: A guideline for South Africa.* Accessed 3 January 2025, https://www.csir.co.za/sites/default/files/Documents/Food waste prevention_LANDSCAPE(EDMS) - 05-02-2021.pdf

Dhulipala RK, Whitbread A, Unger F & Nguyen C (2024) *Digital innovations to support equitable, sustainable, and resilient agri-food systems and last mile delivery.* Consultative Group for International Agricultural Research. Accessed 25 December 2024, https://hdl.handle.net/10568/140793

Dunga H & Mhlanga D (2023) Digital transformation of the agricultural sector in Africa: What are the challenges: A review. *Africagrowth Agenda* 20(2): 14–18. Accessed 25 December 2024, https://ideas.repec.org/a/afj/journ2/v20y2023i2p14-18.html

Food and Agriculture Organization of the United Nations (FAO) (2022) *Food systems profile – South Africa: Catalysing the sustainable and inclusive transformation of food systems.* Accessed 25 December 2024, https://doi.org/10.4060/cc0071en

Fourie J, Engelbrecht K, Govender P, Pillay P & Engel W (2023) *Food loss and waste in farming: Insights from South African farmers.* World Wide Fund for Nature. Accessed 25 December 2024, https://wwfafrica.awsassets.panda.org/downloads/food_loss_and_waste_report.pdf

Hedley C (2015) The role of precision agriculture for improved nutrient management on farms. *Journal of The Science of Food and Agriculture* 95(1): 12–19. Accessed 25 December 2024, https://www.researchgate.net/publication/262197678_The_Role_of_Precision_Agriculture_for_Improved_Nutrient_Management_on_Farms

Javaid M, Haleem A, Singh RP & Suman R (2022) Enhancing smart farming through the applications of Agriculture 4.0 technologies. *International Journal of Intelligent Networks* 3: 150–164. Accessed 25 December 2024, https://doi.org/10.1016/j.ijin.2022.09.004

Kanosvamhira TP (2024) Urban agriculture and the sustainability nexus in South Africa: Past, current, and future trends. *Urban Forum* 35: 83–100. Accessed 25 December 2024, https://link.springer.com/article/10.1007/s12132-023-09480-4#citeas

Levac D, Colquhoun H & O'Brien KK (2010) Scoping studies: Advancing the methodology. *Implementation Science* 5. Accessed 25 December 2024, DOI:10.1186/1748-5908-5-69

Maluleke R (2023) *Assessing food inadequacy and hunger in South Africa in 2021 using the General Household Survey*. Statistics South Africa. Accessed 3 March 2025, https://www.statssa.gov.za/publications/03-00-20/03-00-202021.pdf

Mhlanga D & Ndhlovu E (2023) Digital technology adoption in the agriculture sector: Challenges and complexities in Africa. *Human Behavior and Emerging Technologies* Article ID 6951879, 14 September. Accessed 25 December 2024, https://doi.org/10.1155/2023/6951879

Ministry for Agriculture and Land Affairs (2001) *Land redistribution for agricultural development: A sub-programme of the land redistribution programme*. Accessed 3 January 2025, https://www.gov.za/sites/default/files/gcis_document/201409/land-redistribution-agricultural-development.pdf

Myeni L, Mokhele M & Fyfield T (2023) *Climate-smart agriculture: Evidence-based case studies in South Africa*. Department of Agriculture, Land Reform and Rural Development. Accessed 25 December 2024, https://www.researchgate.net/publication/373135928_Climate-Smart_Agriculture_Evidence-based_case_studies_in_South_Africa

National Agricultural Marketing Council (2019) *Status Report on statutory measures implemented in terms of the Marketing of Agricultural Products Act, Act No. 47 of 1996: 2016 survey*. Accessed 25 December 2024, https://www.namc.co.za/wp-content/uploads/2020/03/2019-Stat-measures-REPORT.pdf

National Planning Commission (2012) *Our future – Make it work: Your guide to the NDP*. Accessed 26 December 2024, https://www.nationalplanningcommission.org.za/assets/Documents/ndp-2030-our-future-make-it-work.pdf

National Planning Commission (2021) *Technical paper on women and gender for NDP*. Accessed 25 December 2024, https://www.nationalplanningcommission.org.za/assets/Documents/Technical Paper on Women and Gender for the NDP Review_03 March 2021.pdf

Olivier DW (2016) Uprooting patriarchy: Gender and urban agriculture on South Africa's Cape Flats. *The Conversation* 10 March. Accessed 25 December 2024, https://theconversation.com/uprooting-patriarchy-gender-and-urban-agriculture-on-south-africas-cape-flats-55882

O'Neill A (2025) *Urbanization in South Africa 2023*. Statista, 14 February. Accessed 6 August 2024, https://www.statista.com/statistics/455931/urbanization-in-south-africa

Parameshwari S (2017) Impact of food waste and its effect on environment. *International Journal of Food Science and Nutrition* 2(4): 184–187. Accessed 25 December 2024, https://www.foodsciencejournal.com/assets/archives/2017/vol2issue4/2-4-47-690.pdf

Pereira L & Drimie S (2016) Governance arrangements for the future food system: Addressing complexity in South Africa. *Environment: Science and Policy for Sustainable Development* 58(4): 18–31. Accessed 25 December 2024, https://doi.org/10.1080/00139157.2016.1186438

Republic of South Africa (2020) National policy for beneficiary selection and land allocation. *Government Gazette* 3 January. Accessed 26 December 2024, https://static.pmg.org.za/BSLA.pdf

Ritchie H, Rosado P & Roser M (2022) Environmental impacts of food production: What are the environmental impacts of food production? How do we reduce the impacts of agriculture on the environment? Our world in data. Accessed 25 December 2024, https://ourworldindata.org/environmental-impacts-of-food

Sihlobo W (2020) South Africa's agricultural exports registered the second-largest level on record in 2020. *SA weekly agricultural viewpoint* 15 February. Accessed 25 December 2024, https://agbiz.co.za/content/open/15-february-2021-agri-market-viewpoint

Sihlobo W & Qobo M (2021) *Addressing constraints to South Africa's agriculture inclusiveness*. Southern Centre for Inequality Studies, University of the Witwatersrand. Accessed 25 December, https://www.wits.ac.za/media/wits-university/faculties-and-schools/commerce-law-and-management/research-entities/scis/documents/AddressingConstraints-to-SAs-AgricultureInclusiveness.pdf

Simelane T, Mutanga SS, Hongoro C, Parker W, Mjimba V, Zuma K, Kajombo R, Ngidi M, Masamha B, Mokhele T, Managa R, Ngungu M, Sinyolo S, Tshililo F, Ubisi N, Skhosana Ndinda C, Sithole M, Muthige M, Lunga W, Tshitangano F, Dukhi NF, Sewpaul R, Mkhongi A & Marinda E (2024) *National food and nutrition security survey: North West province report*. Pretoria: Human Sciences Research Council 16 January. Accessed 25 December 2024, http://hdl.handle.net/20.500.11910/22794

Soto I, Barnes A, Balafoutis A, Beck B, Sánchez B, Vangeyte J, Fountas S, Van der Wal T, Eory V & Gómez-Barbero M (2019) *The contribution of precision agriculture technologies to farm productivity and the mitigation of greenhouse gas emissions in the EU*. Publications Office of the European Union, 29320 EN. Accessed 25 December 2024, https://publications.jrc.ec.europa.eu/repository/handle/JRC112505

Thom A & Conradie B (2013) Urban agriculture's enterprise potential: Exploring vegetable box schemes in Cape Town. *Agrekon* 52(sup 1): 64–86. Accessed 25 December 2024, https://doi.org/10.1080/03031853.2013.770953

United Nations (2015) *Transforming our world: The 2030 Agenda for Sustainable Development. Resolution adopted by the General Assembly on 25 September.* Accessed 26 December 2024, https://www.un.org/en/development/desa/population/migration/generalassembly/docs/globalcompact/A_RES_70_1_E.pdf

Wilson MH & Lovell ST (2016) Agroforestry: The next step in sustainable and resilient agriculture. *Sustainability* 8(6): 574. Accessed 25 December 2024, https://doi.org/10.3390/su8060574

Zaca FN, Ngidi MSC, Chipfupa U, Ojo TO & Managa LR (2023) Factors influencing the uptake of agroforestry practices among rural households: Empirical evidence from the KwaZulu-Natal province, South Africa. *Forests* 14(10): 2056. Accessed 25 December 2024, DOI:10.3390/f14102056

9 The role of technology for marketers in Africa

Winfrida Thadei Kobero

Background

Africa is blessed. Being the second largest continent, it has an abundance of natural resources that gives it the potential not only to provide for people's basic needs but also to trade within individual countries, across Africa, and overseas.

African countries export raw materials overseas where they are processed and products are imported back to Africa and sold at higher prices. For instance, Tanzania exports cotton to China and India, but it imports clothes from these countries. Most of the raw material exported from Tanzania to India and China are in raw state unlike those imported into Tanzania from India and China, hence the higher price (Ubwani 2023).

Many Tanzanian wholesalers, retailers, and even some consumers travel to the United Arab Emirates, China, Turkey, and/or India to purchase products because overseas suppliers in these countries have heavily invested in information and communication technology (ICT) to promote their products. Other African buyers purchase products online on business-to-business (B2B), business-to-consumer (B2C), and consumer-to-consumer (C2C) e-commerce platforms such as Alibaba, Aliexpress, Amazon, eBay, Etsy, IndiaMart, Namshi, and Shein, or social media platforms such as Instagram, Facebook, TikTok, and WhatsApp.

This means that African e-commerce and social media platforms on which African buyers and sellers can connect, communicate, and transact can foster trade in Africa and accelerate the African Continental Free Trade Area Agreement (AfCFTA). Such platforms would also enable African suppliers to connect with and sell to foreigners. The AfCFTA is intended to allow the free flow of goods and services all over Africa by eliminating trade barriers and uniting African countries into a single market, thereby improving intra-Africa trade and Africa's trading situation globally (African Union 2019; East African Community 2021). Rapid ICT growth in Africa since the millennium (Ncube et al. 2013) enables AfCFTA progress.

This study was conducted in Tanzania to determine the role of ICT in accelerating the implementation of the AfCFTA, that is, how the use of electricity, the internet, communication devices, social media, and e-commerce can influence AfCFTA implementation. Such a study had never been conducted in Tanzania. Another aim was to assess Tanzanian traders' awareness of the AfCFTA agreement and its benefits. The results indicated that many traders are not aware of the AfCFTA so ICT could play a significant role in accelerating the implementation of AfCFTA.

Key marketing concepts relevant to this study

Marketing communication mix

The marketing mix – also known as the 4Ps of marketing – is comprised of product, price, promotion, and place (McCarthy 1960). The marketing communication mix consists of promotional tools or methods that traders use to inform, educate, and attract customers to purchase products. These include advertising, direct marketing, sales promotions, personal selling, public relations, and publicity (Kotler & Keller 2009). Other methods that can be used are product packaging and labelling, events, and experiences.

Advertising

Advertising is paid-for, one-way communication to promote a product or service. Advertising can take place on a radio or television (TV) station, in a print publication, or anywhere else that it may catch the public's attention. The message communicated can reach many people in a very short time.

Direct marketing

When traders use this tool, they directly send a message to a customer through a short message service, SMS or text messaging, email, and phone calls. It does not involve paying an advertising agency to promote the products. Communication is two-way between the seller or trader and the customer.

Sales promotion

This involves providing incentives to attract customers to purchase products. For instance, traders can provide discounts and gifts when customers purchase products or organise contests with prizes. Sales promotion can be integrated with other promotional tools to send a message to customers, creating awareness of the incentives to build interest.

Public relations and publicity

Public relations involves relationship and image management between an organisation and its publics. Such publics include customers, employees, the media, the government, intermediaries, and the community. Traders perform public relations through one-way or two-way communication. They can provide donations, conduct charity activities, sponsor events, and/or support environmental well-being. Such acts can attract customers and gain their support through purchases of products and services.

Publicity

Publicity occurs when a third party, without being paid, promotes a product or service to people. It can occur through word of mouth, social media, newspapers, or magazines. A celebrity with a huge following on Instagram or TikTok can post praising the goodness or benefits they get from a product. This can create a buzz, and hence publicity for that product.

Personal selling

In personal selling, sellers directly approach customers and communicate face to face. During the interaction, the benefits of the product are communicated. Merchants can even show the customer how to use the product and demonstrate how it was made. This can make the customer feel special because the interaction is personal and can convince the customer to buy.

Technology acceptance model (TAM)

The technology acceptance model demonstrates the relationship between the perceived usefulness of a product, its perceived ease of use, and its acceptance. This means that a customer or user will use a technology if they see it as useful and easy to use. For example, a creator or inventor of a technology product may believe it is useful and user-friendly, but it will not be accepted if users do not perceive it that way (Davis 1989). Technology can accelerate the implementation of the AfCFTA because ICT communication tools such as computers and mobile phones are easy to use and can deliver multi-media marketing messages across Africa.

Figure 9.1 *Technology acceptance model*

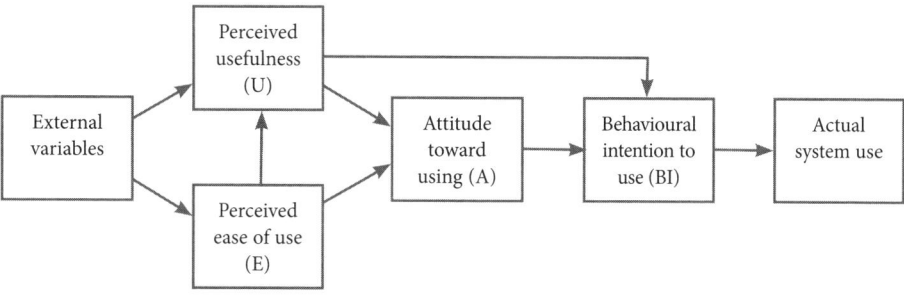

Source: Wikipedia (n.d.)

Benefits of ICT for the AfCFTA

The AfCFTA was created to eliminate trade barriers and boost intra-African trade. It is an ongoing project aiming to unite African countries into a single continental market. One of the tools used to achieve the goals of the AfCFTA agreement is ICT.

The impact of intra-African technology exports is considerable (Kwami 2022), which suggests that access to mobile phones and high-speed internet can help achieve the goals of the AfCFTA. The internet and mobile telephony do not directly influence service exports, but when ICT is linked to foreign direct investment, they positively and significantly affect service exports (Wonyra, Cassama & Gnedeka 2023).

While most of the world lives and participates in a digital economy (Ismail 2020) only 30 per cent of Africans shopped online in 2019, compared to 50 and 45 per cent of Asians and South Americans, respectively (Lemma, Mendez-Parra & Naliaka 2022). The Sustainable Development Goal (SDG) 9 of the United Nations Agenda 2030 was developed to encourage the building of a strong infrastructure and to enhance maintainable industrialisation and innovation for all. Despite the capability of the AfCFTA to improve intra-African trade (Moyo 2020), most African countries have made only minor progress towards the realisation of SDG 9.

The COVID-19 pandemic has directly influenced e-commerce as B2B, B2C and C2C online sales have grown (World Trade Organization 2020) meaning it has also impacted African states. If Africans really want to reap the benefits of the AfCFTA, they should increase ICT usage.

ICT can help run and influence African business success by exchanging relevant information between buyers and sellers. ICT usage can have a positive effect on the performance of micro, small and medium enterprises because it enhances market visibility, marketing effectiveness, and business survivability (Etim, James & Ekong 2023). It also helps to easily calculate the benefits of a business, improve productivity, and minimise operational costs (Magambo, Nyamwesa & Mgulunde 2023).

As many African states struggle to collect enough tax revenue, the adoption and usage of ICT helps to tackle such problems by recognising the tax base, monitoring, and facilitating adherence (Okunogbe & Santoro 2023). Some people use ICT to become technopreneurs (Okune & Mutuku 2023) running, for example, financial technology companies in Tanzania, such as Jumo, Nala Money, AzamPay, and Branch, which compete with traditional financial models for delivering financial services. Farmers in Africa also use ICT to share knowledge that helps improve the agricultural sector.

The results of the Africa Goes Digital consortium show that it brings its members together through communication on WhatsApp and X, sharing knowledge and success stories, and forming partnerships (Ayamga et al. 2023). Other findings show that the expansion of ICT has a constructive effect on renewable energy transition (RET) financing in Africa, while a decline in ICT destroys RET financing (Evans 2023).

African countries should reduce costs by making their telecommunication sector more competitive and improving service quality. Furthermore, investment in ICT should be improved and its usage should be promoted in African states (Kwami 2022) to the advantage of both the AfCFTA and SDG 9.

The role of electricity in business success in Africa

Almost everyone in the world uses electricity. It is vital – not only for using the internet, communication devices, and platforms. All ICT devices require electricity to perform and influence productivity. Unreliable electricity supply is a big problem in developing countries because power outages negatively impact productivity (Kupgiz 2023).

Although there has been a rapid advancement of privately managed solar energy recently, much of non-Mediterranean Africa has limited access to electricity (Baker 2023). Limited or no access to electricity prevents African countries from increasing their degree of financial development with the help of ICT (Owolabi et al. 2021). ICT does not have a significant effect on many African states because of inadequate and unreliable electricity. Many African countries use solar energy to generate electricity for ICT devices, especially in remote rural areas, because it is the most cost-effective technique (Paul & Uhomoibhi 2013).

Electricity is one of the basic needs such as food, clothing, and shelter, and it is essential for personal and business communication, especially internet usage. Using the internet decreases the need to travel, which saves energy and money (Kouton 2019).

Internet and business in Africa

Manufacturing, transportation, agriculture, and other types of technologies are heavily dependent on ICT, and so are humans. The internet has made it easier for people living in different parts of the world to communicate faster. Text messages, videos, audio, and documents can be sent in seconds if a person has a mobile phone with communication software and the internet. People can also communicate through audio and video calls. Some people do not have access to high-speed internet. In Tanzania, high internet costs, the speed of the internet, insufficient bandwidth, and the cost of maintaining internet applications limit the use of the internet (Nantembelele & Gopal 2018).

The internet has made it easier for buyers and sellers to communicate and conduct transactions online while simultaneously reducing costs. Barriers to entering a particular market decrease when there is an increase in access to high-speed internet (Houngbonon, Mensah & Traore 2022). Increased innovation and use of online platforms connect buyers and sellers easily and help reduce costs (Goldfarb & Tucker 2019).

E-commerce platforms such as Amazon, Aliexpress, eBay, Etsy, Alibaba, Flipkart, and Temu connect buyers and sellers for B2B, B2C, and C2C business activities. In addition, sellers use social media platforms such as Facebook, Instagram, X and WhatsApp to promote products and services by connecting directly with potential customers.

All these platforms need the internet to function. Therefore, governments need to create an infrastructure that enables the use of high-speed internet and easy information sharing to help African countries be competitive in business (Darley 2003). A time series analysis showed that both internet utilisation and monetary growth lead to economic growth (Salahuddin & Gow 2016).

Internet use in Africa is rapidly accelerating. Fixed lines, mobile phones, the internet, and websites are the most common technologies adopted by businesses to support their e-business activities. Financial support, personal skills, and experience are important factors affecting the adoption of ICT (Mpofu, Milne & Watkins-Mathys 2013).

Impact of communication devices in Africa

The use of mobile phones and computers has become a part of African culture as people from both urban and rural areas use them consistently (Scott et al. 2004). Mobile phones are not only used to keep in touch with family and friends, but also in business. They can be used to make payments, send money, and promote products and services through e-commerce and social media.

Mobile phone usage in Africa has grown in the last two decades bringing opportunities to Africa (Aker & Mbiti 2010), and greatly reducing the digital disparity with the global north (James & Versteeg 2007). Mobile telephony is widely used for personal and business purposes. Mobile phones are affordable and accessible, and they fulfil the requirements of most businesses, so they are more widely used than the internet, computers, and fixed-line phones (Deen-Swarray, Moyo & Stork 2013). However, since the introduction of smartphones in the past decade, the use of the internet has also increased rapidly, as has the use of AI such as ChatGPT, Alexa by Amazon, Siri by Apple, Google Assistant, Interior.ai, and AI Art generators (Rusdi & Abdullah Sani 2023). The International Telecommunications Union (ITU) estimated that, by the end of 2017, the number of world internet users would be 3.6 billion and forecast that by 2025, the number of internet users in the world would be 4.5 billion (Areppim 2017), as shown in Table 9.1. However, the ITU reported that the number of individuals using the internet in the world was already approximately 5.4 billion at the beginning of 2024 (International Telecommunications Union n.d.).

Table 9.1 *World internet users*

Year	Number[1] (million)		World population	Internet penetration
	Actual	Forecast	Million	% Pop[2]
1990	2.64	58.7	5 295	0.05%
1991	4.4	71.5	5 382	0.08%
1992	7	87.1	5 467	0.13%
1993	10	106.0	5 552	0.18%
1994	21	128.8	5 636	0.37%
1995	40	156.5	5 719	0.70%
1996	74	189.8	5 802	1.28%
1997	117	229.8	5 883	1.99%
1998	183	277.8	5 964	3.07%
1999	275	335.1	6 045	4.55%
2000	390	403.2	6 124	6.37%
2001	489	483.7	6 203	7.88%
2002	616	578.0	6 281	9.81%
2003	721	688.0	6 359	11.3%
2004	867	814.8	6 437	13.5%
2005	1 024	959.6	6 515	15.7%
2006	1 147	1 123.0	6 593	17.4%
2007	1 367	1 304.9	6 671	20.5%
2008	1 547	1 504.4	6 750	22.9%
2009	1 729	1 719.6	6 828	25.3%
2010	1 991	1 947.7	6 907	28.8%
2011	2 184	2 185.0	6 985	31.3%
2012	2 424	2 427.0	7 063	34.3%
2013	2 631	2 669.0	7 141	36.8%
2014	2 880	2 906.3	7 218	39.9%
2015	3 150	3 134.4	7 295	43.2%
2016	3 385	3 349.6	7 371	45.9%
2017	3 578	3 549.1	7 447	48.1%
2018		3 731.0	7 521	49.6%
2019		3 894.4	7 595	51.3%
2020		4 039.2	7 667	52.7%
2021		4 166.0	7 738	53.8%
2022		4 276.0	7 808	54.8%
2023		4 370.3	7 877	55.5%
2024		4 450.8	7 945	56.0%
2025		4 518.9	8 011	56.4%
Average annual growth rate	30.62%	13.21%	1.19%	22.24%

[1] Logistic growth function [2] Internet users as a percentage of world population; actuals until 2017, forecasts thereafter.
Source: Areppim 2017

Spreading of innovation refers to the adoption and acceptance of innovation by members of a particular community (Gikenye 2011). Wakari Gikenye's 2011 study showed that ICTs, such as the internet and computers, were widely adopted by Westerners, while they took much longer to be adopted in developing countries (Gikenye 2011). However, people in both developing countries and the West have widely adopted the use of mobile phones.

Among the benefits that mobile telephony has brought to Africa is the introduction and rise of mobile banking. Examples include, the introduction of money transfer services such as m-pesa, tigopesa, airtel money, halopesa, and t-pesa in Tanzania in the past decade. M-pesa was first introduced in Kenya in 2007 (Gikenye 2011). The rise of fintech companies in Africa helps the African diaspora send money back home. Mobile telephony has also brought benefits in the world of marketing and trading as buyers and sellers can easily connect and conduct business (Goldfarb & Tucker 2019).

Social media marketing in Africa

There is a significant rise in social media usage in Africa. Social media has taken over the world through Facebook, Instagram, X, WhatsApp, Snapchat, and Threads. It is being used worldwide for both personal and business communications.

The introduction and quick adoption of mobile technology has led to a great increase in the usage of the internet and social media, through which marketing communication can take place (Duffet & Wakeham 2016). For instance, Facebook and Instagram users can post pictures or videos of their products and services. They can even pay to boost exposure to their target audience in different locations around the world.

Social media can be used to promote products or services in any industry. The perception of functionality, quality of service, level of information, and customer satisfaction influence the usage of digital marketing tools and platforms (Chamboko-Mpotaringa & Tichaawa 2023). Social media marketing features such as trendiness, entertainment, interaction, customisation, and electronic word-of-mouth impact customers' perceptions and have a direct effect on purchase intention (Bushara et al. 2023; Armawan et al. 2023). This indicates that traders need to draft marketing messages that resonate with their target audiences and sell products relevant to their needs to shape their perspectives and stimulate immediate purchases. The affordability of social media has greatly influenced its adoption in Africa by businesses (Gwala & Mashau 2023).

Impact of e-commerce in Africa

Electronic commerce involves more than just using technology. It is an application of ICT that involves the achievement of business goals through practising business electronically (Wigand 1997). ICTs can boost trade in and between countries, and contribute to economic growth in Africa (Ndonga 2012). E-commerce platforms in Africa include Jumia, Jiji, Konga and Noon.

E-commerce promotes small and large businesses in high-income countries (Cordes & Marinova 2023) so adopting and strengthening ICTs may bestow similar benefits on mid- to low-income countries. E-commerce adoption is positively influenced by organisational resources such as communication, dedication, customer electronic preparedness, and enterprise size (Urban & Van der Putten 2023). Governments need to take action to encourage the adoption of e-commerce by businesses.

Although Tanzania did not have a lockdown during the COVID-19 pandemic, many people relied on online shopping and deliveries. The pandemic greatly affected business relationships that had no formal agreements (Antai & Eze 2023). It also led to the adoption and incorporation of inventive technologies in ICT to promote productivity at the workplace and in business (Enaifoghe & Zenzile 2023).

Due to digital disparity, COVID-19 affected the informal sector more than the formal sector (Anakpo, Hlungwane & Mishi 2023), hence information technology (IT) should be improved, and training programmes should be implemented to increase people's knowledge and understanding of digital communication (Anakpo, Nqwayibana & Mishi 2023). E-commerce adoption and growth are important to African states because they facilitate B2B, B2C, C2C, and other forms of business that promote African economies, and they are significantly connected to government assistance (Chundakkadan & Sasidharan 2023).

Research methodology

This study was conducted using a survey research design, which is used when the researcher wants to collect quantitative or qualitative data from a sample or an entire population of people to describe behaviours, attitudes, characteristics, and opinions. It can include exploratory, descriptive, and causal research methods. The researcher distributed questionnaires to traders and asked them about their knowledge and experiences with ICT in Tanzania. The study was conducted in Dar es Salaam, Tanzania, specifically targeting entrepreneurs from different industries such as food and beverages, fintech, beauty, energy, agriculture, hospitality, textiles, transport, media, fishing, arts and design, telecommunications, and banking. The target population was traders in Dar es Salaam. Tanzania consists of formal registered and informal unregistered businesses. Keeping this in mind, the researcher included traders from both types of business formalities and from large to small businesses.

Variables and their measurements

This study included both independent and dependent variables. An independent variable causes change in the dependent variable. In this study, the independent variables were electricity, internet, communication devices, social media and e-commerce, and the dependent variable was AfCFTA implementation (Figure 9.2).

Questions were generated from five independent variables. The responses of the traders were measured using a 5-point Likert scale, and the researcher analysed their levels of agreement and disagreement (1 = strongly disagree up to 5 = strongly agree). When the response numbers were 4 or 5, the levels of agreement were high, and when the response numbers were 1 or 2, the levels of agreement were low. When the response number was 3, it meant that the respondent did not know or was not sure whether they agreed or not with the questions.

Sample size and sampling technique

The researcher used a purposive or judgemental sampling technique, which is a type of non-probability sampling that involves selecting a sample of people by convenience and focusing on the characteristics the researcher requires. In this study, the main characteristic on which the researcher focused was that the respondents had to be traders. With a non-probability sampling technique, the researcher had an opportunity to intentionally select a sample to reach traders who were available at that time.

The researcher chose to use a non-probability sampling technique because of the nature of the study population. The study included traders from both formal and informal businesses. Therefore, obtaining a reliable sampling frame was a challenge, hence the decision to use non-probability sampling. The sample size was 384, which was calculated using Cochran's formula for an unknown population.

Figure 9.2 *Research framework*

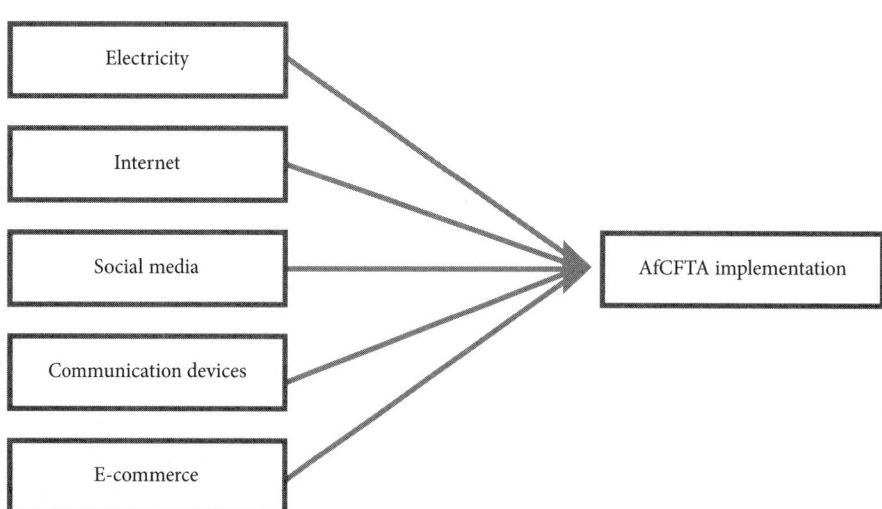

Data collection and analysis methods

Data were collected through questionnaires. The questionnaire was designed using five independent variables: electricity, internet, communication devices, social media, and e-commerce. The questionnaire consisted of 22 closed-ended and 5 open-ended questions that asked traders about their knowledge and experiences with ICT and AfCFTA. The researcher used SPSS version 26 to analyse the data. The variables were coded, and the data were entered in the SPSS tool data sheet. The mean, median, and mode were used as measures of central tendency. The results are shown in Table 9.2, and a summary of the overall frequency and percentage of responses were manually entered in Table 9.3.

Results

Data analysis involved determining the mean, median, and mode of data obtained from the respondents. The analysis led the researcher to compare the results and determine the overall level of agreement or disagreement. The results from qualitative data analysis are also presented. Table 9.2 shows the results for the mean, median, and mode as measures of central tendency. The highest and lowest values of responses for each variable are also shown in the table as well as the range between those values. Table 9.3 shows the frequencies of the responses and their equivalent percentages.

Quantitative analysis results

The total number of respondents was 384. There were no missing data for all questions in all variables.

The codes ELE, INT, COMM, SM, and ECOM stand for electricity, internet, communication devices, social media, and e-commerce, respectively. For each independent variable, traders were provided with questions to measure their level of agreement or disagreement using a 5-point Likert scale.

For the electricity variable, four closed-ended questions were generated. For internet and communication device variables, two closed-ended questions were generated for each, hence four questions. For social media and e-commerce variables, seven closed-ended questions were generated for each variable, making a total of fourteen questions. There were also five open-ended questions. Together the open-ended and closed-ended questions total 27.

The researcher used the mean, median, and mode as measures of central tendency. The mean is the sum of values divided by the total number of those values. The median is the number at the centre of an arranged ascending or descending dataset. The mode is the most frequent value, the one that appears the most in the dataset.

Table 9.2 *The mean, median and mode for each variable*

	Statistics							
	N							
	Valid	Missing	Mean	Median	Mode	Range	Minimum	Maximum
ELE1	384	0	3.88	4.00	4	4	1	5
ELE2	384	0	4.38	4.00	4	3	2	5
ELE3	384	0	4.39	5.00	5	4	1	5
ELE4	384	0	4.71	5.00	5	4	1	5
INT1	384	0	4.39	4.00	4	4	1	5
INT2	384	0	4.74	5.00	5	3	2	5
COMM1	384	0	4.30	4.00	4	4	1	5
COMM2	384	0	4.60	5.00	5	4	1	5
SM1	384	0	3.85	4.00	4	4	1	5
SM2	384	0	4.58	5.00	5	4	1	5
SM3	384	0	4.72	5.00	5	4	1	5
SM4	384	0	4.04	4.00	4	4	1	5
SM5	384	0	4.34	4.00	4	3	2	5
SM6	384	0	3.65	4.00	5	4	1	5
SM7	384	0	4.43	5.00	5	4	1	5
ECOM1	384	0	4.43	5.00	5	4	1	5
ECOM2	384	0	4.06	4.00	4	4	1	5
ECOM3	384	0	4.35	4.00	4	4	1	5
ECOM4	384	0	4.48	5.00	5	4	1	5
ECOM5	384	0	4.18	4.00	4	4	1	5
ECOM6	384	0	3.52	4.00	4	4	1	5
ECOM7	384	0	4.67	5.00	5	4	1	5
Overall	384	0				4.304		

Table 9.2 shows that there were 384 respondents and there were no missing values. Using SPSS, the researcher calculated the mean, median, and mode for each variable and then calculated the overall mean, median, mode, range, and maximum and minimum scores of responses for all variables.

Table 9.3 *Frequencies and percentages of responses*

	Strongly disagree		Disagree		I don't know		Agree		Strongly agree	
	Freq	Pct	Freq	Pct	Freq	Pct	Freq	Pct	Freq	Pct
ELE1	4	1.0	52	13.5	49	12.8	161	41.9	118	30.7
ELE2	0	0	8	2.1	3	0.8	209	54.4	164	42.7
ELE3	11	2.9	36	9.4	12	3.1	57	14.8	268	69.8
ELE4	7	1.8	8	2.1	9	2.3	43	11.2	317	82.6
INT1	1	0.3	5	1.3	5	1.3	205	53.4	168	43.8
INT2	0	0	3	0.8	2	0.5	85	22.1	294	76.6
COMM1	2	0.5	6	1.6	2	0.5	238	62.0	136	35.4
COMM2	2	0.5	2	0.5	10	2.6	118	30.7	252	65.6
SM1	2	0.5	91	23.7	5	1.3	152	39.6	134	34.9
SM2	2	0.5	4	1.0	9	2.8	125	32.6	244	63.5
SM3	1	0.3	5	1.3	4	1.0	82	21.4	292	76.0
SM4	3	0.8	9	2.3	4	1.0	320	83.3	48	12.5
SM5	0	0	2	0.5	2	0.5	245	63.8	135	35.2
SM6	86	22.4	14	3.6	5	1.3	123	32.0	156	40.6
SM7	6	1.6	5	1.3	7	1.8	165	43.0	201	52.3
ECOM1	6	1.6	3	0.8	9	2.3	167	43.5	199	51.8
ECOM2	2	0.5	5	1.3	88	22.9	163	42.4	126	32.8
ECOM3	1	0.3	1	0.3	2	0.5	239	62.2	141	36.7
ECOM4	1	0.3	5	1.3	50	13.0	82	21.4	246	64.1
ECOM5	2	0.5	3	0.8	5	1.3	288	75.0	86	22.4
ECOM6	83	21.6	8	2.1	8	2.1	197	51.3	88	22.9
ECOM7	2	0.5	8	2.1	5	1.3	85	22.1	284	74.0

The data in Table 9.3 show the frequency of responses and their equivalent percentages. They also indicate, out of 384, how many people gave a particular response. The interpretation of the results is as follows:

- ELE1: The variable received a mean or average score of 3.88. The median score was 4.00. The number of responses was 384, which is an even number. This means that the median fell between two values in the middle of the dataset. The mode score was 4. This indicated that 4 was the most frequent answer. All three scores indicated that the respondents agree that there is good electricity supply in Tanzania. The maximum and minimum response values were 5 and 1, respectively, hence a range of 4.
- ELE2: This variable received mean, median, and mode scores of 4.38, 4.00, and 4, respectively. All scores indicated that the respondents agreed that electricity

is available in their areas of business. The maximum response score was 5 and minimum response score was 2. Subtracting the two values, a range of 3 was obtained.
- ELE3: The results in Table 9.2 show that this variable received mean, median, and mode scores of 4.39, 5.00, and 5, respectively. These results indicate that the respondents strongly agreed that when electricity is available, the sales of their businesses are maintained. The maximum response value was 5, and the minimum response value was 1, meaning that even though some respondents strongly agreed, some strongly disagreed. Therefore, the range between the responses was 4.
- ELE4: Many respondents strongly agreed that power outage decreases their sales since the mean, median, and mode scores were 4.71, 5.00, and 5, respectively. Some respondents strongly agreed, and some disagreed hence, the maximum and minimum values were 5 and 1, resulting in a range of 4.
- INT1: The mean score for this variable was 4.39, meaning the respondents agreed that there is good internet in Tanzania. Also, the median and mode scores were 4.00 and 4, respectively. Both scores indicated that the respondents agreed with the statement. The maximum response score was 5, and the minimum response score was 1, making a range of 4.
- INT2: This variable received a mean score of 4.74, a median score of 5.00, and mode was 5. All scores indicated that the respondents strongly agreed that the internet is easily accessible in their areas of business. The maximum response value for this variable was 5, the minimum value was 2, so the range was 3.
- COMM1: This variable received mean, median, and mode scores of 4.30, 4.00, and 4, respectively. All three scores indicated that the respondents agreed that they have excellent skills in using mobile phones or smartphones. The maximum score of responses was 5 while the minimum was 1, hence a range of 4.
- COMM2: The variable received mean, median, and mode scores of 4.60, 5.00, and 5, respectively. These results indicate that the respondents strongly agreed that they have excellent skills in using computers such as desktops and laptops. The range was 4 since the maximum and minimum response values were 5 and 1, respectively.
- SM1: This variable received scores of 3.85 for mean, 4.00 for median, and 4 for mode. These scores indicate that the respondents agree that social media helps their businesses gain exposure in Tanzania. The range was 4 since the maximum and minimum response values were 5 and 1.
- SM2: For this variable, the results were 4.58, 5.00, and 5 for mean, median, and mode, respectively. All scores showed that the respondents strongly agreed that social media helps their businesses gain exposure in other African countries. The maximum value of the response was 5, and the minimum value was 1. Therefore, the range was 4.
- SM3: This variable received a mean score of 4.72, median score of 5.00, and 5 for mode. These results showed that many respondents strongly agreed that social media helps them connect with customers in Tanzania. The maximum value was 5 and the minimum value was 1, hence a range of 4.

- SM4: The variable received a mean score of 4.04, median score of 4.00, and mode score of 4. The scores indicated that many respondents agreed that social media helps them connect with customers from other African countries. The maximum and minimum values in the responses were 5 and 1, respectively. Therefore, the range is 4.
- SM5: Results for this variable were a mean score of 4.34, median score of 4.00, and mode was 4. These scores indicated that many respondents agreed that social media helps them connect with suppliers in Tanzania. The maximum value of response was 5, while the minimum value was 3, hence the range of 2.
- SM6: This variable received a mean, median, and mode score of 3.65, 4.00, and 5, respectively. The mean and median scores indicate that the respondents agree that social media helps them connect with suppliers from other African countries. The mode score indicates that many respondents strongly agreed with the statement, with 5 being the most frequent response. The maximum response value was 5 and the minimum was 1, therefore, the range was 4.
- SM7: The mean, median, and mode scores obtained for this variable were 4.43, 5.00, and 5, respectively. All three scores indicated that many respondents strongly agreed that social media helps them increase customers. The range was 4, with the maximum response value being 5 and the minimum value being 1.
- ECOM1: This variable received mean, median, and mode scores of 4.43, 5.00, and 5, respectively. The results showed that many respondents strongly agreed that e-commerce helps their businesses gain exposure in Tanzania. The range was 4 as the highest and lowest values of response were 5 and 1, respectively.
- ECOM2: Many respondents agreed that e-commerce helps their businesses gain exposure in other African countries. The mean, median, and mode scores were 4.06, 4.00, and 4, respectively. The most frequent response value was 4. The difference between responses was 4 since the maximum and minimum response values were 5 and 1, respectively.
- ECOM3: Many respondents agreed that e-commerce helps them connect with customers in Tanzania. The mean, median, and mode scores were 4.35, 4.00, and 4, respectively. The most frequent answer was 4. The maximum and minimum response values were 5 and 1, making a range of 4.
- ECOM4: A mean score of 4.48, median score of 5.00, and mode score of 5 indicated that many people strongly agreed that e-commerce helps them connect with customers from other African countries. The range was 4 as the maximum and minimum responses were 5 and 1, respectively.
- ECOM5: The mean, median, and mode scores for this variable were 4.18, 4.00, and 4, meaning the respondents agreed that e-commerce helps them connect with suppliers in Tanzania. The maximum response value was 5, and the minimum response value was 1, hence a range of 4.
- ECOM6: The mean, median, and mode score were 3.52, 4.00, and 4, respectively. The results indicated the agreement of respondents that e-commerce helps them connect with suppliers from other African countries. In addition, for this variable, the maximum response value was 5, and the minimum response value was 1. Therefore, the range was 4.

- ECOM7: The mean score was 4.67, median was 5.00, and mode was 5, meaning the most frequent response was 5 which is a strong agreement. Overall, for this variable, many respondents strongly agreed that e-commerce helps them increase customers. The maximum response value was 5, while the minimum was 1, hence a range of 4.
- Overall: The overall average score for all variables was 4.304. The researcher calculated the average mean score to determine the level of agreement among the respondents for all variables. The results showed that the respondents agreed with most of the statements, meaning they agreed that ICT plays an important role in facilitating business activities in Tanzania and Africa in general, hence accelerating the implantation of AfCFTA.

Qualitative analysis results

The questionnaire consisted of four open-ended questions. The researcher collected qualitative data and used a thematic qualitative data analysis technique to obtain the results.

The researcher asked the respondents if they knew about the AfCFTA. Of 384 people, only 57 respondents knew, 311 respondents did not know, and 16 respondents did not answer.

The researcher asked the respondents which social media platforms they use most for business. The platforms that stood out were Instagram, WhatsApp, Facebook, and Tiktok. The respondents described how Instagram, Facebook, and Tiktok help them chat with customers and suppliers through comments or direct messages. They also attach WhatsApp contact numbers or links to the platforms to guide customers.

The researcher also asked the respondents which e-commerce platforms they mostly use for business. Many respondents mentioned Instagram, followed by WhatsApp and Alibaba. Some respondents wrote WhatsApp, not specifying if it was WhatsApp Messenger or WhatsApp Business, but some did. The platforms allow their customers to place orders. They also allow them to place orders with their suppliers.

To the question of whether they generally saw growth in sales due to new technological inventions and advancements such as mobile phones, smartphones, computers, social media, and e-commerce compared to previous years where many businesses did not use such technologies, 304 respondents agreed that they saw growth, 62 respondents did not know, and 18 respondents did not answer.

To the question of whether they saw growth in their sales due to using mobile phones, smartphones, computers, social media, and e-commerce compared to when they do not use them, 372 respondents said, yes, they saw growth in their sales; 9 respondents said no, and 3 respondents did not answer.

Discussion

Quantitative analysis results

The researcher calculated the total percentage for agreement and strong disagreement responses to represent the disagreement level for each variable. The same calculations were done for agreement and strong agreement responses.

ELE – Electricity

The results showed that 72.6 per cent of all respondents agreed that there is a good electricity supply in Tanzania, while 14.5 per cent disagreed. Of all respondents, 97.1 per cent agreed that electricity is available at their location of business, but 2.1 per cent disagreed. Also, 84.6 per cent of respondents agreed that the availability of electricity helps sales, but 12.3 per cent disagreed, and 93.8 per cent of respondents agreed that power outages decrease sales, while 3.9 per cent disagreed.

Tanzania should improve its electricity supply by adding new sources of electricity such as natural gas and solar energy, to stop power outages. The country should ensure that all regions, rural and urban areas, have adequate electrical supply to facilitate not only daily personal activities but also business activities, since the results showed that the availability of electricity helps to maintain sales. Doing so will help businesses to have unlimited connections with suppliers and buyers across Africa, hence succeeding in achieving the goal of being a single market.

INT – Internet

The results showed that 97.2 per cent of all respondents agreed that there is good internet condition in Tanzania, while 1.6 per cent disagreed. Also, 98.7 per cent of all respondents agreed that the internet is easily accessible at their locations of business, but 0.8 per cent of respondents disagreed.

The companies that provide internet package services in the country are Vodacom, Tigo, Airtel, Halotel, and Tanzania Telecommunications Corporation. These telecommunications companies should make sure that customers in all parts of Tanzania have access to high-speed internet. This applies to all African countries. When people have access to high-speed internet, it becomes easier to use websites, social media, and e-commerce platforms to get information about products and services, communicate with buyers or sellers, upload and download files, make audio and video calls, place orders, and write reviews.

COMM – Communication devices

Table 9.3 shows that 97.4 per cent of all respondents agree that they can use communication devices like mobile phones and smartphones, but 2.1 per cent of respondents indicated they do not have the skills. Most of the respondents (96.3 per cent) agreed that they can use laptops and desktop computers, but 1 per cent of respondents do not know how to use them.

The results indicated that many people know how to use communication devices. This puts Tanzania in a good position to connect with other African countries and achieve the AfCFTA goals. Traders and entrepreneurs should be educated on how to use communication devices because it is the only way to easily connect with buyers and sellers from other African countries. Governments in Africa should encourage business individuals to have such skills to accelerate knowledge sharing and the flow of goods among African states. E-commerce and social media platforms can only be used if one has a mobile phone, smartphone, or computer, so education is necessary.

SM – Social media

The results show that
- 24.2 per cent of the respondents disagreed that social media helps their businesses get exposure in Tanzania, but 74.5 per cent of respondents agreed.
- 96.1 per cent of respondents agreed that social media helps their businesses get exposure in other African countries, but 1.5 per cent of respondents disagreed.
- 97.4 per cent of respondents agreed that social media helps them connect with customers in Tanzania, but 1.6 per cent of respondents disagreed.
- 95.8 per cent of all respondents agreed that social media helps them connect with customers from other African countries but 3.1 per cent of respondents disagreed.
- 99 per cent of all respondents agreed that social media helps them connect with suppliers in Tanzania, but 0.5 per cent of respondents disagreed.
- 72.6 per cent of all respondents agreed that social media helps them connect with suppliers from other African countries but 26 per cent of respondents disagreed.
- 95.3 of respondents agreed that social media helps them increase customers but 2.9 per cent of all respondents disagreed.

Social media may help to accelerate the AfCFTA because many respondents agreed it helps their businesses get exposure, connect with buyers and sellers, and increase customers. Through social media, advertisements for products and services can reach many people in Africa in a short time, suppliers can directly message customers, and publicity for products and services is quick and easy. Therefore, African businesses should largely focus on using social media to connect with customers and suppliers to achieve a single market.

ECOM – e-commerce

The results showed that
- 95.3 per cent of all respondents agreed that e-commerce helps their businesses gain exposure in Tanzania but 2.4 per cent of all respondents disagreed.

- 75.2 per cent of all respondents agreed that e-commerce helps their businesses gain exposure in other African countries but 1.8 per cent of respondents disagreed.
- 98.9 per cent of respondents agreed that e-commerce helps them connect with customers in Tanzania but 0.6 per cent of respondents did not agree.
- 85.5 per cent of all respondents agreed that e-commerce helps them connect with customers from other African countries but 1.6 per cent of respondents disagreed.
- 97.4 per cent of respondents agreed that e-commerce helps them connect with suppliers in Tanzania but 1.3 per cent of respondents didn't agree.
- 74.2 per cent of all respondents agreed that e-commerce helps them connect with suppliers from other African countries but 23.7 per cent of respondents disagreed.
- 96.1 per cent of all respondents agreed that e-commerce helps them increase customers but 2.6 per cent of respondents disagreed.

These results indicate that e-commerce has a big influence on accelerating business activities in Africa because it also helps businesses gain exposure, connect with customers and suppliers, and increase customers. This helps to grow African economies. Therefore, Africans should be encouraged to use e-commerce platforms to advertise and sell their products. In addition, they should not rely on e-commerce platforms from overseas but should use local e-commerce platforms. African e-commerce platforms should be developed to help Africans connect and conduct business, hence accelerating the implementation of the AfCFTA.

Qualitative analysis results

Results showed that 81 per cent of all 384 respondents knew nothing about the AfCFTA agreement. This means Tanzanians are not sufficiently well informed. Therefore, the government should educate people about the AfCFTA, for instance in schools and universities.

The results indicated that the social media platforms traders use most for business are Instagram, Facebook, Tiktok, and WhatsApp, while the e-commerce platforms they mostly use are Alibaba, Instagram, and WhatsApp. These platforms connect traders with customers worldwide but some, for example, Alibaba serves mostly Chinese suppliers. To connect with fellow African suppliers or customers, ICT experts in Africa should be encouraged to create more platforms on which African suppliers can sell products.

Of the respondents, 79 per cent agreed that sales grew compared to previous years due to new technological inventions and advancements. In addition, 97 per cent of all respondents agreed that their sales grew when they started using new technologies of communication such as mobile phones, smartphones, computers, social media, and e-commerce. This indicates that the introduction of new communication technology has accelerated trade activities tremendously, and may help to accelerate the implementation of the AfCFTA.

Conclusion, policy implications, and recommendations

ICTs such as electricity, internet, communication devices, social media, and e-commerce play an important role in accelerating the implementation of the AfCFTA. Africa depends on ICT, so all African states should have adequate electricity supply, high-speed internet, and access to communication devices with social media and e-commerce platforms to facilitate communication across Africa. ICT is one of the important requirements for business in Africa because it can help Africans achieve the goal of creating one African market. Communication devices can only be used when electricity is available, so governments should ensure they have more than one way of generating electricity. Africans should have access to high-speed internet to enable social media and e-commerce platforms to perform and facilitate smooth communication between traders and customers. Communication cannot occur if there are no facilitating devices and the skills to use them. Therefore, people who conduct business should have communication devices and sufficient skills. Those who do not have skills should learn because it is the only way they can communicate with buyers and sellers in Africa. The researcher also recommends that all businesses should use social media and e-commerce platforms to create one African market. E-commerce platforms where customers can easily place orders should be created in each African country. This will help to minimise imports of products from overseas since African countries will be able to exchange goods with each other. The African Union should create an e-commerce platform on which African suppliers can sell products to African customers.

Recomendations arising from these results include increasing awareness of policies such as AfCFTA. This can be done through addressing these issues in schools and universities, professional associations, and the media. Each African should be aware of the agreement and project goals. Electric supply companies must ensure that there are no power outages, and if so, there must be a good reason for the situation, and it must be communicated immediately before it happens. Telecommunication companies should provide high-speed internet services to customers to facilitate good communication and speed up business activities. Each member of the AfCFTA agreement should create an e-commerce platform and encourage experts in their countries to do the same. The platforms will help connect African buyers and sellers. They can also create opportunities to export goods overseas.

Limitations of the study and areas for further research

The limitations of this study are that there was no generalisation of the results since the study was conducted in Dar es Salaam, Tanzania only. The researcher did not collect data in other regions of the country or other African countries. However, the results showed the importance of ICT to African countries in accelerating the implementation of AfCFTA. Other limitations included the time taken to collect data, transportation costs and difficulties faced by the researcher in finding traders and administering the questionnaires. However, these limitations are insignificant compared with the importance of conducting this study. In the future, the same study could be conducted in other regions of Tanzania and/or in other African countries to assess the views of traders in other parts of Africa, because business environments are not the same. Researchers can use questionnaires, interviews, and focus groups, and compare results.

Also, the same study could be conducted with respondents from other professions or industries. This will help to get insights of how they think ICT facilitates their activities and accelerate the implementation of the AfCFTA. Furthermore, apart from ICT there are other technologies such as mechanical, manufacturing, transportation, financial, and agricultural technologies that are used in business operations. Therefore, researchers can conduct studies to determine their role in accelerating the implementation of the AfCFTA.

References

African Union (2019) *CFTA: Continental free trade area*. Accessed 27 December 2024, https://au.int/en/ti/cfta/about

Aker JC & Mbiti IM (2010) Mobile phones and economic development in Africa. *Journal of Economic Perspective* 24(3): 207–232. Accessed 27 December 2024, https://www.aeaweb.org/articles?id=10.1257/jep.24.3.207

Anakpo G, Hlungwane F & Mishi S (2023) The impact of COVID-19 and related policy measures on livelihood strategies in rural South Africa. *Africa Growth Agenda* 20(2): 4–7. Accessed 27 December 2024, https://ideas.repec.org/a/afj/journ2/v20y2023i2p4-7.html

Anakpo G, Nqwayibana Z & Mishi S (2023) The impact of work-from-home on employee performance and productivity: A systematic review. *Sustainability* 15(5): 4529. Accessed 27 December 2024, https://doi.org/10.3390/su15054529

Antai I & Eze NL (2023) Impact of the COVID-19 pandemic on business-to-business relationships in digital ecosystems: An African perspective. *Information Technology & People* 36(8): 69–93. Accessed 27 December 2024, https://www.emerald.com/insight/content/doi/10.1108/itp-05-2022-0346/full/html

Areppim (2017) *Mobile cellular phones global market penetration 1980–2025*. Accessed 14 January 2025, https://stats.areppim.com/stats/stats_mobilexpenetr.htm

Armawan I, Sudarmiatin S, Hermawan A & Rahayu WP (2023) The effect of social media marketing, SerQual, eWOM on purchase intention mediated by brand image and brand trust: Evidence from Black Sweet Coffee Shop. *International Journal of Data and Network Science* 7(1): 141–152. Accessed 27 December 2024, DOI: 10.5267/j.ijdns.2022.11.008

Ayamga M, Lawani A, Akaba S & Birindwa A (2023) Developing institutions and interorganizational synergies through digitalization and youth engagement in African agriculture: The case of 'Africa goes digital'. *Land* 12(1): 199. Accessed 27 December 2024, DOI: 10.3390/land12010199

Baker L (2023) New frontiers of electricity capital: Energy access in sub-Saharan Africa. *New Political Economy* 28(2): 206–222. Accessed 27 December 2024, https://doi.org/10.1080/13563467.2022.2084524

Bushara MA, Abdou AH, Hassan TH, Sobaih AEE, Albohnayh ASM, Alshammari WG, Aldoreeb M, Elsaed AA & Elsaed MA (2023) Power of social media marketing: How perceived value mediates the impact on restaurant followers' purchase intention, willingness to pay a premium price, and E-WoM? *Sustainability* 15(6): 5331. Accessed 27 December 2024, https://doi.org/10.3390/su15065331

Chamboko-Mpotaringa M & Tichaawa TM (2023) Domestic tourists' perceptions of the intention to use digital marketing tools and platforms. *GeoJournal of Tourism and Geosites* 46(1): 9–18. Accessed 27 December 2024, DOI:10.30892/gtg.46101-995

Chundakkadan R & Sasidharan S (2023) The role of government support on e-commerce and firm innovation during pandemic crisis. *Economic Analysis and Policy* 78: 904–913. Accessed 27 December 2024, https://doi.org/10.1016/j.eap.2023.04.021

Cordes DL & Marinova D (2023) Systematic literature review of the role of e-commerce in providing pathways to sustainability for poverty alleviation in sub-Saharan Africa. *Discover Sustainability* (Article 7). Accessed 27 December 2024, https://doi.org/10.1007/s43621-022-00109-3

Darley WK (2003) Public policy challenges and implications of the internet and the emerging e-commerce for sub-Saharan Africa: A business perspective. *Information Technology for Development* 10(1): 1–12. Accessed 27 December 2024, DOI:10.1002/itdj.1590100102

Davis FD (1989) Perceived usefulness, perceived ease of use, and user acceptance of information technology. *MIS Quarterly* 13(3): 319–340. Accessed 27 December 2024, https://www.jstor.org/stable/249008

Deen-Swarray M, Moyo M & Stork C (2013) ICT access and usage among informal businesses in Africa. *Info* 15(5): 52–68. Accessed 27 December 2024, DOI:10.1108/info-05-2013-0025

Duffet RG & Wakeham M (2016) Social media marketing communications effect on attitudes among millennials in South Africa. *The African Journal of Information Systems* 8(3): 20–44. Accessed 27 December 2024, https://www.researchgate.net/publication/304152202_Social_media_marketing_communications'_effect_on_attitudes_among_Millennials_in_South_Africa

East African Community (2021) *African Continental Free Trade Area (AfCFTA) Agreement.* Accessed 27 December 2024, https://www.eac.int/trade/international-trade/trade-agreements/african-continental-free-trade-area-afcfta-agreement

Enaifoghe A & Zenzile N (2023) The rapidly evolving situation of employee work-from-home productivity and the integration of ICT in post-COVID-19 pandemic. *Scientific African*, 20: e01709. Accessed 27 December 2024, https://doi.org/10.1016/j.sciaf.2023.e01709

Etim GS, James EE & Ekong JE (2023) Information and communication technologies (ICT) and performance of micro, small and medium enterprises (MSMEs) in Nigeria. *African Journal of Economics and Sustainable Development* 6(3): 89–112. Accessed 27 December 2024, DOI:10.52589/AJESD-WYE3IERI

Evans O (2023) The investment dynamics in renewable energy transition in Africa: The asymmetric role of oil prices, economic growth and ICT. *International Journal of Energy Sector Management* 18(2): 229–247. Accessed 27 December 2024, DOI:10.1108/IJESM-03-2022-0002

Gikenye W (2011) *The diffusion of mobile phones for business and information management in Kenya.* Paper presented at the International Conference on Information Management and Evaluation, Reading, UK April 2011. Accessed 27 December 2024, https://www.proquest.com/docview/1010335837?sourcetype=Conference Papers & Proceedings

Goldfarb A & Tucker C (2019) Digital economics. *Journal of Economic Literature* 57(1): 3–43. Accessed 27 December 2024, https://www.aeaweb.org/articles?id=10.1257/jel.20171452

Gwala RS & Mashau P (2023) COVID-19 and SME adoption of social media in developing economies in Africa. In SA Qalati, D Ostic & R Bansal (Eds) *Strengthening SME performance through social media adoption and usage.* Hershey PA: IGI Global Scientific Publishing

Houngbonon GV, Mensah JT & Traore N (2022) *The impact of internet access on innovation and entrepreneurship in Africa.* Policy Research Working Paper 9945. World Bank Group. Accessed 27 December 2024, https://openknowledge.worldbank.org/server/api/core/bitstreams/5cb7fdd3-ea2e-5392-b6d5-77baec4dbb9a/content

International Telecommunications Union (n.d.) *Statistics: Individuals using the internet.* Accessed 14 January 2025, https://www.itu.int/en/ITU-D/Statistics/pages/stat/default.aspx

Ismail Y (2020) *Mobilising e-commerce for development in Africa through AfCFTA.* Geneva: CUTS International. Accessed 27 December 2024, https://www.cuts-geneva.org/wp-content/uploads/2023/09/eAfCFTA-Study-E-Commerce_in_the_AfCFTA-1.pdf

James J & Versteeg M (2007) Mobile phones in Africa: How much do we really know? *Social Indicators Research* 84: 117–126. Accessed 27 December 2024, DOI:10.1007/s11205-006-9079-x

Kotler P & Keller KL (2009) *Marketing management* (13th edition). Upper Saddle River: Pearson Prentice Hall

Kouton J (2019) Information communication technology development and energy demand in African countries. *Energy* 189: 116192. Accessed 27 December 2024, https://doi.org/10.1016/j.energy.2019.116192

Kupgiz N (2023) Power outages, firm productivity, and generator ownership in East Africa. *Journal of African Business* 24(2): 280–300. Accessed 27 December 2024, https://ideas.repec.org/a/taf/wjabxx/v24y2023i2p280-300.html

Kwami WO (2022) Digitalisation as a driver of intra export promotion under African continental free trade area (AfCFTA). *Social Science Research Network* 22 January. Accessed 27 December 2024, https://papers.ssrn.com/sol3/papers.cfm?abstract_id=4014847

Lemma A, Mendez-Parra M & Naliaka L (2022) *The AfCFTA: Unlocking the potential of the digital economy in Africa.* ODI Report. Accessed 27 December 2024, https://odi.org/en/publications/afcfta-unlocking-the-potential-of-the-digital-economy-in-africa/

Magambo EF, Nyamwesa AF & Mgulunde AA (2023) Factors influencing ICT adoption among incubated small businesses in SIDO Mwanza. *African Journal of Applied Research* 9(1): 78–91. Accessed 27 December 2024, https://www.ajaronline.com/index.php/AJAR/article/view/522

McCarthy JE (1960) *Basic marketing: A managerial approach*. Homewood, IL: Richard D Irwin

Moyo T (2020) The African Continental Free Trade Agreement. *Africa Insight* 50(1): 54–75. Accessed 27 December 2024, https://journals.co.za/doi/abs/10.10520/ejc-afrins-v50-n1-a5

Mpofu KC, Milne D & Watkins-Mathys L (2013) *ICT adoption and development of e-business among SMEs in South Africa*. Buckinghamshire New University Faculty of Enterprise & Innovation. Accessed 27 December 2024, https://bnu.repository.guildhe.ac.uk/id/eprint/9583/1/Mpofu,%20Knowledge%20ICT%20adoption.pdf

Nantembelele FA & Gopal S (2018) Assessing the challenges to e-commerce adoption in Tanzania. *Global Business and Organizational Excellence* 37(3): 43–50. Accessed 27 December 2024, 10.1002/joe.21851

Ncube M, Lufumpa CL, Murinde V & Kayizzi-Mugerwa S (2013) *The Africa Infrastructure Development Index (AIDI)*. Infrastructure Consortium for Africa. Accessed 27 December 2024, https://www.icafrica.org/fileadmin/documents/Knowledge/AFDB/Economic_Brief_-_The_Africa_Infrastructure_Development_Index_01.pdf

Ndonga D (2012) E-commerce in Africa: Challenges and solutions. *African Journal of Legal Studies* 5(3): 243–268. Accessed 27 December 2024, DOI:10.1163/17087384-12342009

Okune A & Mutuku L (2023) Becoming an African techpreneur: Geopolitics of investments in 'local' Kenyan entrepreneurship. *Engaging Science, Technology and Society* 9(1). Accessed 27 December 2024, DOI: https://doi.org/10.17351/ests2023.1095

Okunogbe O & Santoro F (2023) Increasing tax collection in African countries: The role of information technology. *Journal of African Economies* 32(Supplement 1): 57–83. Accessed 27 December 2024, https://www.ictd.ac/publication/increasing-tax-collection-in-african-countries-the-role-of-information-technology/

Owolabi OA, Oku A-R, Alejo A, Ogunbiyi T & Ubah I (2021) Access to electricity, information and communications technology (ICT), and financial development: Evidence from West Africa. *International Journal of Energy Economics and Policy* 11(2): 247–259. Accessed 27 December 2024, https://www.researchgate.net/publication/348954762_Access_to_Electricity_Information_and_Communications_Technology_ICT_and_Financial_Development_Evidence_From_West_Africa/citation/download

Paul DI & Uhomoibhi J (2013) Solar electricity generation: Issues of development and impact on ICT implementation in Africa. *Campus-Wide Information Systems* 31(1): 46–62. Accessed 27 December 2024, DOI:10.1108/CWIS-05-2013-0018

Rusdi SD & Abdullah Sani NZA (2023) The rise of artificial intelligence: A savior or saboteur. *RISE: Catalysing Global Research Excellence* 3(27): 1–3. Accessed 27 December 2024, https://ir.uitm.edu.my/id/eprint/87535/

Salahuddin M & Gow J (2016) The effects of internet usage, financial development and trade openness on economic growth in South Africa: A time series analysis. *Telematics and Informatics* 33(4): 1141–1154. Accessed 27 December 2024, https://doi.org/10.1016/j.tele.2015.11.006

Scott N, Batchelor S, Ridley J & Jorgensen B (2004) *The impact of mobile phones in Africa*. Commission for Africa. Accessed 3 March 2025, http://gamos.org/publications/Impact of Mobile Phones in Africa_Commission for Africa_Report 2004.pdf

Ubwani Z (2023) RC: How to boost Tanzania's exports to India. *The Citizen* 20 March. Accessed 27 December 2024, https://www.thecitizen.co.tz/tanzania/news/national/rc-how-to-boost-tanzania-s-exports-to-india--4165420

Urban B & Van der Putten W-F (2023) The importance of e-commerce adoption to boost small enterprise growth in the South African tourism industry. *International Journal of Entrepreneurship and Small Business* 50(1): 1–22. Accessed 27 December 2024, https://ideas.repec.org/a/ids/ijesbu/v50y2023i1p1-22.html

Wigand RT (1997) Electronic commerce: Definition, theory, and context. *The Information Society* 13(1): 1–16. Accessed 27 December 2024, DOI:10.1080/019722497129241

Wikipedia (n.d.) *Technology acceptance model*. Accessed 27 December 2024, https://en.wikipedia.org/wiki/Technology_acceptance_model

Wonyra KO, Cassama BLS & Gnedeka KT (2023) Towards the operationalization of the AfCFTA in service protocol: Do FDI and ICT enable trade in services for ECOWAS countries? *European Journal of Development Studies* 3(1): 42–51. Accessed 27 December 2024, https://ej-develop.org/index.php/ejdevelop/article/view/195

World Trade Organization (2020) *World Trade Organization report looks at role of e-commerce during the COVID-19 pandemic*. Accessed 27 December 2024, https://www.wto.org/english/news_e/news20_e/rese_04may20_e.htm

10 Survival strategies of Nigerian youth when things fall apart

Oluwafunmilayo Olarewaju Aminu, Babatunde Raphael Ojebuyi, Oluwabusolami Oluwajulugbe, Oluwaseun Ayomipo and Ridwan Abiola Kolawole

Introduction

The phase of youth can be described as the period of life between childhood and adulthood. According to the United Nations (2007), youth is a transition period from the dependence of childhood to adulthood and is defined as being aged between 15 and 24. A youth is between 15 and 29 years of age according to the Commonwealth (n.d.), while the African Youth Charter defines a youth as between 15 and 35 (African Union Commission 2013). In Nigeria, people between 18 and 35 are regarded as youths according to the 2009 National Youth Policy, but the updated 2019 National Youth Policy categorises individuals between 18 and 29 as youths (Federal Ministry of Youth and Sports Development 2019). However, in the context of this study, the term 'youth' refers to people between the ages of 15 and 35 as defined by the African Youth Charter. It has been argued that youths should not be defined by age alone but by the distinctness of existing culture and social processes that indicate the transitioning of a person from childhood to adulthood (Unini 2020).

The inadequacy of using age to define youth is revealed by the fact that most youths have not met the aspirations they set when young. Youth is when people have the energy and drive to achieve their goals and fulfil their dreams. Aspirations are dreams, set goals, plans, purposes, ideas, earnest desires, and longings geared toward the attainment of great success and a good life in the future (University of Minnesota Extension 2023). It is believed that the aspirations of youth are how young men and women hope, imagine, and envision their intended future lives. Youth aspirations can be politically, economically, socially, or educationally motivated.

Aspirations are drivers of youth choices in education, employment and job-seeking efforts (Costa, Contreras-González & Palacios-Lopez 2022). Young people's aspirations are indispensable to their human capital investment, educational choices and labour market outcomes (Gardiner & Goedhuys 2020). Youth aspirations can be influenced by personal interest or motivation, enabling environment, acquaintances, family, friends, educational instructors, societal values, and culture. Youths aspire to becoming responsible citizens who can contribute to the advancement of their communities. Unfortunately, these aspirations are often not fulfilled, largely due to the vulnerabilities of youths to uncertainties mostly beyond their control.

The vulnerabilities of youth are revealed in their poor quality of life. Millions of Nigerians, including young people, are affected by unsatisfactory educational status, poor health results, and poor housing conditions, among others (Chukwuemeka 2024). The array of constraints militating against youth aspirations include unemployment, information gap, and lack of or inadequate infrastructure. An enabling environment based on good infrastructure is necessary for youths to achieve their aspirations.

However, Nigeria's poor state of the infrastructure had thwarted youth advancement and entrepreneurial development (Kwentua 2022), and contributed to the high youth unemployment rate. Youths need good educational facilities, constant power supply, access to good water, good health facilities, serviceable roads, and credit facilities, among others, to realise the good life they envisioned. The availability of the aforementioned infrastructure is crucial to the creation of job opportunities for the youth and the improvement of their quality of life. It will also help in decreasing unemployment, depression, and frustration.

Despite the challenges faced by the youth, they remain resilient and continue to try to realise their aspirations by employing creative strategies to ensure survival. The youth are not deterred in their quest for knowledge but they are handicapped by the unfavourable Nigerian economy, lack of infrastructure, inadequate capacity building, and unemployment. A study of youths from 15 to 35 conducted across all the states in rural and urban Nigeria identified poor infrastructure as a major problem limiting youth potential (Danne Institute for Research 2021).

The poor state of infrastructure limits economic opportunities available to all Nigerians, including youths – the focus of this study. This study promotes cross-cultural understanding as it provides a point of reference for researchers on a global discourse on youth development, empowerment, and survival strategies in the face of infrastructural challenges. It is crucial to the attainment of sustainable development goals as it helps to find ways to support the aspirations of Nigerian youths despite infrastructural challenges. The survival strategies of Nigerian youths, their resilience, adaptive capacity, and resourcefulness in the face of challenges portray a positive image of youth capabilities in Nigeria. The study is an eye-opener to the lived experiences of youths in Nigeria and it contributes to the existing body of knowledge on research on youth development and the effects of poor infrastructure on youth aspirations. Moreover, there is a dearth of studies on the nexus of youth aspirations, survival strategies, and infrastructure challenges in Nigeria. So, the four objectives of this study are understanding youth aspirations in Nigeria, identifying the major challenges to youth aspiration actualisation in Nigeria, elucidating the effects of poor infrastructural development on youth aspirations, and describing the survival strategies employed by youth in Nigeria.

Literature review

Youth aspirations are life ambitions, goals, desires, hopes, or dreams that youths have for their future. According to the University of Minnesota Extension (2023), youth aspirations can be defined as a process by which young people hope and imagine what their lives will become in the future. In the opinion of Cherry (2021), aspirations are hopes, ambitions, or dreams to attain a life goal. Hence, aspirations are aimed at the future, with elements of positivity and success driving youths to be relentless in the pursuit of their aspirational achievement. Some factors influencing youth aspirations include family dynamics, level of education, culture, socioeconomic background, societal expectations, and peer relationships. These factors influence the choices, decisions, and actions of youths as they gradually transition to adulthood. Aspirations are believed to be shaped by interests brought about by the interactions of youths with other people, institutions, schoolmates, family members, and neighbours (University of Minnesota Extension 2023). Young men and women in Nigeria have many different aspirations and plans for their lives. According to a nationwide survey of Nigerian youths aged 18 to 35 by the British Council, the three topmost youth aspirations were positive and values-driven – leadership, economic security and prosperity, and education (Danne Institute for Research 2021).

Understanding youth aspirations is crucial to meeting their infrastructure challenges. In a dialogue session with the UN Deputy Secretary-General Amina Mohammed, a youth participant stated that 'you cannot create a future for people, if you do not understand their needs, their aspirations, and goals' (United Nations Nigeria 2020). The evident infrastructural challenges in Nigeria have important implications for the attainment of youth aspirations. According to a report by Danne Institute for Research (2021), youths believed that the array of infrastructural challenges in Nigeria is due to bad leadership, corruption, and incompetence. Nigeria is ranked 130th out of the 141 economies surveyed for quality infrastructure facilities according to the 2019 Global Competitive Index Report (Babatunde 2023). In the 2019 Global Competitive Index Report, out of the maximum score points of 100, Nigeria scored 48.33, implying that the country has an infrastructure deficit over 50 per cent. According to the International Trade Administration (ITA) of the US Department of Commerce (2022), the total infrastructure stock in Nigeria amounts to 30 per cent of GDP, which is 40 per cent below the international standard of 70 per cent set by the World Bank.

Furthermore, of the 54 countries in Africa, Nigeria ranked 24th in the Africa Infrastructure Development Index (AIDI) in 2020 (Babatunde 2023). One of the notable infrastructural challenges in Nigeria is insufficient road network (International Trade Administration 2022). Inadequate infrastructure facilities such as erratic power supply, poor road network, poor ICTs, and poor water supply hinder the sustainable development of youths in Nigeria and the viability of businesses. The state of infrastructure development in Nigeria affects investor confidence, business investment, individual quality of life, national economic growth, sustainable development, entrepreneurial development, and employment opportunities. This makes realising youths' aspirations more difficult.

Despite the many challenges to youth aspirations, youths are navigating their way through by employing a number of survival strategies. Youths in Nigeria have the drive to succeed, which is evident in the way they use their creativity and ingenuity to get what they desire (Nwaeze 2023). According to recent studies, youths' survival strategies in Nigeria include point of sale businesses, home lessons, e-book sales, affiliate marketing, home cleaning services, sales agencies, graphic design, devising new strategies, mentorship, seeking scholarship opportunities, digital skill acquisition, agribusiness, and food businesses (Ndubuisi-Okolo & Obinna 2022; Uzoamaka & Nwagbala 2023). A pilot study in Nigeria by the Challenge Fund for Youth Employment (2021), revealed that proposed solutions to youth aspiration challenges include vocational training institutions establishment, provision of infrastructures, free online skills training, adult education, empowerment programmes by the government with training, and the provision of loans with little or no interest. This shows that Nigerian youths need assistance and, according to the Partnership for African Social and Governance Research, the lack of opportunities and resources prevent most Nigerian youths from attaining their full potential (Badru 2023). Nevertheless, Nigerian youths can navigate challenging situations successfully through resilience and persistence.

Methodology

Study area

The study was conducted in Nigeria, located on the western coast of Africa. Nigeria is bounded in the west by the Republic of Benin, in the east by Chad and Cameroon, in the north by Niger, in the south by the Gulf of Guinea, and the northeast by Lake Chad. It is situated in the tropics and has an area of 923 768 km². The two prominent seasons are the rainy and dry seasons. Nigeria's population are from diverse ethnic groups, and it has numerous resources including coal, natural gas, lead, tin, arable land, and iron ore. Nigeria is the most populous country in Africa, with youth accounting for the greatest proportion. Most Nigerian youths are employed in the technology or agriculture sectors.

Sampling

Respondents interviewed were youths aged 15 to 35 years from civic society (YF1, YM1, etc.) as well as stakeholders from government and non-government organisations.

Data collection

This study employed a qualitative method of data collection to allow respondents to freely express their opinions. A total of 12 in-depth interviews (IDIs) were conducted using the IDI interview guide developed. The views represent the opinions of youths aged 15 to 35 years in Nigeria based on their knowledge, experiences, and dealings with other youths. Data collected were transcribed and the responses of the interviewees were critically and objectively examined in line with the stated objectives. The report was drawn up based on the findings from the study. Additionally, secondary sources such as online articles were used to corroborate findings from this study.

Discussion

Youth aspirations in Nigeria

The aspirations of Nigerian youths are diverse, and include security, dignified employment, education, a decent standard of living, political stability, and freedom of movement.

Security

Youth aspirations are plagued with uncertainties arising from the current insecurity in the country. The study revealed that youth want a secure environment in which they can actualise their aspirations. Youths are in search of greener pastures. Thus, they aspire for safe mobility and freedom to go about their daily business without fear and tension. One respondent stated,

> The youth want a country that is secure enough for them to move
> around so that they can exploit the economic potentials in the country.
> (Government stakeholder, National Orientation Agency)

Dignified employment

The study discovered that a good job is a major aspiration for most youths. A good job is one that is well-paying. According to a government stakeholder interviewed, the youth want

> not just any job, at least a well-paying job that could make youths live
> a good life and have an internationally acceptable standard of living.
> (Government stakeholder, National Orientation Agency)

> Most youths aspire for white-collar jobs, jobs that have good pay. (YM2, male, 31)

A reasonable salary is needed to pay for necessities like comfortable accommodation, a good car, a house, getting married, and sending children to good schools. Another aspect of dignified employment is that graduate youths aspire to jobs where they can put into practice the skills acquired from tertiary institutions.

> When youths graduate, they hope to have jobs and settle down. They are now faced with a very terrible reality after graduation. The jobs they're expecting are not forthcoming, they become frustrated, and they are coming from a society that emphasises so much on money, everybody is looking for money instead of value creation. (Government stakeholder, Industrial Training Fund)

Economic independence

Youths aspire to be economically self-reliant.

> Less than 15 per cent of Nigerian youths can boast of economic independence. As a result, it is affecting youths in the area of optimal development. (Non-government stakeholder, Joint National Association of Persons with Disabilities)

> The youth want to be someone that is respected in the society, not dependent on others, even youths in school want to be economically independent. (Non-government stakeholder, Mental Hub Nigeria)

Women, too, aspire to good jobs.

> Gone are the days where women are classified as housewives; modern day women want good jobs too. (Government stakeholder, National Orientation Agency)

> In the past, women were more domesticated, they were restricted to childbearing and kitchen activities, but young women now often help young men via the provision of food, clothing and shelter. (Government stakeholder, National Directorate of Employment)

Standard of living

Youths desire to at least have a minimum standard of living achievable through financial independence. They want to be able to feed themselves adequately and have access to basic amenities.

> We want a future that is assured in terms of a better life, enabling environment that will enable us to exhibit our potentials, creativity, talent … the atmosphere that assures the security of people, lives and properties. (Non-government stakeholder, Joint National Association of Persons with Disabilities)

> The first and basic aspiration for every young [person] out there is survival. When I say survival, I mean food, clothing and shelter. (Government stakeholder, National Directorate of Employment)

Stable political climate

Youths believe they have the potential to make society a better place to live in, but they are denied platforms that can give them freedom of expression. Some youths believe that they could be change agents who could bring hope for a better future in Nigeria and the world at large.

> The youth wants a political climate that is good enough for them to participate as youths. (Government stakeholder, National Orientation Agency)

> Even in politics youths want to play active roles, for instance, some want to be in some key political positions. One of the things that is hindering youths from active participation in politics is the economy. (Non-government stakeholder, Joint National Association of Persons with Disabilities)

Marriage

Youths in Nigeria want to get married and look forward to having a comfortable home, which requires financial security. Some male youths believe that marriage is more important to women than to men.

> Young women aspire to live a meaningful life and be gainfully employed, they are enterprising, but they are also looking forward to marrying a responsible man. (YM1, male, 35)

Education

Youths are concerned about educational success.

> Men want to get to the peak of their career as a fully professional family man but as we have it now women too are getting to that level. (Non-government stakeholder, Center for Support of Women in Unpaid and Informal Employment)

Though being a graduate does not guarantee automatic employment, youths in Nigeria are not deterred in pursuing their educational goals. This is apparent in the astronomical rise in the number of students writing Joint Admissions and Matriculation Board exams (Alabi 2022; Idoko 2019). Also, there is an increase in the number of people going to the National Youth Service Corps (Ogundare 2021). The increase in Nigeria's population might also contribute to this.

Migration

Youths aspire to travel abroad because they feel the situation in the country is unbearable with no hope of better opportunities.

> Youths want job security. They prefer to go abroad and get a job that will last – at least that will give them the kind of standard of living they want. (Non-government stakeholder, Center for Support of Women in Unpaid and Informal Employment)

> Some youths want to stay in Nigeria but the kind of leadership and system we have is forcing them to go outside the country. They aspire to build their life in the country if the country is conducive enough. (Non-government stakeholder, Center for Support of Women in Unpaid and Informal Employment)

Youths want to migrate if they have the financial resources and opportunities. Migration is seen as an escape route from hardships and a means of achieving their aspirations. Surprisingly, many youths want to migrate abroad despite being aware of the many challenges they may face overseas (Nwosu et al. 2022). The voluntary migration of youths from Nigeria is believed to be inspired by important factors such as better career opportunities, improved security, a better future for one's children, and superior governance (Peterside 2022).

Zero gender discrimination

Young women want their voices heard, especially in the political sphere.

> Young women want a society where all the gender biases can be eliminated. (Government stakeholder, National Orientation Agency, female)

> Young women aspire to be politically involved, they want to have social, political and economic freedom. We have the problem of male dominance over their female counterparts, so the female counterparts are agitating for empowerment so that they will be free to have control over their lives: economic control, political control. For instance, female youths are marginalised when it comes to political matters, they are not involved politically, they are not engaged in decision-making, especially the decisions that affect them. (Government stakeholder, Ministry of Youths and Sports Oyo State Nigeria, female)

This is crucial to the shrinking of the civic space for women and some female youths believe they have the potential to make a difference that will spur Nigeria into becoming a desirable place to live. So, some young women want to be given a chance to showcase their potential.

Contribution to society

The study revealed that youths aspire to make meaningful contributions to their society. They do not want to constitute a nuisance in their communities, be liabilities to their elders, or be dependent on their parents. Youths believe that they are the leaders of tomorrow and, as such, a measure of responsibility is expected of them. They believe they are expected to begin to exhibit leadership abilities from a young age if indeed they are going to take the stage from the elders someday. Youths want to be responsible citizens and contribute to the growth and development of their respective communities. The study found that youths need money to achieve this. Youths aspire to represent their communities in matters relating to politics and also to fight for the rights of their communities such as access to basic amenities. If a community decides to attend to some community basic needs such as road repairs, sinking of boreholes, or repairs, youths intend to be able to contribute their share.

Differences between the aspirations of men and women

To some of the interviewees, aspirations are the same generally for youths irrespective of gender, while others consider them to differ.

> There are no differences between the aspirations of young men and young women in the sense that the present economic situation has put both genders at par in terms of responsibilities. I can say the responsibilities of upkeep of homes had become shared responsibilities of both genders. (Government stakeholder, National Directorate of Employment, male)

> Aspiration is the same generally because we are all living by a certain standard. Each and every one of us has a particular standard that we are aspiring to attain. Everybody wants to be somebody who is respected in the society, someone who is not dependent on others. You realise that in this generation, even those in school right now, you discover that everybody is trying to be independent, not to be dependent on anybody. Everybody wants some measure of respect for themselves, so it cuts across. (Non-government stakeholder, Mental Hub Nigeria, male)

> Young women aspire for marital fulfilment more than young men. Most young men are mainly concerned about making money, becoming prosperous, and becoming wealthy. (Government stakeholder, National Orientation Agency, female)

> Most young women want to get married. thinking marriage is an escape route from all the hardships that they have been facing. (YF2, female, 29)

> There are variations in the aspirations of male and female youths. For instance, most male youths preferred ICT-based empowerment schemes, but the female counterpart dwells more on skill acquisition. For instance, in developing a programme for the youths, you need to take care of the needs and interests of male and female youths. Engineering aspect too, there are more male youths than young women. Most female youths prefer vocations like fashion designing, hairdressing, etc., while male youths

prefer web design and different kind of ICT-based trainings. (Government stakeholder, Ministry of Youths and Sports Oyo State Nigeria, female)

Most young men concentrate more on building their financial capability because they see themselves as the head of the home, so they tend to strive to earn better income, while young women try to build on their entrepreneur or vocational skills. (YM1, male, 35)

In terms of political leadership, young men seem to have more interest than young women. Young men and young women have similar interests in the entertainment industry. In terms of fashion, young women's interest tends to be higher than that of young men. (Non-government stakeholder, Joint National Association of Persons with Disabilities, male)

Young men are eager to assume better positions than young women. Before, it was believed that women end their career in the kitchen, but nowadays things are changing. (Non-government stakeholder, Youth Wing of Christian Association of Nigeria, male)

Major challenges to the actualisation of youth aspirations

Factors hindering the realisation of youth aspirations include economic barriers, poor infrastructure, security issues, lack of information, unfavourable government policies, unemployment, and psychological issues.

Economic barriers

The biggest challenge militating against youth aspirations as revealed in this study is money. Youths have realistic goals, ambitions, and ideas that they cannot achieve because of lack of finance. Youths want enterprises that can also employ others. It was found that some youths who have completed vocational training lack funds to establish ventures and youths who are established lack money to expand their businesses. The study found that this was particularly the case for male youths because they believed that they were the carriers of home responsibilities and that women only provided support. Youths aspiring to engage in small and medium enterprises require financial support to survive in Nigeria. Helping youths in this way can reduce unemployment and ensure stable prices for goods and services. It is practically impossible for youths who source capital from financial institutions at a high interest rate to sell their products at low prices. Because they will be struggling to repay loans, they will have to increase the prices of their goods and services.

> Most youths believed in white collar jobs and the white-collar job is not forthcoming but most of them are diversifying now, and are taking skill acquisition as alternatives. Unfortunately, some of them that trade don't have the equipment. After training, they don't have the capital. Some of

them have viable business plans, but no funds to implement them. Both male and female youths need empowerment. Even some youths after starting their businesses, they have the problem of sustainability. So, youths need managerial skills to sustain their businesses. (Government stakeholder, Ministry of Youths and Sports Oyo State Nigeria)

Poor infrastructural development

Missing or poor infrastructure makes it impossible for enterprising youths to start and/or grow their businesses. They have to struggle with the high costs of production and low productivity because the absence or poor state of essential infrastructure makes it difficult for businesses to thrive. Thus, youths are hampered in running their own businesses. Also, the lack of basic infrastructure is putting youths in occupations they do not necessarily want to pursue. For instance, youths are discouraged from engaging in businesses that require electricity. Adanlawo and Vezi-Magigaba's (2021) study on the effect of electricity outages on small to medium enterprises in Nigeria established that poor electricity supply has significant effects on these businesses. Abur (2020) reported that inadequate infrastructure hinders small and medium business development in Nigeria, thereby reducing income, profitability of businesses, and government revenue, and exacerbating unemployment.

Security

Recently in Nigeria, there has been a continuous rise in criminal activities such as kidnapping, banditry, and conflict between farmers and herders. Roads are no longer safe and most youth cannot afford air transportation so they are afraid to change location, expand their businesses beyond their current location, and market their goods to other areas owing to the lack of security in the country. Youths do not want to go to volatile zones owing to vulnerability to bandit attacks. They do not see such areas as promising green pastures to expand their businesses or realise their aspirations, even if there are opportunities. This study revealed that the farmer–herder conflicts prevented some youths from pursuing promising agricultural initiatives. Some youths are still suffering from irreparable losses caused by farmer–herder conflict, so they cannot farm in susceptible communities even if they have the resources. Therefore, constant farmer–herder conflict has led to fear, tension, and limited access to productive farmlands. Nigeria's security challenge is worsening every day which is revealed in heightened societal tensions fuelled by the activities of kidnappers, bandits, secessionists, terrorists, and other miscreants (Peterside 2022). Available statistics in 2021 showed that the death toll reached 8 281 within 9 months and 3 490 people were kidnapped within 8 months, indicating the dire state of Nigeria's security situation (Peterside 2022).

Lack of information

The study discovered that youths were often not aware of opportunities meant for them.

> The government still needs to make sure that as many youths as possible get to know about their programmes because there is no point having a scheme if the majority of people that are to benefit from it are not even aware of it. (Government stakeholder, National Orientation Agency)

> Most times when you look at these empowerment schemes and you measure their impact, you discover that there is little or no impact. Why? Because the implementation strategies are wrong. Most youths are not even aware of these opportunities, they don't get to hear about them. Yes, they appeared in the paper, but how many youths are aware? Who are those getting empowered? Is there a monitoring and evaluation scheme to monitor and ensure where the lapses are and how to measure up so that the right set of people are taking up the opportunity? Things like that are not properly done … so it's not the right set of people who are taking up the opportunity. There's even one that I heard of – somebody that could afford N150 000 a month just for feeding taking up grants for cooking all in the name of empowerment – but there are youths out there who cannot even afford N10 000 in months. So how do you measure up that corruption here and there? If there could be advocacy, I think there will be improvement. (YF1, female, 25)

There are empowerment opportunities from government and non-government organisations but, even if youths are aware, some are not fortunate to be among the beneficiaries. This is because available resources can only cater for a limited number of beneficiaries. Also, favouritism and nepotism cannot be completely ruled out when selecting beneficiaries for empowerment programmes.

Unfavourable government policies

Unfavourable government policies coupled with the shrinking of the civic space for youths have reduced their opportunities. In a workshop organised by the Partnership for Africa Social and Governance Research and the Mastercard Foundation, a team of researchers from Nigeria found that youths demand government policies that align with their life aspirations, apply to their livelihoods, and can save them from persistent unemployment (Makokha & Otieno 2023). Depriving youths of their right to resources needed to actualise their aspirations is disheartening. The report recommended that government should 'address corruption and other social ills that hinder youth capacities for development and create inequalities in accessing work opportunities [and] channel resources recovered from corruption to supporting youth-specific programmes' (Makokha & Otieno 2023: 4).

High unemployment rate

The study revealed that some youths were doing jobs that were not commensurate with their educational qualification just to get money to survive. These included BSc and MSc graduates who had become commercial motorcycle, *okada*, and tricycle riders to earn a living. The untold hardships in the country affected both young men and young women. In Nigeria, some young women are now commercial drivers of cabs and tricycles in a bid to survive the harsh economy, even though it is generally believed that these jobs are meant for men. A stable source of income is key to actualising aspirations. Unfortunately, most youths are unable to secure formal employment or get money to establish an informal source of income. A study carried out by Jobberman in collaboration with Young Africa Works and the Mastercard Foundation revealed that, of the 122 million people in Nigeria, 46 million were employed, 43 million were informally employed, and only 3 million (about 2.3 million being men) were formally employed (George 2022). Most youths that had graduated had resigned themselves to the fact that government jobs are no longer forthcoming. Besides, the increase in population makes it impossible for the labour market to absorb the copious number of graduates produced by Nigerian universities every year. Hence, the increasing number of unemployed youths. Nigeria's youth unemployment rate was projected to be about 57 per cent in 2023 (Trading Economics 2022).

Psychological/emotional imbalances

Deviant behaviours attributable to joblessness are common amidst the youth. The inability to find a stable source of income deters them from pursuing positive aspirations and manifesting the good values expected of them in society. Psychological and emotional imbalances put youths in the wrong frame of mind to think of or concentrate on positive survival strategies to achieve their goals. Some youths experience stress and depression as they struggle through life, especially if they have family responsibilities. Thus, youths need psychological and emotional therapy to reach their potential. Psychosocial support and counselling can help young people harness their talents to actualise their aspirations (Sarkar, Sahatqija & Kyo 2021). Financial stress coupled with societal pressure can result in mental instability and even depression. Thus, economic barriers are one of the factors that subject youths to avoidable psychological stress.

Effects of poor infrastructural development on youth aspirations

In 2022, 70 per cent of the Nigerian population was under 30 years of age (Chukwuemeka 2024). So, developing physical, social, institutional, and agricultural infrastructure to meet the needs of the youth is essential for their survival and the nation's development. The study found that most youths are incapacitated by the poor state of infrastructure in the country, and they lack the financial resources to improvise. The infrastructural needs of the youth include physical, social, and institutional structures. The most important infrastructural issues negatively impacting youth aspirations are those relating to transport, power, and water. Availability and reliability of these utilities would go a long way to hastening the achievement of youth aspirations. A good road network would facilitate the movement of goods and services, and facilitate timely delivery of commodities. Youth in productive communities with poor roads are not encouraged to engage in productive ventures, so they do not realise their aspirations. This is corroborated by reports that indicate that inadequate and poor infrastructure does not motivate youths to greatness (Ekpimah 2020).

Additionally, erratic power supply affects informal jobs including clothes manufacturing, printing businesses, café business, hairdressing, laundry, tailoring, cold drink sales, baking, and agricultural processing. Some businesses cannot thrive due to inconsistent electricity because reliance on alternative sources of power such as generators would escalate operational cost, thereby reducing returns.

> It's not easy, just look at what is currently happening. If you have a small [barber's] salon … no electricity … if you want to use a generator … it's not easy to get money to get generator … fuel. Even people who want to patronise you don't even have money, the purchasing power is too poor, they don't have money to come and patronise you. So, what do you do? How do you survive? (Government stakeholder, Industrial Training Fund)

> There is no form of assistance from anywhere, you must generate your own electricity, build your company by yourself, do everything by yourself and it's really very difficult. So, in as much as youth try to help themselves, the situation is not in any way making things easy for them. (Government stakeholder, Industrial Training Fund)

> Youths want to have minimum standard of living. They want employment, to be useful to the community, to be useful to society. In the process of doing that they are also able to feed themselves, have access to electricity and potable water.

> Youth are not happy about what is going on in the country. Presently there is lack of electricity power supply and things are not going well. (Non-government stakeholder, Mental Hub Nigeria)

Youth survival strategies

Young men and women employ various strategies to survive the harsh economy in the country. This study revealed that the survival strategies employed by youths are both positive and negative.

Positive youth survival strategies

Multiple streams of income

It was found that youths are combining multiple streams of income to make ends meet.

> COVID-19 opened the eyes of everyone. Everybody can be at home and be working and earning. It also helped me to realise that one job is no longer enough in Nigeria again. Youths have to be multitasking. That is why many young people in Nigeria are buying and selling one thing or another – they are doing make-up, affiliate marketing, digital marketing, graphics. They are just into something, just to meet their goals – and what is the goal? To have some money so that they can be self-sufficient. (Non-government stakeholder, Mental Hub Nigeria)

Thus, the pandemic has helped youths understand that one job is no longer sufficient for human survival in Nigeria, especially in the face of increasing prices of essential and non-essential commodities. Most youths are marketing various products that are profitable. Multiple streams of income are crucial to boosting youth's financial resources and enhancing their ability to meet their daily needs and aspirations. The COVID-19 National Longitudinal Phone Survey revealed that 22 per cent of youths between the ages of 15 and 22 aspire to becoming traders and business owners when they turn 30 (Mba 2021).

> Most of the youths are multitasking, they are engaging in many things at a time. Some are teaching and also doing their personal business. Nowadays, youths are conversant with the internet, creating blogs, writing articles. Youths are learning trades, vocations, because with the current happenings, [for] most people their salary doesn't serve them. Youths also engage in farming, poultry, and the likes to survive. (Non-government stakeholder, Youth Wing of Christian Association of Nigeria)

Migration

Some youths believed that the situation in Nigeria is not favourable for the attainment of their aspirations.

> A popular statement among the youth is, 'I want to japa'. Young people struggle to make extra money so that they can travel abroad. Just last week, I had a couple that relocated to UK, another one is going very soon now, just waiting for her mother to get some extra money so that she can go. (Non-government stakeholder, Mental Hub Nigeria)

Most youths travel abroad in search of greener pastures. A study conducted among Nigerians aged 18 to 35 about their aspirations had established that 'young, healthy, educated and skilled Nigerians are leaving the country' (Danne Institute for Research 2021).

Entrepreneurship skill development

The study shows that, owing to a dearth of white-collar jobs, youths are building their entrepreneurial skills in fields including fashion designing, hairdressing, dry cleaning, make-up, barbering, masonry, photography, videography, cake making, and catering. Some are acquiring farming-related entrepreneurship skills in poultry, piggery, crop production, crop processing, fishery, and others. The study envisages that youths can become independent if they master these skills, and can even employ other people, thereby contributing to the reduction of youth unemployment in Nigeria.

> I have one who is about to complete his law programme. He is really into entrepreneurship and it's fetching him money. Now he too has become [an] employer of labour. When I interacted with him last, he was saying law school can wait for now, and that he will go to law school at his own convenient time because he already sees something he can actually build on for the future. What he is doing is not even in line with what he studies in the university. I have a boy reading engineering who is into creative arts. (Non-government stakeholder, Center for Support of Women in Unpaid and Informal Employment)

> In line with our mandate we try as much as possible to emphasise the importance of skills acquisition. We are in a country that is very blessed, but we can only utilise the resources if we have the technical know-how. We encourage youths, we let them see how well-endowed this country is and what they really need to do to be able to take advantage of the wealth that God has blessed this country with. So, we have different programmes aimed at doing that. For instance, we managed the Students Industrial Work Experience Scheme which exposes Nigerian students to technical processes in industry. Some can even set up small-scale businesses, production businesses that they can do without necessarily looking for jobs after graduation. The government is also trying as much as possible to encourage youth to go into skills acquisition. One of the things we do is that we identify trade areas in different locations in different states of the country, then we carry out skills training for these youths. After training, we give them start-up kits, something that they use to start their businesses, and as they grow in the business they can expand, we guide them into setting up their businesses, we monitor them, and then they are on their own. (Government stakeholder, Industrial Training Fund)

Openness to change

The study established that young men and women who embrace change have a better chance of survival. Accepting change that will bring about positive results is invaluable. The current situation in the country calls for timely adjustment to the status quo in order to survive. Youths are not afraid to venture into new enterprises if they bring in money. The dissatisfaction of young people with the current economy in Nigeria inspires them to pursue alternative means of achieving their aspirations.

> Like 10 years ago, you hardly see women driving 'keke napep' [tricycles], it's changing now. I have seen a couple of women driving 'keke napep', motorcycles due to the economic adversity that we are experiencing. Even some women seem to be more hard-working than men. Some women are working as bricklayers. Things are changing. I have seen female painters, carpenters. I think that women are now exploring previously unthinkable professions. (Non-government stakeholder, Joint National Association of Persons with Disabilities)

Alternative jobs

We discovered that youths do not mind changing jobs.

> Nigerian youths are some of the most resilient youths in the world. You see graduates who studied engineering, for example, after university they will not mind doing any work available. At least they will not be idle, it will not be as if they are not doing anything. (Government stakeholder, National Orientation Agency)

> Then, most of these Uber drivers are youths. If you interact with them, you will find out that most of them are graduates. The days of graduates' leaving university and waiting for government jobs is not practicable any longer. As soon as they leave university, they look for what they can do. It is part of what they were advised to do by the National Orientation Agency – that youth should be hard-working, diligent and self-reliant. (Government stakeholder, National Orientation Agency)

> I have seen youths who are lawyers, degree holders, even master's holders, after leaving university, they have to learn make-up, gele [a fabric headdress] tying, cooking, doing online business, they are doing all these to survive. (Government stakeholder, National Orientation Agency)

> Even there are medical doctors that are into entertainment now because it's the fastest way for them to get money. My nephew that read a course in arts now works in a bank. So, it is the job available that the youths are doing now so far it brings in money. (Non-government stakeholder, Center for Support of Women in Unpaid and Informal Employment)

> They are also going into farming now, most of them are going into agri-business. (Non-government stakeholder, Center for Support of Women in Unpaid and Informal Employment)

> Many people have developed a lot of strategies just to cope with the situation. Some have to pick up menial jobs [or an] extra job in order to cope. (YF1, female, 25)

> The hope of youths … is that a tiny drop makes a mighty ocean. In the last two or three years, the way Nigerian youths are moving into business, whether you are a student or not has increased … just to survive … be able to overcome the hash economic realities that is currently being experienced as a result of COVID-19. (Non-government stakeholder, Mental Hub Nigeria)

Digital skills acquisition

The study established that the rate at which youths are acquiring digital skills is increasing day by day. Youths are acquiring digital skills such as computer literacy, freelance writing, data entry, data analytics, web design, graphic design, video editing, cyber security, content creation, digital marketing, and others. Some of these skills can be used for wealth creation in the comfort of their homes and they can be combined to increase income. The use of digital skills is not limited to Nigeria alone – youths can get international jobs without having to travel outside the country.

Circle of friends and families

The maintenance of circles of friends and families is important for psychological health because it enables youths to cope with stress brought about by unexpected circumstances.

> One of the things that young people are using to cope with the situation in Nigeria is circles of friends, bonding with family, friends. The African way of living, community upbringing, is actually the way I can say has helped young people generally. Because, looking at our generation right now, we have a lot of depressed people, people committing suicide. Youths are depending on one another to survive. A circle of friends is essential to meet emotional needs and to offer solutions. There is an adage that says 'Two heads are better than one'. So, when somebody is having a problem and we can talk about it and I think I have the solution, then the aspect of networking comes in. (Non-government stakeholder, Mental Hub Nigeria)

In this way, there is a chain of helpful connections and networking. This can resolve problems and help some youths get out of trouble. The study revealed that friends and family are rendering assistance in their own ways if they know about a person's plight.

Emotional intelligence

Youths are learning and understanding their emotions in order to avoid stress.

> Everybody is raising their emotional intelligence. Somebody does not have to open his or her mouth that he is broke [not having money] before you know the person is broke. (Non-government stakeholder, Mental Hub Nigeria)

Thus, it is not until somebody speaks out that it is known that the unpalatable situation in the country is hitting them hard. Emotional intelligence is important to help youths who are in distress, experiencing depression, or entertaining suicidal thoughts to become positive about their lives.

Prudent spending

Owing to the economic crisis in the nation, young people are now living within their means.

> Many youths are now cutting their coat according to their arm's length because this is not the time to be spending money extravagantly on things that you don't need. You need to spend money based on your need, one need at a time. Now everybody has become budget minister, budgeting and planning on how to manage money. Youth are now spending the money based on hierarchy of needs – most important need for now. (Non-government stakeholder, Mental Hub Nigeria)

Thus, the current situation has necessitated spending money based only on what is needed, not extravagantly on unnecessary items. Judicious spending of available money is paramount.

> Some people reduce their feeding, some people even resort to eating twice daily. You hear a family say, 'Before I could afford fishes, but these days I have to reduce it to one.' (YF1, female, 25)

Online businesses

The study revealed that youths are forward-looking, and have taken to online businesses as a survival strategy. It was discovered that some run online stores and services that also create jobs for dispatch drivers. Youths use web platform for displaying their various products, and customers can place orders that will be delivered to their homes. In this way, young men and women are promoting their products and services. For instance, some youths showcase their cooking skills by advertising various delicacies they can make on WhatsApp, Instagram, and Facebook. People place orders for the delicacy, and it will be delivered to them at their homes.

> Youths had to absorb entrepreneurship skills both online and offline. Youths go for online training, forex training. Most youths are working from home, attending Zoom meetings. Most shifted to vocational and entrepreneurship training both online and offline. (Government stakeholder, National Directorate of Employment)

Reliance on God

The spiritual nature of some youths helps them survive.

> In social work, there is what is called spiritual buffer and it is very scientific because research has shown that those who are more religious tend to survive better than their counterparts who are not, because they hope that one day it's going to get better, they keep pushing hard, working hard, trying to create opportunities … their comfort is in the fact that God is going to help them … that spirituality aids their survival rate a lot. (Non-government stakeholder, Mental Hub Nigeria)

When you look at the rate of those who are depressed and those who are not depressed, the research shows that one factor that makes a difference is belief in God – either as a Muslim or as a Christian.

> Personally, it's been God that has been taking care of me. (YF2, female, 29)

Government opportunities

Some people are exploiting empowerment opportunities from government, non-government organisations, philanthropists, and religious organisations but the number of people benefitting from such programmes is minimal relative to the teeming population of unemployed youths in Nigeria. Moreover, the weakened economy does not allow the government to create optimal youth development programmes.

> There should be an enabling environment. Let the country first of all be habitable for our youth, let it accommodate their aspirations and fulfilment. If government has the right thing in place, youths will have that peace of mind to stay in the country and make the best use of whatever will help them to achieve their aspirations in life. (Non-government stakeholder, Center for Support of Women in Unpaid and Informal Employment)

Negative survival strategies

The constraints of the Nigerian economy are hitting the youths hard and inspiring unscrupulous behaviour among some youths.

Because of some youth's attitude to materialism, instead of engaging in decent work, they are now exploring illegal means such as internet fraud, etc. There are more young men into social vices than women. (Non-government stakeholder, Joint National Association of Persons with Disabilities)

Youths that are God-fearing have been very consistent, very resilient but the truth is that the weak ones are looking for shortcuts. If they cannot get it through the hard way, whichever way they can get it, even if it is through the illegal means, they don't mind. That is why you see a lot of them taking up crime. (Government stakeholder, Industrial Training Fund)

The rate of internet fraud is increasing, also ritual killing and hooliganism. Where I stay presently, five, six, seven years ago there was no issue of thuggery but now there is. Then, the issue of scammers is increasing. I lived in Sabo, there is [an] increase in youth beggars. (Non-government stakeholder, Youth Wing of Christian Association of Nigeria)

The negative approaches of youths towards the achievement of their aspirations needs attention.

Conclusion and policy implications

The majority of the youths in Nigeria have integrity and aspirations that are relevant, promising, and realistic. Despite the downturn in the Nigerian economy, youths are resilient, but some survive by employing negative survival strategies to cope with the harsh economy. Most believe that their current survival strategies are just temporary, and they do not find them satisfying. The efforts of youths to survive are frustrated by inadequate infrastructure. Thus, the limitations of the infrastructure in Nigeria hinders the attainment of youth aspirations. The study indicates that the current Nigerian infrastructure does not create a favourable environment for youths to showcase their potential. This study has important implications for policy development on youths in Nigeria. Youth aspiration challenges should be the fulcrum for the development of youth policies in Nigeria. If the aspiration of youths is not considered when developing youth policies, it is apparent that policies targeted at meeting the life goals of youth and reducing unemployment will continue to fail. It is hoped that his study will serve as an eye opener to policymakers about the challenges of youth aspirations in the light of poor infrastructure. The outcome of this study suggests designing policies and interventions aimed at improving infrastructure and the overall development of the youth in Nigeria. Poor or inadequate infrastructure limits access to quality education and entrepreneurial development. A close examination of youths' survival strategies can stimulated important deliberations about education and youth entrepreneurship policies to enhance learning and skills development among youths.

Recommendations

1. Youth policies in Nigeria should be based on their aspirations.
2. Government should place a high premium on youth infrastructural needs in Nigeria.
3. Access to credit should be provided by the government for youth with no collateral, and interest rates should be controlled to make such loans accessible.
4. The security situation needs proactive government intervention.
5. Entrepreneurship efforts by the government, non-government organisations, and philanthropists should be intensified locally and internationally to reach more beneficiaries.
6. Information on government empowerment programmes should be widely disseminated to reach a wider youth audience.
7. Effective community counselling services are crucial for assisting youths in need of psychological or emotional support.

References

Abur CC (2020) Infrastructure deficit and the performance of small and medium-sized enterprise in the post COVID-19 Nigerian economy. *International Journal of Advanced Studies in Business Strategies and Management* 8(1): 1–11. Accessed 24 December 2024, DOI: 10.48028/iiprds/ijasbsm.v8.i1.01

Adanlawo EF & Vezi-Magigaba M (2021) Electricity outages and its effect on small and medium scale enterprises (SMEs) in Nigeria. *The Business and Management Review* 12(1): 98–105. Accessed 24 December 2024, DOI: 10.24052/bmr/v12nu01/art-09

African Union Commission (2013). *African Youth Charter*. Accessed 21 December 2024, https://www.youthpolicy.org/library/documents/african-youth-charter

Alabi M (2022) 2022 UTME: JAMB registers 1.8 million candidates, rakes in N8.6 billion. *Premium Times*. Accessed 11 December 2024, https://www.premiumtimesng.com/news/headlines/520140-2022-utme-jamb-registers-1-8-million-candidates-rakes-in-n8-6-billion.html

Babatunde F (2023) Nigeria's infrastructure deficit is 40 per cent short of World Bank standard, 15 June. Accessed 11 December 2024, www.dataphyte.com/latest-reports/nigerias-infrastructure-deficit-is-40-short-of-world-bank-standard/

Badru A (2023) Nigerian youth aspirations will not nosedive if … PASGR. *Vanguard*, 4 December. Accessed 4 March 2025, https://www.vanguardngr.com/2023/12/nigerian-youth-aspirationsll-not-nosedive-if-pasg

Challenge Fund for Youth Employment (2021) *Youth aspiration report: Nigeria*. Accessed 11 December 2024, https://fundforyouthemployment.nl/wp-content/uploads/2021/11/Youth-Aspiration-Nigeria-2021-Challenge-Fund-for-Youth-Employment.pdf

Cherry K (2021) What are aspirations? *Verywellmed*, 6 May. Accessed 11 December 2024, https://www.verywellmind.com/what-are-aspirations-5200942

Chukwuemeka ES (2024) Countries with the highest youth/young population 2024: Top 13. *Bscholarly*, 17 February. Accessed 5 January 2023, https://bscholarly.com/countries-with-the-highest-youth-young-population-2022-top-9/

The Commonwealth (n.d.) *Year of youth: 2023/24.* Commonwealth Secretariat. Accessed 3 January 2025, https://thecommonwealth.org/our-work/youth-2023

Costa V, Contreras-González IM & Palacios-Lopez A (2022) What do you want to be? Youth aspirations in the time of the COVID-19 crisis. *World Bank Blogs.* Accessed 11 December 2024, https://blogs.worldbank.org/opendata/what-do-you-want-be-youth-aspirations-time-covid-19-crisis

Danne Institute for Research (2021) The aspirations of the next generation of Nigerians. Accessed 12 December 2024, https://danneinstitute.org/publications/the-aspirations-of-the-next-generation-of-nigerians/

Ekpimah E (2020) Nigeria has poor infrastructure to encourage youths: Abdullahi. *Punch*, 15 February. Accessed 12 December 2024, https://punchng.com/nigeria-has-poor-infrastructure-to-encourage-youths-abdullahi/

Federal Ministry of Youth and Sports Development (2019) National youth policy: Enhancing youth development and participation in the context of sustainable development. Accessed 21 December 2024, https://www.prb.org/wp-content/uploads/2020/06/Nigeria-National-Youth-Policy-2019-2023.pdf

Gardiner D & Goedhuys M (2020) Youth aspirations and the future of work: A review of the literature and evidence. *International Labour Organization* Working Paper 8. Accessed 12 December 2024, https://www.ilo.org/employment/Whatwedo/Publications/working-papers/WCMS_755248/lang--en/index.htm

George G (2022) Experts kick as unemployed Nigerians hit 23 million. *Punch*, 27 August. Accessed 4 March 2025, https://punchng.com/experts-kick-as-unemployed-nigerians-hit-23-million/

Idoko C (2019) Why we recorded increase in candidates' registration: JAMB. *Nigerian Tribune*, 7 March. Accessed 12 December 2024, https://tribuneonlineng.com/why-we-recorded-increase-in-candidates-registration-jamb/

Kwentua S (2022) Lack of infrastructure hinders entrepreneurial viability: Ajadi asserts. *Vanguard*, 7 July. Accessed 12 December 2024, https://www.vanguardngr.com/2022/07/lack-of-infrastructure-hinders-entrepreneurial-viability-ajadi-asserts/

Makokha R & Otieno J (2023) *In the throes of limited opportunities: How African youth navigate their aspirations for dignified and fulfilling work.* Policy Brief September 2023. Partnership for African Social and Governance Research. Accessed 4 March 2025, https://www.pasgr.org/wp-content/uploads/2022/08/PASGR_AYAR_In-the-throes-of-limited-opportunities_Policy-brief.pdf

Mba C (2021) 22 per cent of Nigerian youths aspire to become traders or business persons when they turn 30. *Dataphyte*, 5 September. Accessed 12 December 2024, https://www.dataphyte.com/latest-reports/development/22-of-nigerian-youths-aspire-to-become-traders-or-business-persons-when-they-turn-30-years-old-policy-implication-for-achieving-sdgs/

Ndubuisi-Okolo PU & Obinna O (2022) Nigeria youths and survival strategies. Paper presented at the Catholic Youth of Nigeria Youth Summit 2022, Awka, Nigeria

Nwaeze N (2023) Potentials of the Nigerian youth. *Medium*, 7 October. Accessed 12 December 2024, https://medium.com/@nonsonwaezeapu/potentials-of-the-nigeria-youth-f9cd67f468bc

Nwosu IA, Eteng MJ, Ekpechu J, Nnam MU, Ukah JA, Eyisi E & Orakwe EC (2022) Poverty and youth migration out of Nigeria: Enthronement of modern slavery. *SAGE Open* 12(1). Accessed 12 December 2024, https://journals.sagepub.com/doi/pdf/10.1177/21582440221079818

Ogundare F (2021) NYSC Tasks FG on approval of trust fund. *ThisDay*, 22 December. Accessed 12 December 2024, https://www.thisdaylive.com/index.php/2021/12/22/nysc-tasks-fg-on-approval-of-trust-fund/

Peterside D (2022) Exodus of the next generation: Time for real concern. *Premium Times*, 3 October. Accessed 12 December 2024, https://www.premiumtimesng.com/opinion/557517-exodus-of-the-next-generation-time-for-real-concern-by-dakuku-peterside.html

Sarkar U, Sahatqija H & Kyo M (2021) The impact of COVID-19 on young people. *Generation Unlimited*, 15 June. Accessed 12 December 2024, https://www.generationunlimited.org/stories/impact-covid-19-young-people

Trading Economics (2022) Nigeria youth unemployment rate. Accessed 12 December 2024, https://tradingeconomics.com/nigeria/youth-unemployment-rate

Unini C (2020) Who is a youth in Nigeria? Why the definition by the national youth policy 2019 is not acceptable. *The Nigerian Lawyer*, 31 October. Accessed 12 December 2024, https://thenigerialawyer.com/who-is-a-youth-in-nigeria-why-the-definition-by-the-national-youth-policy-2019-is-not-acceptable/

United Nations (2007) *Young people's transition to adulthood: Progress and challenges.* United Nation World Youth Report. Accessed 5 January 2025, https://www.un.org/esa/socdev/unyin/documents/wyr07_complete.pdf

United Nations Nigeria (2020) *Listen to us, understand our concerns and aspirations: Nigerian youths*, 17 November. Accessed 4 March 2025, https://nigeria.un.org/en/104992-listen-us-understand-our-concerns-and-aspirations-nigerian-youths

University of Minnesota Extension (2023) *Youth aspirations for higher education.* Accessed 12 December 2024, https://extension.umn.edu/youth-learning-and-skills/youth-aspirations-higher-education

Uzoamaka N-OP & Nwagbala SC (2023) Survival strategies for Nigerian youths. *South Asian Journal of Social Studies and Economics* 18(1), 25–29. Accessed 12 December 2024, https://doi.org/10.9734/sajsse/2023/v18i1648

11 Assessing the efficiency of indigenous soil and water conservation methods

Gideon Monday

Introduction

Water and soil have very strong ties with human physical and spiritual well-being. Regardless of tradition or background, every person depends on water and soil. Many communities and religions believe that water is a way to ritually cleanse people before their gods, and that humans come from the earth so they must return to soil. This means that the traditional teachings of religious and traditional institutions have a direct or indirect influence on the way soil and water resources are managed and these informal rules can govern the success of formal ones (Behailu, Pietila & Katko 2016). No matter how useful they are, new ideologies usually face resistance because people are usually loyal to their traditional ways of life. This failure to heed local knowledge, customs, and traditions partly explains the failure of many years of top-down planning and imposed approaches to managing soil and water resources (Loucks et al. 2005). This is particularly the case in the study area, where many people think that maintenance of soil and water conservation (SWC) systems under a top-down planning and management approach by the central government, leading to their breakdown and subsequent failure. This calls for a shift from a top-down to a bottom-up approach to planning and management of soil and water resources for the sustainability of the systems, which requires a proper understanding of the performance of the indigenous practices of SWC. The indigenous people of Bufumbira/Kisoro have traditional ways of managing soil and water resources that have served them for many years. However, they still face challenges such as flash floods, soil erosion and water shortages. The efficiency of these management practices is assessed in this chapter so that they can be adopted or adapted for use in the design of modern systems intended to serve them, to ensure sustainability, or as improvements.

Statement of the problem

Kisoro is a high rainfall area that receives more rain than the average for Uganda – sometimes in excess of 1 200 mm per year, and often in the form of short-duration, high-intensity rains. The region is hilly, which contributes to flash floods, water pollution and severe soil erosion, especially on the steep slopes (Figure 11.1a–d) due to the high volume of runoff. Karamage et al.'s (2017) research reveals that the Kisoro district loses 3.8 tonnes of soil/ha/year which is greater than the national mean annual soil erosion loss of 3.2 tonnes/ha/year; and Uganda loses 12 per cent of its natural resources annually due to natural resource degradation, of which 85 per cent is accounted for by soil erosion. Soil erosion significantly affects agricultural productivity in Uganda generally and even more so in Kisoro, where many people depend on agriculture. This, in turn, accelerates poverty and hunger, making it difficult to achieve sustainable development goals.

Also, despite the high rainfall, there is a limited supply of safe water, especially in the hilly areas, due to inefficient traditional methods of rainwater harvesting (Uganda Ministry of Water and Environment 2009). This leaves people with little or no water for agriculture or domestic use in dry periods, so people have to walk down into the valleys to fetch water and carry it uphill. Women and children are most affected because they are traditionally responsible for fetching water. This results in loss of household productivity, poor academic performance, water-borne diseases, and accidents. There is a history of conflict in Uganda so people who are forced to make these water-gathering trips run the risk of violence, including rape.

Figure 11.1a–d *Soil erosion (a), river flooding (b, c) and water pollution (d) in the study area*

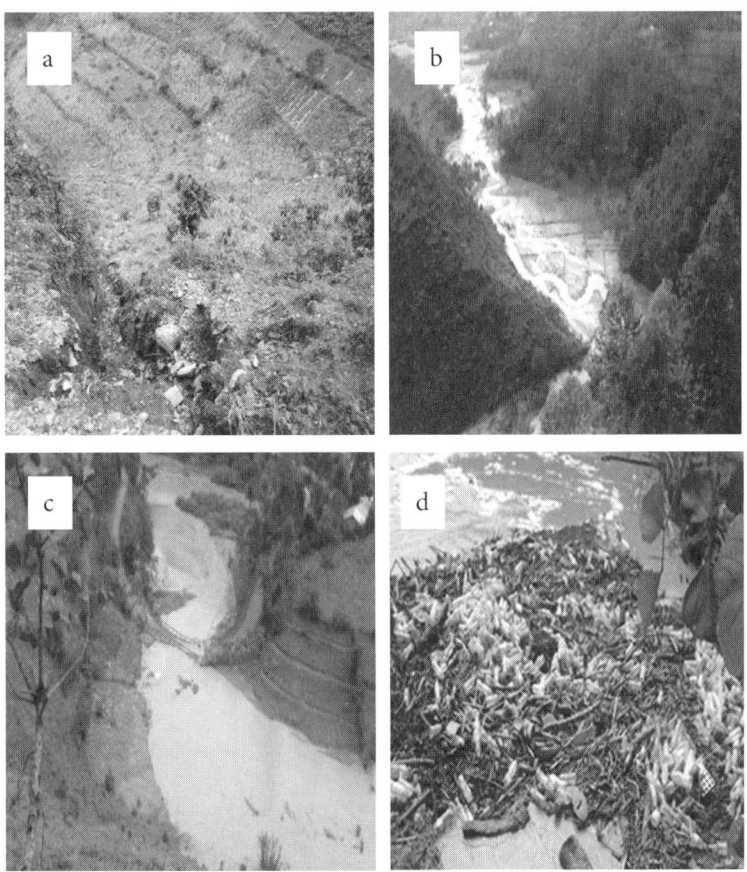

Objective of the study

The objective of the study was to assess the efficiency of indigenous soil and water conservation methods used in the study area.

Materials and methods

The study area

The study was carried out in Nyamiyaga village, Kisoro district, in south western Uganda, about 510 km from the capital Kampala (see Figure 11.2). The area lies between 1°14′S and 1°23′S, and 29°35′E and 29°41′E, at an approximate altitude of 1 811 m above sea level. The catchment is highly populated (with a population density of 286 persons per square kilometre), and annual population growth is 2.8 per cent per year (Uganda Bureau of Statistics 2016).

Climate

The climate is warm and temperate. Rainfall is significant, with precipitation sometimes in the driest months. The average annual rainfall is estimated at 1 368 mm and its pattern is bimodal with peaks during long rains of March–May and September–December. Temperature varies from 10.6 °C in July to 23.7 °C in January, and relative humidity between 40 per cent and 80 per cent (Weatherspark n.d.).

Figure 11.2 *Map of Kisoro District showing the study area*

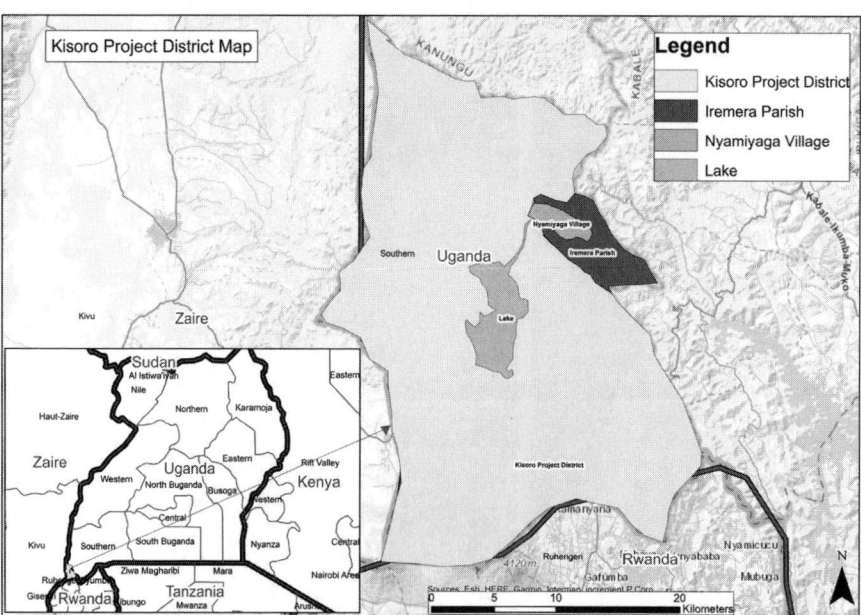

Sampling procedure

The study used systematic sampling. The family names of all the heads of households were listed alphabetically, and every third name was chosen. This technique was used because it ensures a fair representation of all households in the catchment based on probability. A total of seventy (70) out of two hundred and seven (207) households with an average of six (6) members were interviewed, of which 58.6 per cent were female and 41.4 per cent were male.

The sample size, S for the study area was estimated from Yamane's (1967) equation, which applies to qualitative studies.

$$S = \frac{N}{1+N(\alpha^2)}$$

where S represents the sample size, $N = 207$ represents the total number of households in the sub-catchment and $\alpha = 10$ per cent, the error margin or level of precision. Using this formula, the sample size obtained was 67.4, which was approximated to 70 households. Only mature household heads were interviewed.

Data collection and analysis instruments/techniques

Data collection tools included a questionnaire, key informant interviews, discussions with farmers, field experiments, and a literature survey. The main data analysis tools were the Statistical Package for Social Scientists for the analysis of data on soil and water conservation, Microsoft Excel, Hydrological Engineering Centre Statistical Software Package for rainfall data, and Arc Geographical Information Systems for soil and land use mapping.

Rainfall data analysis

Raw data was imported as a text document into Excel and converted into tabular form. Data was then sorted into dates, months and years. The daily, monthly and annual aggregates were tabulated. The years of missing data (1970–1973, 1976–1992, 1996, and 1998–2000) were excluded during data screening, and the aggregated annual rainfall graphs were plotted. The annual time series, which are essential for determining the rainwater harvesting period, were obtained by plotting the scatter of the aggregated monthly to annual rainfall data.

Catchment delineation and establishment of runoff plots

The catchment was delineated into four basins (Figure 11.3) using a digital elevation model, and runoff plots of 3 metres by 15 metres were established randomly. The physical characteristics – soil type, slope and vegetation – were representative of the different sites within the project area, so surface runoff could be quantified under controlled conditions for different rainfall events as shown in Figure 11.4.

Gerlach troughs were used to estimate soil loss and sediment delivery. These troughs are rectangular stainless steel boxes measuring 600 mm by 400 mm and 500 mm high. They were installed in each of six experimental plots with different land uses (Table 11.1 and Figures 11.4 and 11.5). In the second phase of the experiments, the Gerlach troughs were installed in similar plots in areas where traditional methods of SWC were being used. Runoff and sediment suspension from each plot were collected in the Gerlach trough for every rainfall event. Following every storm, the volume of the soil and water collected in the Gerlach trough were measured. Thereafter they were completely emptied of any silt and water and reinstalled.

Table 11.1 *Description of silt traps installed in the project area*

Gerlach troughs	Land description
Silt trap – 1	Placed on gently sloping bare land
Silt trap – 2	Placed on gently sloping grass land
Silt trap – 3	Placed on gently sloping cultivated land
Silt trap – 4	Placed on steeply sloping cultivated land
Silt trap – 5	Placed on steeply sloping bare land
Silt trap – 6	Placed on steeply sloping grass land

Figure 11.3 *Micro catchment delineation*

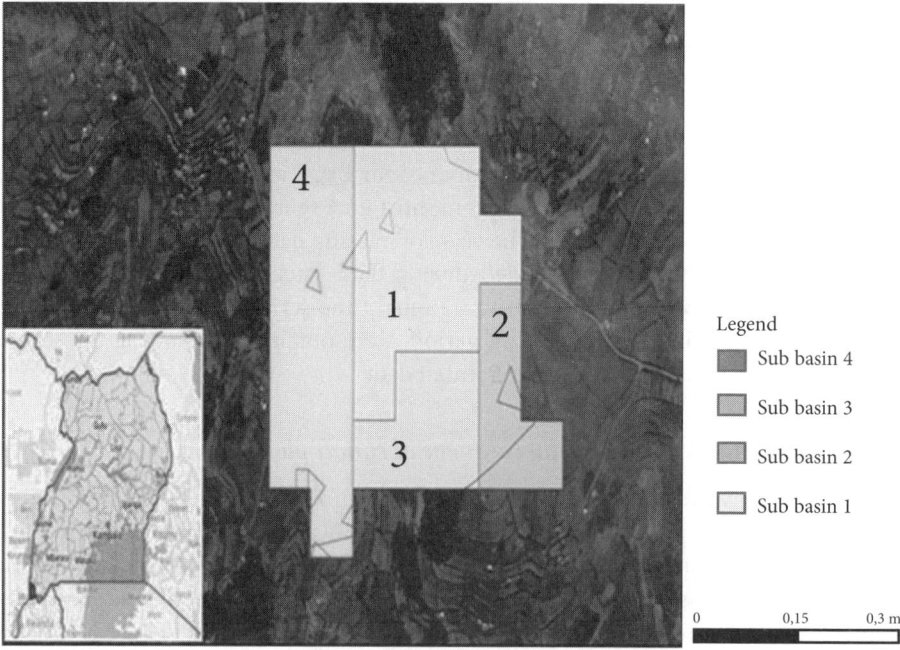

Figure 11.4 *Runoff plots at representative sites*

Figure 11.5 *Installation of silt traps on plots*

Gently sloping bare land: Silt trap 1

Gently sloping grass land: Silt trap 2

Gently sloping cultivated land: Silt trap 3

Steeply sloping cultivated land: Silt trap 4

Steeply sloping bare land: Silt trap 5

Steeply sloping grass land: Silt trap 6

Soil sampling and analysis

Soil samples were taken using a hoe at depths of 0–20 cm and 20–30 cm from different locations using a cluster sampling method due to differences in terrain and land use. A total of six samples were taken for the area where the run-off plot was to be established. These were mixed up to form composite samples which were later packed, labelled, and then carefully transported to the laboratory for analysis. A routine analysis was conducted for the availability of nitrogen, phosphorous, and potassium; secondary nutrients such as magnesium and calcium; soil acidity or alkalinity (pH); organic matter; electrical conductivity; and texture.

Water quality assessment

The water quality of surface runoff collected from runoff plots in silt traps was assessed to obtain baseline conditions for temporal and spatial comparisons (Figure 11.6). Soil erosion was also considered during the baseline survey because it could affect surface water quality through increased sediment load, siltation, and/or increased turbidity. Water quality was assessed after rainfall events, and an average concentration from the silt traps was determined for inference. In-situ water quality assessment was done using a multi-parameter water quality meter (Figure 11.7) measuring dissolved oxygen, conductivity and resistivity, soil acidity or alkalinity, temperature, and salinity.

Figure 11.6 *In-situ sampling in the troughs*   **Figure 11.7** *Multi-parameter water quality meter*

Soil erosion assessment

Soil erosion potential was assessed to ascertain the amount of soil that could be washed from the hills causing river bed shift and increasing the risk of flooding. The soil erosion potential was assessed based on the revised universal soil loss equation (RUSLE) (Food and Agriculture Organization of the United Nations n.d.):

$$A = (R * K * LS * C * P)$$

The RUSLE model uses the rainfall factor R as a measure of erosive energy of rainfall; soil erodibility factor K as a measure of the soil's inherent susceptibility to erosion; topographic factor LS, which combines slope steepness and slope length; and vegetation and management factor C which is used to determine the relative effectiveness of soil management in terms of vegetation cover and crop residue or artificial protection cover. The last factor considered by the RUSLE model is the support factor P, which measures the effects of practices designed to modify flow patterns, grade or direction of runoff and thus reduce soil erosion.

Sedimentation and siltation

The sediment delivery ratio (SDR) method was used to determine sediment accumulation. It provides realistic levels of sediment accumulation and is suitable for the estimation of sediment yields and prediction of the influence of land treatment measures on future sediment yields. The method employs the following equations:

$$Y = E \ (SDR)$$

Where: Y = Sediment Yield (tonnes/acre/year) and E = Gross Erosion (tonnes/acre/year), but

$$SDR = 0.51A^{-0.11}$$

where A is the catchment area in square miles.

Results and discussion

General characteristics of respondents

The study revealed that all the respondents were mature farmers (Figure 11.8a) who had experienced soil erosion on their farms. Seventy-six per cent had stayed in the area for more than 20 years (Figure 11.8b). This indicates that agriculture is a traditional practice in this community, so people have a wider understanding of the traditional practices of soil and water conservation.

Figure 11.8a *Age of respondents*

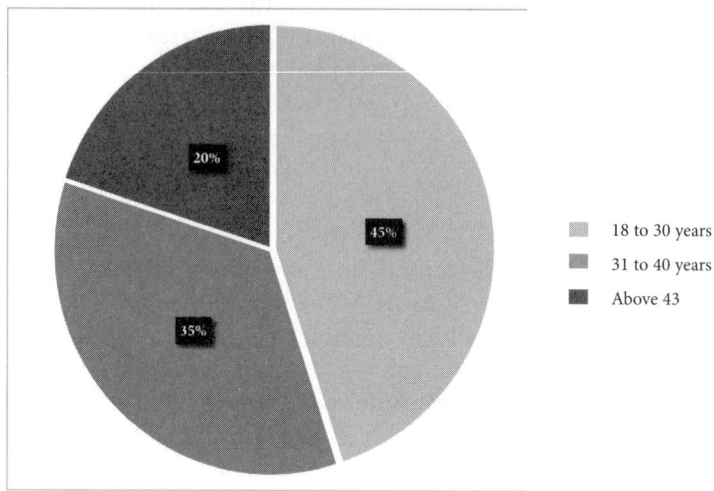

Figure 11.8b *Duration of stay in the study area*

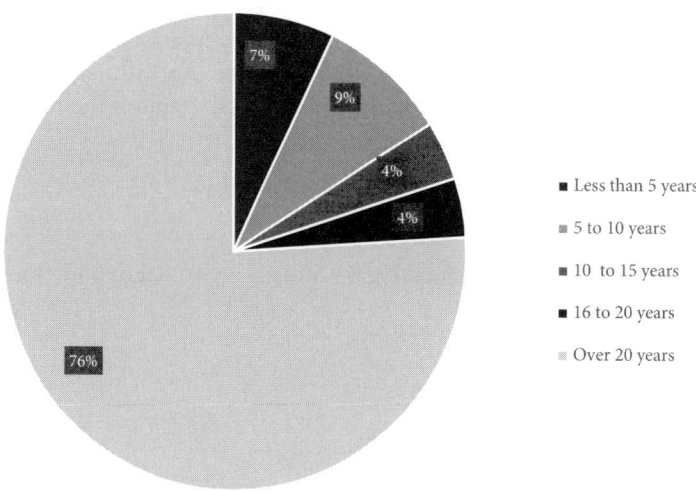

Causes of soil erosion in the area

Respondents identified different factors that were responsible for soil erosion in the study area. These factors can be classified into proximate and underlying causes (Karamage et al. 2017; Nkonya 2002).

ASSESSING THE EFFICIENCY OF INDIGENOUS SOIL AND WATER CONSERVATION METHODS

Proximate factors, which cause soil erosion directly, include topography (the place is hilly), type of soil (the soil is loose), climate (the place receives heavy rains), and human activities such as deforestation, bush burning, overgrazing, mining and poor farming methods.

Underlying factors, which cause soil erosion indirectly, include poverty, population pressure, lack of knowledge about soil conservation by farmers, institutional framework, poor land tenure systems, and poor infrastructure and services.

Controlling soil erosion

The local practices of soil erosion control as identified by farmers in the study area (Figures 11.9a–d) include fallowing, tree planting, contour bunds, stone bunds, terracing, fanya juu terraces, slit fences, ridge cultivation, and water retention trenches. The analysis revealed that bench terraces (23.40 per cent) dominated the indigenous SWC measures, followed by tree planting (17.1 per cent), slit fences (16 per cent), and water retention trenches. Stone contour bunds dominated in fields with plenty of stones.

Figures 11.9a–d *Soil erosion control by tree planting (a), fallowing (b), ridging (c) and contour bunds (d)*

Effects of soil erosion

Farmers reported that soil erosion leads to the destruction of growing crops, loss of topsoil and agricultural land, and water pollution. This further leads to low incomes and creates food insecurity in the area, leading to famine, and making it difficult to achieve sustainable development goals.

Water conservation

The three main sources of water identified by respondents were rainfall, streams, and springs. Water sources are limited in the area, with rainfall being the major water source, so it should be effectively harvested.

Traditional water management

The traditional ways of managing water resources in the study area include traditional rainwater harvesting tanks, run-off harvesting ponds, rainwater harvesting clay pots, wooden troughs, and fencing of water sources (Figures 11.10a–d) (Uganda Ministry of Water and Environment 2009).

Figure 11.10a–d *Traditional rainwater harvesting tank (a), rainwater harvesting pond (b), clay pot (c) and wooden trough (d)*

Soil and runoff results from Gerlach troughs

Soil and runoff from Gerlach troughs were measured after every rainfall event in each plot for different types of slopes. The results were plotted as shown in Figures 11.11a–f.

Gently sloping bare land and gently sloping grassland

In Figure 11.11a, the volume of runoff collected in the silt trap increased with the volume of soil collected. The correlation, R, was positive and high, which implies a high soil erosion rate. In Figure 11.11b, more runoff was collected in the silt trap but no or very little soil was collected. The correlation, R, was very low and negative, which implies a low soil erosion rate.

Gently sloping cultivated land and steeply sloping cultivated land

In Figure 11.11c, the volume of runoff collected in the silt trap fluctuated with an increase in the volume of soil collected. The correlation, R, was negative and low. This implies a low soil erosion rate. Figure 11.11d shows the highest volume of runoff and soil collected in the silt trap. The correlation, R, was positive and very high. This implies a high soil erosion rate.

Steeply sloping bare land and steeply sloping grassland

In Figure 11.11e, the volume of runoff collected in the silt trap increased with the volume of soil collected. The correlation, R, was positive and very high implying a high soil erosion rate. Figure 11.11f shows that very little soil and runoff were collected. The correlation, R, was very low and negative, implying a low soil erosion rate.

Figure 11.11a *Gently sloping bare land*

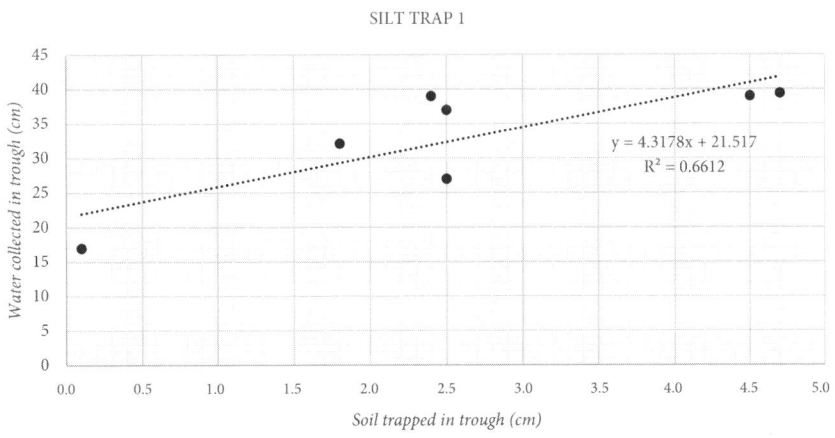

Figure 11.11b *Gently sloping grassland*

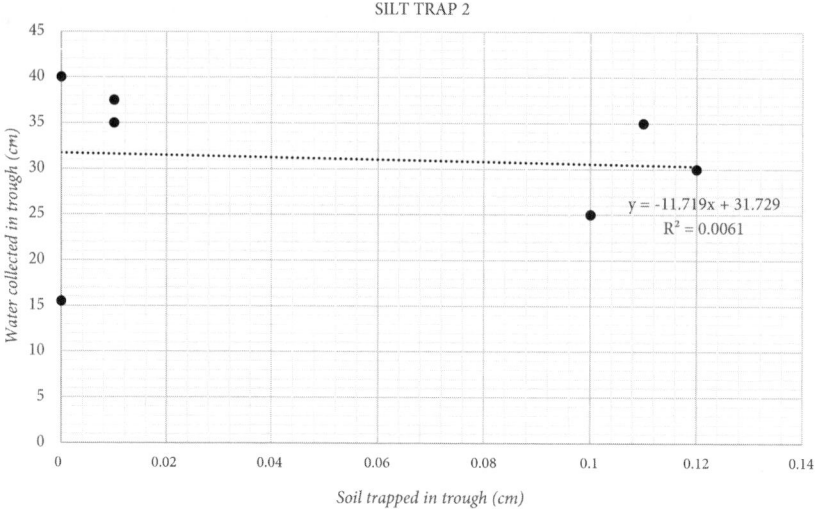

Figure 11.11c *Gently sloping cultivated land*

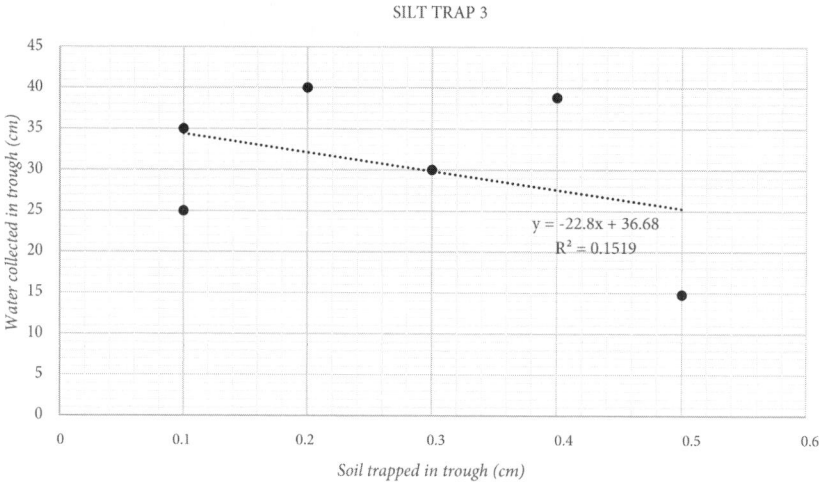

Generally, silt traps 1 and 4 exhibited high silt accumulation over the run-off plot. Silt trap 1 was on gently sloping bare land that had been prepared for the planting season. Silt trap 4 was on steeply sloping cultivated land that was in the early stages of plant growth. This accumulated a lot of silt because the soils had been disturbed

ASSESSING THE EFFICIENCY OF INDIGENOUS SOIL AND WATER CONSERVATION METHODS

Figure 11.11d *Steeply sloping cultivated land*

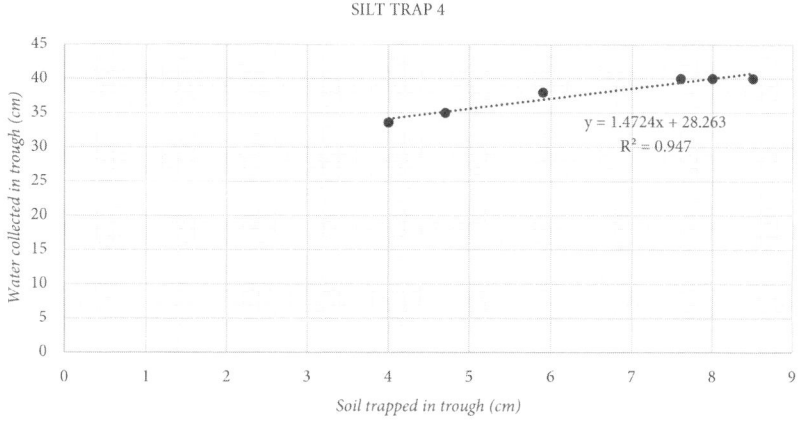

Figure 11.11e *Steeply sloping bare land*

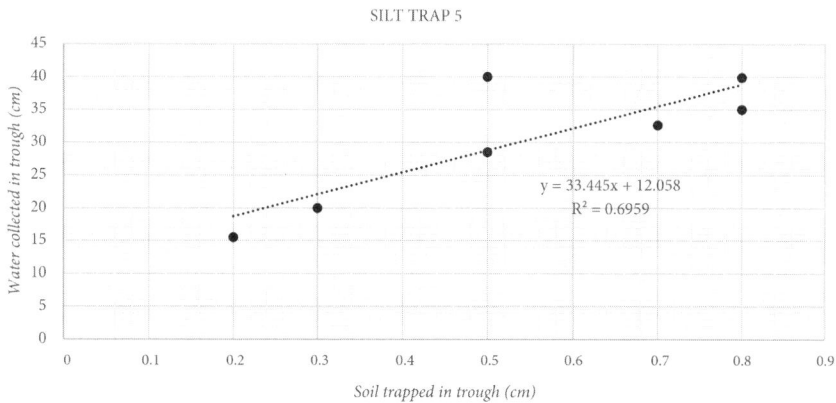

so more silt was transported away from the agricultural plots when it rained. The volume of runoff and soil collected in the silt trap was the lowest in silt trap 2 (gently sloping grassland). This is because grass is good at trapping the soil, and hence controlling soil erosion.

Figure 11.11f *Steeply sloping grassland*

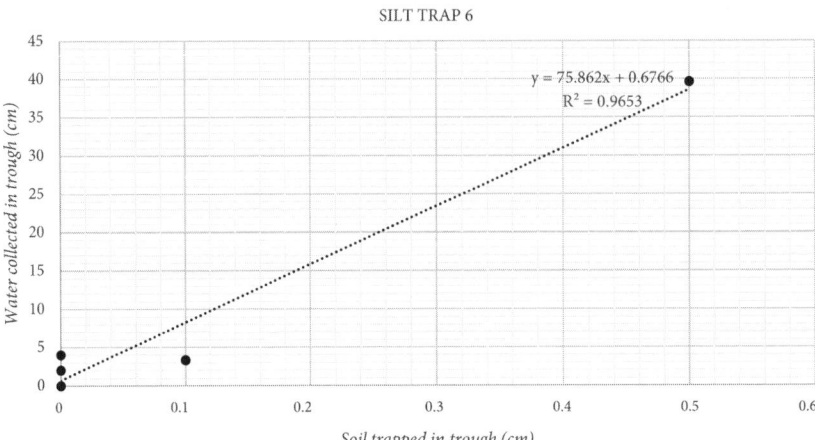

Soil sampling and analysis

The laboratory results show that the level of phosphorus in pilot areas is high due to fixation by acidity. Small quantities of nitrogen were observed in all silt traps, implying that it is being lost through soil erosion. Potassium and nitrogen levels are quite low in both areas, probably due to erosion and leaching because of the high rainfall intensities, steep slopes, and over-cultivation. Such nutrient depletion leads to low fertility. The proportion of sand, clay, and silt was not balanced, implying a high risk of erosion.

Water quality assessment

The samples from the silt traps revealed that the water was dirty and brown with clay sediment. The colour, turbidity, and suspended solids significantly impacted the water's aesthetics. The detected levels of nitrates in the sampled sources complied with the WHO drinking water standards (Table 11.2), so they do not present a health risk. The nutrient concentrations in the silt traps (total nitrogen, ammonia, iron, nitrate and phosphorus) point to a loss of minerals from the soil through erosion.

Table 11.2 *Water quality analysis*

Sample ID/ parameter	Silt trough A	Silt trough B	Silt trough C	Silt trough D	Silt trough E	Silt trough F	WHO drinking water standards	NEMA effluent discharge standards
Apparent colour	19 960	1 096	2 028	2 880	1 344	933	ns*	50
Turbidity	365	46	255	3 245	230	84	5	300
Total suspended solids (mg/l)	3 954	236	443	221	3 491	684	n	100
Nitrates (mg/l)	0	5.6	3.7	0	0	0	50	45
Ammonia (mg/l)	0.264	0.268	0.783	1.33	1.35	0.13	ns	10
Nitrogen (mg/l)	0.060	0.061	0.177	0.302	0.331	0.11	ns	10
Phosphorus (mg/l)	5.182	0.01	2.064	2.064	0.204	0.12	ns	10
Iron (mg/l)	0.02	0.01	0.1	0.04	0.08	0	0.3	

Note: ns = no standards

Soil erosion rate

Soil erosion potential was assessed based on RUSLE (Karamage et al. 2017) to ascertain the amount of soil being lost. The average annual soil loss values for the micro catchment areas in Nyamiyaga were found to be between 460.632 and 110.502 t ha^{-1} yr^{-1} which is significantly above the soil loss tolerance of 10 t ha^{-1} yr^{-1} (Table 11.3).

Table 11.3 *Annual soil erosion rates for micro catchments 1, 2, 3 and 4*

Micro catchment	Annual soil erosion rate (t ha^{-1} yr^{-1})		Severity class
	Average	Maximum	
1	230.316	460.632	Very severe
2	159.5375	319.075	Very severe
3	136.182	272.364	Very severe
4	110.502	221.004	Very severe

Siltation

The sediment delivery ratio method was used to determine sediment accumulation. Annual sediment yield was between 283.40 – 67.24 t yr^{-1} and 67.24 t yr^{-1} (Table 11.4).

Table 11.4 *Annual sediment yield in micro catchments 1, 2, 3 and 4*

Micro catchment	Annual sediment yield (t yr^{-1})	
	Average	Maximum
1	141.70	283.40
2	111.59	223.18
3	91.76	183.51
4	67.24	134.49

Sediment trap efficiency of the indigenous SWC structures

Trapping efficiency of indigenous SWC measures was influenced by several parameters, including sediment size distribution, the time and rate of water inflow past the structure, type and width of vegetation cover, and the particle size of the sediment (coarser sediments are more likely to be trapped than medium or fine particles). The trapping efficiency for biophysical structures was estimated to be 'fair' using the revised Brune's formula, as shown in Table 11.5. The equipment used was not well maintained, which significantly reduced its performance, leading to severe soil erosion.

Table 11.5 *Trapping efficiency of indigenous soil and water conservation measures*

Micro catchment	Trapping efficiency (TE)%
1	75.23
2	76.44
3	73.67
4	77.11

Conclusion

The study assessed the efficiency of traditional methods of SWC in Nyamiyaga village, Kisoro District – a mountainous part of Uganda. The study used a questionnaire, field experiments, and field studies to reveal that soil erosion is significant in the study area, affecting farmers directly and indirectly by destroying crops, washing away topsoil, and polluting water sources. Soil erosion causes were identified as proximate and underlying factors. The efficiency of commonly used traditional SWC practices such as fallowing, water retention trenches, stone bunds, bench terrace, and slit fences, was found to be at 75 per cent. This is considered to be fair, but the equipment was not properly maintained, which reduced its efficiency, and therefore the efficacy of the SWC methods. Fallowing was found to be the most efficient traditional method of SWC with an average efficiency of 87 per cent. Soil erosion rate was highest in micro catchment 1 with 460 t ha^{-1} yr^{-1} and lowest in micro catchment 4 with 110.5 t ha^{-1} yr^{-1}. All these soil losses were found to be in the 'very severe' category. Similar studies should be done in other mountainous regions of Uganda and Africa in general.

Limitations and recommendations for further study

This study assessed traditional methods of soil and water conservation in mountainous regions of Uganda. Due to time and financial constraints, Nyamiyaga village in Kisoro District was used as a case study, but it represents a very small part of the catchment area, so further studies should be conducted on other slopes of Kisoro, Uganda, and Africa in general.

Also, the study reveals that women have not been empowered in conservation although they are actively involved in utilising these resources. This partly explains why conservation of these resources has not been a success, so the gendered aspects of soil and water conservation should be studied.

Another avenue of potential research is the willingness of farmers to incorporate traditional and/or indigenous knowledge in the design of improved soil and water conservation in the catchment. Such studies would supplement efforts by the planning authorities to improve soil and water conservation for sustainable agriculture and water resources management.

References

Behailu BM, Pietila PE & Katko T (2016) Indigenous practices of water management for sustainable services: Case of Borana and Konso, Ethiopia. *SAGE Open* 6(4): 1–11. Accessed 10 January 2025, DOI:10.1177/2158244016682292

Food and Agriculture Organization of the United Nations (n.d.) *Revised universal soil loss equation*. Accessed 26 December 2024, https://www.fao.org/land-water/land-governance/land-resources-planning-toolbox/category/details/en/c/1236444/

Karamage F, Zhang C, Lui T, Maganda A & Isabwe A (2017). Soil erosion risk assessment in Uganda. *Forests* 8(2):52. Accessed 26 December 2024, DOI:10.3390/f8020052

Loucks DP, Van Beek E, Stedinger JR, Dijkman JPM, Jozef PM & Villars MT (2005) *Water resources systems planning and management: An introduction to methods, models and applications*. UNESCO. Accessed 10 January 2025, https://unesdoc.unesco.org/ark:/48223/pf0000143430

Nkonya E (2002) *Soil conservation practices and non-agricultural land use in the south-western highland of Uganda*. Strategic Criteria for Rural Investments in Productivity, Programme of the USAID Uganda Mission. Accessed 26 December 2024, https://pdf.usaid.gov/pdf_docs/Pnacy474.pdf

Uganda Bureau of Statistics (2016) *The national population and housing census 2014*: Main report. Accessed 26 December 2024, https://www.ubos.org/wp-content/uploads/publications/03_20182014_National_Census_Main_Report.pdf

Uganda Ministry of Water and Environment (2009) *Handbook on rainwater harvesting storage options*. Accessed 26 December 2024, https://www.mwe.go.ug/sites/default/files/library/Rain Water Harvesting Handbook.pdf

Weatherspark (n.d.) *Climate and average weather year round in Kisoro, Uganda*. Accessed 10 January 2025, https://weatherspark.com/y/95896/Average-Weather-in-Kisoro-Uganda-Year-Round#google_vignette

Yamane T (1967) *Statistics: An introductory analysis* (2nd Edition). New York: Harper and Row

About the authors

Editors

Lavhelesani R Managa is a senior research specialist at the Africa Institute of South Africa in the Human Sciences Research Council. He is dedicated to conducting evidence-based research to enhance Africa's inclusive growth and sustainable development.

Nicasius Achu Check is a Golden Key scholar, a chief research specialist, and Acting Director of Research in the Governance, Peace, and Security research programme of the Africa Institute of South Africa. He is also an extraordinary professor in the Faculty of Humanities at North-West University, South Africa.

Vuyo Mjimba is a chief research specialist at the Africa Institute of South Africa in the Human Sciences Research Council.

Chapter authors

Oluwafunmilayo Olarewaju Aminu teaches at Olusegun Agagu University of Science and Technology, Nigeria. Her research interests include gender and youth studies and rural sociology.

Oluwaseun Ayomipo is a doctoral student in the Department of Communication and Language Arts at the University of Ibadan, Nigeria. He specialises in applied communication.

Joseph Francis is a full professor and the current Director of the Institute for Rural Development at the University of Venda. His expertise encompasses local governance, innovation-driven development, participatory action research, and livestock science.

Winfrida Kobero is an assistant lecturer at Mzumbe University in Tanzania, teaching and helping students achieve their research and career goals in entrepreneurship, marketing, and public relations. She is passionate about business and the development of Africa.

Ridwan Abiola Kolawole is a doctoral student in the Department of Communication and Language Arts, University of Ibadan, Nigeria. He teaches at Fountain University, Osogbo, Nigeria.

Lufuno Kone and **Phellecy Lavhelani** are both affiliated with the OR Tambo Institute of Governance and Policy Studies at the University of Venda, and specialise in public administration, local government, and development.

Phemelo Michelle Mashamaite is a PhD candidate in public management and governance at North-West University and a Golden Key member. She is working as a research trainee at the Africa Institute of South Africa in the Human Sciences Research Council.

Gideon Monday is a civil engineer, educator, and environment auditor at the National Environment Management Authority (Uganda), and Director of the Universal Climate Change Organization (UCCO).

Collin Olebogeng Mongale is a PhD candidate in social sciences with political studies in the Department of Political Studies and International Relations at the North-West University. He is a PhD research trainee in the Developmental, Capable and Ethical State research division at the Human Sciences Research Council.

Jacqueline Nakaiza is a political scientist at Makerere University. Her research interests focus on resolving terrorist insurgencies, militaries and security, African peace and security architecture, gender, conflict-induced migrations, conflict transformation, and sustainable peace. She is a 2021 Next Generation Women in International Security Fellow.

Awelani Jeanette Nemathithi is an emerging researcher focused on local governance, community development, and food security. She holds an MA in Rural Development from the University of Venda and was previously an intern in the Africa Institute of South Africa at the Human Sciences Research Council.

Boikanyo Collins Nkwatle is an emerging researcher who is currently working as a research intern within the Coalitions in Africa Research Project at the African Centre for the Constructive Resolution of Disputes.

Babatunde Raphael Ojebuyi teaches at the Department of Communication and Language Arts, University of Ibadan, Nigeria. His research interests include media studies and journalism.

Oluwabusolami Oluwajulugbe is a doctoral student in the Department of Mass Communication at Redeemer's University, Ede, Nigeria. Her research interests include gender and youth studies.

Keaobaka Tsholo is a PhD student at the International Studies Group at the University of Free State. Tsholo was previously a junior researcher at the Institute of Pan-African Conversation & Thought at the University of Johannesburg.

Index

advertising 140
AfCFTA 11, 66, 98, 139
   barriers to leveraging 111–112
   benefits of leveraging 109–111, 113
   leveraging for critical minerals 105–107
   and ICT 142–143, 158–159
African Charter on Democracy, Elections and Governance (ACDEG) 15–16, 25
African Continental Free Trade Area *see* AfCFTA
African Peer Review Mechanism 6–7
African Renaissance 65
African Transition Mission in Somalia *see* AMISOM
African Union (AU)
   Convention on Preventing and Combating Corruption 76
   founding 5
   Mission in Somalia see AMISOM
   and multidimensional development 11
   needs 'teeth' 79
   response to coups 28
   see *also* OAU
Agenda 2063 5, 65–66
   aspirations 66–67
   challenges 12
   flagship projects 6, 66
   and food security 121
   goals 6
   hindered by coups 15
   problems in meeting targets 75–76, 78
   and SDGs 67
agriculture
   and market access 125, 127, 130, 132, 132
   and racial disparity in South Africa 122–123, 123
   technology and innovation 131–133
   technology vs employment 133
   and traditional SWC 197–198, 197, 198
   urban see urban agriculture
   women and youth 127–128
agroforestry 119
Al-Shabaab 36, 40–46

controlling Somalia 37–38
aluminium 105, 106–107, 112
   in Guinea 72–73
AMISOM 36
   failure to silence the guns 42–47
   missions 40–42
Arab Spring 19
artisanal miners 106
AU *see* African Union

Boko Haram 4, 5, 22, 73
broken window theory 54
Burkina Faso 15, 72, 73
   coup 21, 25–26

Cabo Delgado *see* Mozambique
Cameroon 106–107
capabilities approach 70
carbon emissions 98, 99, 100, 101, 103, 112
catchment delineation 191–192, *191*
cell phones and willingness to communicate 53
Central African Republic 4–5
Chad 24–25
China 28–29, 139
   mining investment 75
climate change 98
   and food security 118, 133
   voluntary pledge to combat 101–102, 103
coal-fired power generation 98–99, 101
cobalt 105, 106, 112
cocoa 74
Cold War 3, 4, 27, 28
communication *see* willingness to communicate
community 181
Compaoré, Blaise 21, 22, 25–26
Comprehensive Agricultural Support Programme (CASP) 126
confirmatory factor analysis 58–59, *59*, 60–61
conflicts 73–74
   in Africa 4, 5
   asymmetric 5, 21–22

farmer–herder 174
global 3
proxy 16
over resources 17
COP 15 99, 101, 103
correlational analysis 59–60, *60*
corruption 76, 175
   potential of REDZ 111
Côte d'Ivoire 74
coups 14, 71–73
   between 1956 and 2001 19
   AU response 28
   belt 14, 29
   Burkina Faso 21, 25–26
   capital of the world 15
   good and bad 16
   Guinea 27
   influence of hegemons 28–29
   Mali 21, 26–27
   and political fragility 19–20
   Sahel 15–16
   Sudan 20–21
   types of 16
   zero tolerance 71–72
   Zimbabwe 71–72
COVID-19 72–73, 74
   and e-commerce 142, 147
   opportunities 178
   and unemployment 122
crime 174
   prevention in Nigeria 54
critical minerals 99
   barriers to leveraging 111–112
   benefits of leveraging 109–111, 113
   insecurity of supply 99–100
   security in SA 102, 103–105, 104, 105
   need for trade agreements 107
cross-sectional surveys 56–57

Darfur 20
data collection and processing 149–154, *150, 151*, 167, 191
Deby, Idriss and Mahamat 24–25
democracy 7
   reversals 18–19
   see also elections

Democratic Republic of the Congo (DRC) 106
development 69–70
   multidimensional 9–11
   paradigms 4
   rural 10
   sustainable *see* sustainable development
digital skills 181
dignified employment 168–169
direct marketing 140
disorder 54

e-commerce 139, 149, *150, 151*, 153–154
   impact in Africa 146–147
   qualitative results 154, 157
   quantitative results 156–157
economic
   barriers to youth aspirations 173–174
   diversity 10
   global conditions 4
   independence for women and youth 169
   transformation 122, 133
economic growth
   and energy transition 103
   and food security 118
   multidimensional approach 9–10
   and sustainability 79, 98–99
ECOWAS 20, 28, 78, 79
education in Nigeria 170
elections 71
   contested 71
   entrenching democracy 77
   and inflation 71
   rigging 7
electric vehicles 106
Electricity 149, *150,* 151–152, *151*, 154
   importance for business 143, 174, 177
   qualitative results 154, 157
   quantitative results 155
embracing change 179–180
emotional intelligence 182
employment *see* dignified employment; unemployment
empowerment 66, 68
   community 86, 87–88, 129
   farmers 126–128
   of women 70, 128, 174

youth 165, 167, 172, 174, 175, 183
entrepreneurship 179
    funding 173–174, 185
environment, society, and governance (ESG) of mining 112
Eskom 100, 102
    decentralising 102
    dysfunction 111–112
exploratory factor analysis 58, *59*, 60–61
exports 139

farmer–herder conflict 174
floods *189*
food
    insecurity 121–122
    waste 123–124, *124*
food production
    resilience 124–125, 133
    sustainability and equity 125–126
    need for transformation 121–122, 133
    urban *see* urban agriculture
food security 119, 128
    and Agenda 2063 121
    and climate change 118, 133
fossil fuels 98, 102
frugality 182

G-5 Sahel military arrangement 29
Gambia 78
gender 9
    differences in aspirations 172–173
    discrimination 171
    see also women
Gerlach troughs 199
Ghana 71, 73, 106
gold smuggling 73
governance 7, 67–68
    impact on Agenda 2063 74–75
    since Agenda 2063 70
    and corruption 73
    vs management 68
    and peace 5
greed
    as a driver of coups 24–25
    vs grievances 16–18, 24, 25–28
green energy *see* renewable energy
grievances *see* greed

Guinea 72–73
    coup 27
    critical minerals 106–107

Ha-Mashau village 89
    data collection 90
    sampling 89–90
Horn of Africa 73
    see also Somalia
human development index 70

inclusive economic growth 10
India 139
indigenous knowledge in conflict resolution 4
inequality 11
    horizontal 18
informal businesses 148
information, communication and technology (ICT) 139–140, 141
    and AfCFTA 142–143, 158–159
    business advantages 142–143
insurgency 25–26, 74
internet 149, *150, 151*, 152, 154, 155
    fraud 184
    importance for business 143–144
    qualitative results 154, 157
    quantitative results 155
    usage 144–146, *145*
Islamic State 22, 26, 73

Jameh, Mammah 78
jihadists 22–23, 37

Kenya 71, 73
Kisoro 188–189, *190*
    climate 190
    farmers 195–196, *196*

Lake Chad Basin 20
Land Redistribution for Agricultural Development (LRAD) 126
land reform 126–127, 133
law
    entrenching 77–78
    equal access to 8, 12
    rule of 7–8
leadership 85

and personality traits 87
servant see servant leadership
types 87
Libya and NATO war 29
literature reviews 119–120, *120*, 165–166
lithium 105, 106, 112
living standards 169
local government 85
   community participation 85–86
   Municipal Structures Act 85
Lomé Declaration 15–16, 25

Mali 72
   and Russia 28
   coup 21, 26–27
   critical minerals 106
marginalised groups 9, 11
marketing 140–141
marriage 170
Mauritius economic diversity 10
migration as a survival strategy 170–171, 178
military 45, 47
   need for alternative 48
   coups see coups
   function of 23
mineral resources 73–75
mobile banking 146
mobile communication 149, *150, 151*, 152, 154
   impact 144–146
   qualitative results 154, 157
   quantitative results 155–156
Mozambique 73–74
   critical minerals 106–107
multitasking as a survival strategy 178
Museveni, Yoweri 14, 40–42, 44

Namibia critical minerals 106
National Development Plan and food
   security 121, 128
Native Land Act 122
NATO war with Libya 29
neo-colonialism 28–29
   vs international sanctions 78
neopatrimonialism 16, 18
New York crime reduction study 54

Niger 73
Nigeria 22, 71, 73, 167
   conflict in 5
   empowerment programmes 183, 185
   police see police
   poor infrastructure 165
   youth aspirations 168
Nkrumah, Kwame 5, 29
Nyamiyaga village see Kisoro

OAU see Organisation of African Unity
Omar Al-Bashir 20, 72
online businesses 182–183
online retail see e-commerce
Organisation of African Unity (OAU) 5
   see also AU

Pan-Africanism 28–29, 65
Paris Agreement 99
peace 70–71
peacebuilding strategies 3
piracy on Somali coast 37
police
   cooperation with 54
   corruption 52, 56
   effectiveness 54–55
   interaction with citizens 52
   morals and ethics 55–56
political stability 170
power of the brick 21
precision farming 118
presidents for life 14
private security in Somalia 37–38
procedural justice 55, 58
profits, planet, and people 69
public relations 140

questionnaires 154

R2P see responsibility to protect
rainfall data analysis 191
raw materials exports 139
regional economic communities 10–11
relative deprivation 17–18
religion 183
renewable energy 98

in Africa 102–103
critical minerals see critical minerals
research and partnerships 107
Renewable Energy Development Zones (REDZ) 100, 102, 109–111
challenges 111
Renewable Energy Independent Power Producer Procurement Programme (REIPPPP) 100, 104–105
research methodology 89, 101–102, 119, 147–149, *147*, 167
resource wars 17
responsibility to protect 36, 38–40
retail *see* e-commerce
rule of law 7–8
entrenching 77–78
run-off 188–189, *189*
capture 191–193, *193*
capture *see also* Gerlach troughs
rural development 10
Russia 28–29

SADC and strategic minerals 100, 102–103, 104, 107, 110–112
Sahel 14
coups in 15–16
drone bases 29
lack of good governance 20
political fragility 20–23
sampling 148, 167, 191
security 70–71
in Nigeria 168
sediment trap efficiency *204*
sedimentation 194
servant leadership 87–88
service delivery 74–75
sex work 184
silencing the guns 40
failure 30, 42–47
silt trapping 191–193, *192, 193*
results 199–202, *199, 200, 201, 202*
siltation 194, *204*
skills development 179, 181
social media 149, *150, 151*, 152–153, 154
and retail 139
marketing 146
qualitative results 154, 157

quantitative results 156
socioeconomic development 74
soil 188
sampling 194
and water conservation (SWC) 188
soil erosion 188–189, *189*
assessment 194
causes 197
controlling 197
effects 198, 205
measuring 199–202, 199, 200, 201, 202
rate *203*
solar PV 99
growth of market 103
research and partnerships 107
Somalia 15, 36
district commissioners 38
private security 37–38
state failure 37
war ecology 37–40
South Africa 71
service delivery protests 74
Southern African Power Pool (SAPP) 100, 102–103, 104, 107, 110–112
special economic zones (SEZ) 10, 100, 108–109, 109–111
state failure 65
Somalia 37
state institutions 7–8
strong man rule 14
Sudan 65, 72
2019 coup 20–21
survival strategies 177
negative 183–184
positive 178–183
sustainability/sustainable 69
resource use 75
development 8–9, 69, 79, 98–99
Sustainable Development Goals 6, 9

Taliban 48
Tanzania 139, 140
technology acceptance model (TAM) 141, *141*
terrorists 21–22, 73–74, 174
vs governments 22–23
top-down planning 188
township infrastructure 109

trade agreements 107
traditional SWC practices 195, *198,* 204–205
traditions 188
two-term limits 14

uber drivers 180
Uganda 14, 188
    People's Defence Forces (UPDF) 36, 40–42
    see *also* Kisoro
UN Security Council 36
    Resolution 1744 40
unemployment
    constraining youth aspirations 176
    psychological impacts 176
urban
    agriculture 128–131, *130–131*
    land tenure 129
USA 28–29

violence 25, 26, 47
    violence and corruption 65
    and inequality 18
    state-sponsored 19
    against women and children 189

ward committees 85
    captured 88
    need for effective leadership 88–89
    roles 86
    youth vs adult opinions 92
ward committee members
    accessibility 92, 94
    ideal attributes 90–93, *91*
    communication skills 92, 94
    education 90–91, 93
    gender 93
    personalities 93–94
wars *see* conflicts
water 188
    conservation 198
    fetching 189
    management 198

quality assessment 194, 202, *203*
West Africa 14
West Rand SEZ and REDZ 109–111
white collar jobs 173–174
willingness to communicate
    intercultural 53–54
    with police 52–53, *57*
willingness to communicate with police on duty (WTCWPOD) 53, 54–56, 61
    procedure 56–58, *56, 57*
    scale 53–54, 60–61
    validity 54
women 9, 11
    in agriculture 127
    weaponizing 22
    see *also* gender

youth 9, 11
    in agriculture 127
    aspirations 166–167
    bulge in Somalia 37
    challenges 164–165, 173–177
    changing jobs 180
    constrained by government policies 175
    need to contribute to society 171–172
    need for counselling 176, 185
    empowerment schemes 175
    as defined in Nigeria 164
    opportunities policy 185
    recruitment into insurgency groups 37–38
    resilience 184
    in the Sahel 23
    survival strategies *see* survival strategies

Zambia 71
    indebted to China 75
Zimbabwe 65
    critical minerals 106
    elections and coup 71–72
    indebted to China 75
    service delivery protests 74–75